SOUTH-WESTERN

Personal &
Professional
KEYBOARDING

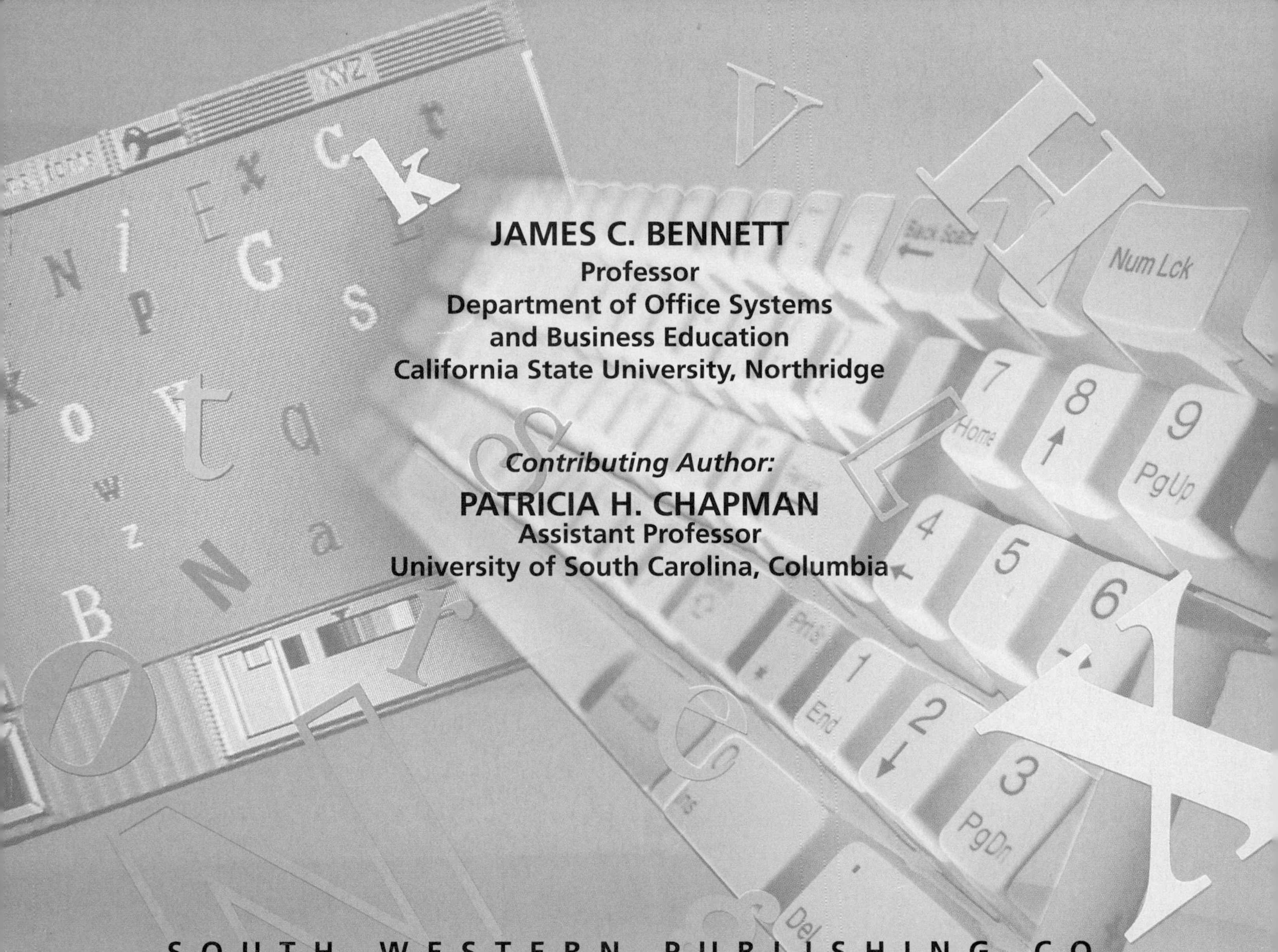

JAMES C. BENNETT
Professor
Department of Office Systems
and Business Education
California State University, Northridge

Contributing Author:
PATRICIA H. CHAPMAN
Assistant Professor
University of South Carolina, Columbia

SOUTH-WESTERN PUBLISHING CO.

Executive Editor: Karen Schmohe
Developmental Editor II: Richard Adams
Coordinating Editor: Susan Richardson
Production Manager: Deborah Luebbe
Senior Production Editor: Jane Congdon
Associate Editor: Dawn Goodman
Design: South-Western Publishing Company
Photo Researcher: Kathryn Russell
Product Manager: Al Roane

Photo Credits:
p. x and xi: Courtesy of International Business Machines Corporation

Copyright © 1995
by SOUTH-WESTERN PUBLISHING CO.
Cincinnati, Ohio

ISBN: 0-538-62021-8

2 3 4 5 6 7 8 9 10 H 03 02 01 00 99 98

I⟨T⟩P

International Thomson Publishing

South-Western Publishing Co. is an ITP trademark is used under license.

PREFACE

OBJECTIVES

Students who complete this book should achieve several objectives. They should be able to:

1. Use the typewriter or computer keyboard as a basic communication tool;
2. Use the touch system to develop effective keystroking skills appropriate to individual abilities;
3. Format a variety of personal and professional papers;
4. Improve basic skills of spelling, grammar, punctuation, capitalization, and proofreading.
5. Use critical thinking skills through composing and editing directly at the keyboard.

The revised title of PERSONAL AND PROFESSIONAL KEYBOARDING, Seventh Edition, reflects a more contemporary approach for the preparation of typed or computer generated material. This new edition also emphasizes the transition from the teaching of keyboarding only on typewriters to the teaching of this skill on computers, and this edition is designed to be used in teaching with electric and electronic typewriters as well as with computers.

ORGANIZATION

This seventh edition has been organized into three parts with seventy-five carefully developed lessons designed for a one-semester course; however, the book can be adapted to meet a variety of instructional programs. The lessons are organized into fourteen units, each of which expands the skills developed in the preceding unit. The successful elements from the previous editions have been retained, and many new features have been added. Many of the modifications are based on data received through a learner verification research (LVR) study.

Skill-building and problem activities progress from the basic to the advanced in a logical sequence as the students develop a mastery of keystroking and formatting skills. In addition, emphasis is placed throughout the book on the improvement of skills in communicating, composing, editing, and proofreading. The vocabulary of this edition reflects expanding technologies as well as areas of special interest to students.

● **Part One—Developing Keyboarding Skills**

This part contains five units which are concerned with the letter keys, punctuation keys, number keys, symbol keys, basic operations, and keystroking continuity. Careful attention is given to the building of basic techniques. The drill lines stress only one new key at a time in order to focus the student's attention on that key. Composing and critical thinking skill development begin early in Part One and continue throughout the book.

● **Part Two—Developing Personal Communication Skills**

The five units in this part are designed to help students apply their basic keying proficiency to the formatting of a variety of personal papers. These include announcements, invitations, outlines, short and long reports, personal business letters, and employment documents. An effective learning sequence is established for problem copy. The first time a student encounters a problem, it is keyed from a visual model. Similar problems are then keyed from copy which has been partially arranged or not arranged at all. Enrichment Assignments are given at the end of each unit for students who finish their work ahead of schedule or who wish to enhance their keyboarding skills with challenging problems.

● **Part Three—Developing Professional Communication Skills**

The final four units of the book emphasize the application of keying proficiency to the formatting of a variety of business and professional papers. These are the types of material most frequently encountered in the business office as well as in other professional situations and include letters, memorandums, and reports. The problems in this unit give students an opportunity to sample career applications and provide a transition to a more advanced keyboarding course leading to an occupational goal. Enrichment Assignments are also given at the end of each unit in this part.

SPECIAL FEATURES

A number of special features are emphasized in this edition.

● **Technique and Keyboarding Skill Building Drills**

A wide variety of these drills is found throughout the book. Many are designed to enable the teacher to provide for individual differences in student abilities. The various parts of each lesson are controlled for time to aid in lesson planning.

● **Timed Writings**

Extensive one-, three-, and five-minute timed writing copy is provided. Both speed and accuracy are emphasized. To provide for reliable skill measurement, all of the 5' timings in Part 3 have been triple controlled for syllable intensity, average word length, and percentage of high-frequency words.

● **Communication Skill Development**

Drills and problems emphasize the importance of spelling, grammar, punctuation, and capitalization.

● **Critical Thinking Skill Development**

Emphasis has been expanded in the area of composing, editing, and proofreading. Composing at the keyboard is developed through a logical sequence beginning with simple word response and progressing to the composing of complete papers.

● **Computer Applications**

A stronger coverage is given to varied word processing operations.

● **Formatting Employment Documents**

An expanded unit is presented on the job search process and includes a resume, an application letter, and an interview follow-up letter. This unit also includes critical thinking skill development in which the student prepares his/her own personal resume and a letter of application in response to a job advertisement.

● **Revised Format and New Copy**

A clearer format is emphasized, and over 50% of the copy is new. This new copy deals with topics of special interest to students and it also gives a perspective on the "information age."

● **Enrichment Assignments**

Additional problems are given at the end of all units in Parts 2 and 3. These problems provide students with added experience in composing papers similar to problems that have already been covered.

● **Reference Guide**

For convenience, an expanded reference guide which contains frequently needed explanations and illustrations is presented in the preliminary pages.

● **Special Index**

An expanded index to special drills is included. This index provides easy reference to a wide variety of activities that can be used in all aspects of skill development.

● **Unit on Ten-Key Numeric Keypad**

A new unit of five lessons on the operation of the ten-key numeric keypad appears in the Appendix.

● **Tests**

Tests are provided for use at the end of each of the three parts of the book and as a final exam.

● **Supplementary Drills**

These drills provide additional copy to aid students in developing keying skills.

● **Template Disks and Blackline Masters**

These are now available. They include letterheads and memo headings.

● **Glossary**

This addition to the book gives important terminology relative to keyboarding, word processing, and using computers.

ACKNOWLEDGEMENTS

I appreciate the comments and suggestions received from teachers and students who have used previous editions of this book. They were very helpful in the preparation of this seventh edition. I also appreciate the excellent work of Dr. Patricia H. Chapman as a contributing author. She prepared all of the new material for Part 3.

My deep gratitude is extended to Dr. S.J. Wanous, who was the original author of this book. His basic concepts and principles continued to guide me in this revision.

James C. Bennett

CONTENTS

◀ **INDEX**   vii

◀ **INDEX TO SPECIAL DRILLS**   ix

◀ **PARTS OF THE ELECTRONIC TYPEWRITER**   x

◀ **PARTS OF THE MICROCOMPUTER**   xi

◀ **REFERENCE GUIDE**   RG-1

PART 1
Developing Keying Skills

◀ **UNIT 1**   **Lessons 1-10**   **Learning the Letter Keys**   2

L1 Home Keys; Space Bar; Return/Enter; Ending the Lesson **L2** Machine Adjustments; H and E; I and R **L3** O and T; N and G **L4** Left Shift; Period (.) **L5** U and C; Correct Posture and Position **L6** W; Right Shift Key **L7** B and Y; M and X **L8** P and V; Q and Comma (,) **L9** Z and Colon (:); Caps Lock and Question Mark (?) **L10** Tab Key, Paragraphs; Proofreading

◀ **UNIT 2**   **Lessons 11-13**   **Building Keying Skill**   24

L11 Word-Response Keystroking; Sentence Guided Writings; Paragraph Keying **L12** Sentence Guided Writings; Keying in All Capital Letters; Word Response **L13** Composing; Sentence Guided Writings; Timed Writing

◀ **UNIT 3**   **Lessons 14-18**   **Learning the Number Keys**   30

L14 8 and 1; Continuity Practice **L15** 9 and 4; Keystroking from Dictation; Sustained Skill Building **L16** 0 and 5; Keying from Script **L17** 7 and 3; Keying from Dictation; Sustained Skill Building **L18** 6 and 2; Sentence Guided Writings; Composing

◀ **UNIT 4**   **Lessons 19-22**   **Learning the Basic Symbol Keys**   39

L19 Diagonal (/) and Dollar Sign ($); Continuity Practice; Timed Writings **L20** Percent (%), Hyphen (-), and Dash (--); Number/Pounds (#) and Ampersand (&); Timed Writings **L21** Left and Right Parentheses: (and) ; Apostrophe (') and Quotation Marks ("); Timed Writings **L22** Backspace Key; Underline (_) and Asterisk (*); Additional Symbols; Critical Thinking Skill; Speed Ladder Paragraph

◀ **UNIT 5**   **Lessons 23-25**   **Building Keying Continuity**   47

L23 Symbol and Number Review; Word Response Keystroking; Exclamation Mark (!); Paragraph Guided Writings **L24** Tabulator Control; Number and Symbol Spacing; Timed Writings; Proofreader's Marks **L25** Spacing after Punctuation; Keying from Corrected Copy; Critical Thinking Skill—Composing

PART 2
Developing Personal Communication Skills

◀ **UNIT 6**   **Lessons 26-30**   **Formatting Announcements and Invitations**   55

L26 Keying Book Titles; Keying Corrected Copy **L27** Speed Ladder Sentences; Horizontal Centering **L28** Problem Formatting—Invitation, Announcement **L29** Centering Vertically—Announcement—Reading Position, Invitation **L30** Centered Invitation; Poem; Enrichment Assignment—Horizontal and Vertical Centering

PART 3
Developing Professional Communication Skills

▶ **UNIT 7 Lessons 31-36 Formatting Outlines and Short Reports**   66

L31 Communication Skill—Spelling; Horizontal and Vertical Centering L32 Spelling Checkup; Timed Writings; Formatting Outlines L33 Correcting Errors L34 Formatting Short, Unbound Reports; One-Page Unbound Reports L35 Formatting a Book Report; One-Page Unbound Report L36 Critical Thinking Skill—Composing and Formatting a One-Page Report

▶ **UNIT 8 Lessons 37-41 Formatting Multiple Page Reports**   82

L37 Carrier/Cursor Return and Tabulator Control; Numbers and Symbols L38 Communication Skill—Quotation Marks; Bibliographical Card, Note Card L39 Communication Skill—Titles of Articles; Learning to Format Leftbound Reports; First and Second Page L40 Leftbound Report with Internal Citations; Title Page L41 Enrichment Assignment—Reports

▶ **UNIT 9 Lessons 42-46 Formatting Personal Business Letters and Envelopes**   96

L42 Sentence Guided Writings L43 Formatting Personal Business Letters, Letter Placement Guide; Personal Business Letter in Block Style with Open Punctuation L44 Problem Formatting—Personal Business Letters L45 Personal Business Letter—Modified Block Style; Formatting Envelopes L46 Composing and Formatting a Personal Business Letter

▶ **UNIT 10 Lessons 47-50 Formatting Employment Documents**   108

L47 Communication Skill—Spelling L48 Correcting Errors by Squeezing Words; Formatting Employment Documents—Resume L49 Spreading Words; Composing and Formatting a Resume L50 Composing Your Personal Resume

▶ **UNIT 11 Lessons 51-58 Business Letters**   119

L51 Proofreading—Spelling Errors L52 Business Letter Formatting Guide; Block Letter Style; Envelopes L53 Modified Block Letter Style L54 Transposition Errors L55 Script; Spelling Checkup L56 Attention Line, Subject Line L57 Business Letter Postscript L58 Second Page of Letter

▶ **UNIT 12 Lessons 59-62 Interoffice Memorandums**   141

L59 Communication Skill—Spelling L60 Communication Skill—Colons; Interoffice Memorandums L61 Difficult Copy; Spelling Checkup L62 Critical Thinking Skill—Revising a Memo

▶ **UNIT 13 Lessons 63-67 Formatting Tables**   151

L63 Sustained Skill Building L64 Formatting a Table L65 Three-Column Tables L66 Use of Parentheses; Two-Column Tables L67 Table with Blocked Headings; Source Note

▶ **UNIT 14 Lessons 68-75 Formatting Professional Reports and Documents**   163

L68 Numbers and Symbols L69 Leftbound Report with Footnotes L70 Title Page, Bibliography; Report with Side Headings and Endnotes L71 Report with Internal Citations and Table L72 Spelling of Names L73 Report in Memorandum Form with Table L74 News Release, Itinerary L75 Rough Drafts—Letter, Itinerary, Table

▶ **APPENDIX**   Learning the Numeric Keypad   A-1

▶ **GLOSSARY**   A-8

INDEX

A, location of, 3
Abbreviations: spacing, with periods, 10, 14; two-letter state ZIP Code, RG-6
Address: in business letters, 123
Adjustments, machine, RG-1, RG-2, 5
Alignment of paper, 104
Ampersand (&): location of, 42
Announcement: centered, 59, 60, 63, 65; illustration of, on half sheet, 62
Apostrophe ('): guides for use of, RG-10, 170; location of, 43; spacing for, 43, 50
Application letter, RG-16, 111
Articles, keying titles of, 86, 171
Asterisk (*): in footnotes, 161
Attention line, in business letters, 135
Average word length (awl), 121

B, location of, 15
Backspace key, x, 45
Bibliographical card, 85
Bibliography, 171
Block style letters: SEE: Letters
Book report: formatting guides, 70
Books, keying titles of, 27, 56, 91, 171
Bottom margins, setting, RG-4
Business letters: SEE: Letters

C, location of, 11
Capitalization guides, RG-9
Capital letters, shifting for, 9, 13, 19
Carbon copies: preparing, RG-5
Cards: bibliographical, 85; note, 85
Center point: elite, RG-2, RG-3, 58; leftbound reports, 87; of odd-size paper, RG-11; pica, RG-2, RG-3, 58
Citations, internal, in a report, 87, 89
Clauses, independent: and placement of commas, 116
Colon (:): guides for use of, RG-10, 143; in mixed punctuation, 102; location of, 19; spacing after, 19, 52
Columnar headings, blocked, 161
Columns, centering in a table, RG-17, 154
Comma: guides for use of, RG-10, 116; in mixed punctuation, 102; location of, 17; placement of, between independent clauses, 116; spacing after, 17
Complimentary close: capitalization guides for, 122; in business letters, 123; in personal business letters, 99
Computer: care of, RG-6; default settings on, defined, RG-1
Correcting errors, RG-5, 74, 77; by spreading letters, 113; by squeezing letters, 111; on carbon copies, RG-6
Correction liquid, use of, RG-5, 74, 77
Correction tape, use of, RG-5, 74, 77

D, location of, 3
Dash (--), guides for use of, RG-10; how to key, 41; spacing, 41, 50, 52
Dateline: in business letters, 123; in personal business letters, 99

Decimal (.), location of
Default settings, on a computer, RG-2, A-8
Diagonal (/), location of, 39; spacing, 39
Direct quotation, 87, 89, 168, 169
Disk drive, defined, A-8
Diskette: care of, RG-6; defined, A-8
Dividing words, guides for, RG-9, 73
Dollar sign ($), location of, 39

E, location of, 6
Eight (8), location of, 30
Electronic typewriter: care of, RG-6
Electronically set margins, RG-4
Elite type, RG-2; center point for, RG-2, 58; setting side margins for, RG-3
Ellipsis, use of, 92
Employment documents, formatting, 111
Enclosure notation: in business letters, 123, 124; in interoffice memorandums, 144; in personal business letters, 99, 106
Endnotes, RG-16, 167, 172, 173
Envelopes: addressing, RG-7, 104, 105; folding letters for large, RG-7, 126; folding letters for small, RG-7; proper size, for business letters, 123
Eraser, using to correct errors, RG-5, 74
Errors, correcting, RG-5, 74, 77; by spreading letters, 113; by squeezing letters, 111; on carbon copies, RG-6
Exclamation point (!): guides for use of, RG-10, 139; how to make, 48

F, location of, 3
Five (5), location of, 34
Folding letters: for large envelopes, 126; for small envelopes, RG-7
Footnotes: formatting guides, RG-16, 167; in reports, 168, 169; in tables, 161
Formal memorandums, 144
Formatting guides, RG-11-RG-17
Four (4), location of, 32
Fractions (made), spacing with, 39, 50
Function keys, xi; defined, A-8

G, location of, 8
Gwam (gross words a minute), 14

H, location of, 6
Hands, position on keys, RG-5, 1, 12
Headings: columnar, blocked, 161; for second page of letters, 139; main, in tables, 155; secondary, in tables, 159
High frequency words (hfw), 121
Home keys, location of, 3
Horizontal alignment of paper, 104
Horizontal centering, RG-11, 58, 154
Hyphen (-), location of, 41 ; spacing for, 41, 50; using, to make a dash, 41

I, location of, 6
Indenting paragraphs, 21
Independent clauses: and placement of commas, 116

Internal citations, in a report, RG-8, RG-16, 87, 89, 167, 175
Invitation, centered, 59, 60, 62, 64
Itinerary, 181; illustration of, 183

J, location of, 3

K, location of, 3
Key-set margins, RG-4
Keystroking: finger-action, 16; in all capital letters, 19; on ruled lines, 116

L, location of, 3
Learning new keys, procedures for, 6
Leftbound reports: SEE: Reports
Left margins, setting, RG-3
Left parenthesis (: location of, 43
Letter placement guide, 99
Letters: address in, 99, 123; application, RG-16, 111, 115; attention line in, 135; block style, RG-8, 100, 125; business, formatting guides, RG-13, 123; business, in block style, RG-8, 125; business, in modified block style, 128; capitalization in, 122; company name in, 123; complimentary close in, 99, 122, 123; copies of 123; dateline in, 99, 123; enclosure notation in, 99, 106, 123; and envelopes, addressing, RG-7, 104, 105; and envelopes, folding for, RG-7, 126; formatting guides, RG-12, RG-13, 99, 123; headings for second page, 139; interview follow-up, RG-16, 111; margins in, 99, 123; modified block style, RG-8, 103, 128; name of writer in, 99, 122, 123; personal business, formatting guides, RG-12, 99; personal business, in block style, 100; personal business, in modified block style, RG-8, 103; personal titles in, 100, 122; postscript in, 137; reference initials in, 123; return address in, 99; salutation in, 99, 122, 123; stationery for, 123; subject line in, 135; two-page, 139
Line space selector, x, 3; setting, RG-2

M, location of, 15
Machine adjustments, RG-1, RG-2, 5
Magazines, keying titles of, 27, 91, 171
Margins: electronically set, RG-4; key-set, RG-4; left, RG-3; placement guides for, 2, 55, 99, 123; push-button, RG-4; push lever, RG-4; right, RG-3; side, RG-3; top and bottom, RG-4
Margin stops, setting, RG-4: for business letters, 123; for interoffice memorandums, 144; for leftbound reports, 87; forpersonal business letters, 99; for tables, 154; for unbound reports, 76
Memorandums: formal, 144; simplified, RG-14, 144; used as a report, 179
Mixed punctuation, 102, 103, 123
Modified block style letters: business letter, 128; illustrated, RG-8, 103, 128; personal business letter, RG-8, 103

N, location of, 8
Name of writer: in business letters, 122
Newspapers, keying titles of, 27
News release, 181; illustration of, 182
Nine (9), location of, 32
Note card, 85
Number-expression guides, RG-9
Number/pound symbol (#): location of, 42
Numeric keypad, xi; defined, A-8

O, location of, 8
Odd-size paper, finding horizontal center of, RG-11
One (1), location of, 30
Open punctuation, 99, 100, 123, 131
Operator's Guide, defined, A-8
Outline, topic: formatting guides, 70

P, location of, 17
Page numbering, in leftbound reports, 87
Paper: alignment of, 104; inserting into type-writer, RG-1
Paragraphs, indenting, 21
Paraphrase, how to format, 103, 168
Parentheses: guides for use of, RG-10, 159; location of, 43; spacing for, 43, 50
Parenthesis: left, 43; right, 43
Percent (%): location of, 41
Period (.): guides for use of, RG-10; location of, 10; spacing after, 10, 13, 14, 18, 52; use with quotation marks, 44, 84
Personal titles: in interoffice memorandums, 144; in letters, 100,122
Pica type, RG-2; center point for, RG-2
Placement guide, for margin settings, 2, 55, 99, 123
Poem, centered on a full sheet, 65
Position of hands: at the keyboard, RG-5, 1, 12; on the numeric keypad, A-2
Postscript, in a letter, 137
Posture: at the keyboard, 1, 12; at the numeric keypad, A-2
Proofreader's marks, RG-6, 51, 52
Proofreading techniques, 22, 120
Punctuation guides, RG-10, 181
Punctuation marks, spacing with, RG-9, 52
Punctuation styles: mixed, 102, 103, 123; open, 99, 100, 123, 131

Q, location of, 17
Question mark (?): guides for use of, RG-10; location of, 19; spacing after, 19
Quotation marks ("): guides for use of, RG-10, 44; location of, 43
Quotations: and the ellipsis, 92; short, in a report, 87, 89, 168; long, in a report, 87, 89, 169

R, location of, 6
Reading position, RG-11, 61, 158
Reference initials: in business letters, 123; in interoffice memorandums, 144

Reference note, in a table, 161
References, in a report, RG-8, RG-16, 87, 90, 91, 167
Removing paper, 5
Report: bibliographical cards for writing a, 85; bibliography for, 171; book, formatting guides, 70; book, illustrated, 79; endnotes for, 167, 172; footnotes in, 167, 168, 169; formatting guides, RG-15, 70, 75, 87; in memorandum form, 179; internal citations in, RG-8, 87, 89, 167, 175; leftbound, first page of two-page, 89, 168; leftbound, formatting guides, RG-15, 86; leftbound, illustrated, RG-8, 89, 90, 168, 169; left-bound, two-page, RG-8, 89, 90, 168, 169; note cards for writing a, 85; references in, RG-8, 87, 90, 167; side headings in, 172; tables in, 175; title page for, 93; unbound, formatting guides, 75; unbound, from rough draft, 80; unbound, illustrated, 76
Resume: formatting guides, RG-16, 111; illustrated, 112
Return address: in personal business letters, 99
Return/Enter key, x, xi, 3
Returning at line endings, 3
Right parenthesis): location of, 43
Ruled lines, keying on, 116

S, location of, 3
Salutations: capitalization guides for, 122; in business letters, 123
Semicolon (;): guides for use of, RG-10, 134; location of, 3; placement of, between independent clauses, 134
Seven (7), location of, 36
Shift lock: depressing for capitals, 19; depressing for underlining, 45
Shifting for capital letters, 9, 13, 19
Simplified memorandums, RG-14, 144
Single spacing, RG-2, 3
Six (6), location of, 37
Source note, in a table, 161
Spacing: after a colon, 19, 52; after a comma, 17, 18, 52; after a dollar sign, 39, 50; after end-of-sentence punctuation, RG-9, 52; after a number/pound symbol, 42, 50; after a period, 10, 13, 14, 18, 52; after a question mark, 19; after a semicolon, 4, 52; before and after an ampersand, 42, 50; before and after an apostrophe, 43, 50; before and after an asterisk, 50; before and after a dash, 41, 50, 52; before and after a diagonal, 39; before and after an exclamation point, 48; before and after a hyphen, 41, 50; before and after parentheses, 43, 50; before and after a percent sign, 41, 50; before and after quotation marks, 44, 50; before Zip Code numbers, 100, 104; double, 7; fractions, 39, 50; guides for, RG-9, 50, 52; setting, RG-2; single, 3; quadruple, 7
Spreading letters, to correct errors, 113

Squeezing letters, to correct errors, 111
State ZIP Code abbreviations, RG-6
Stationery, for business letters, 123
Stroking: finger-action, 16
Subject line, in business letters, 135
Syllable intensity (si), 23
Symbols: keystroking special, 46; spacing with, RG-9, 50

T, location of, 8
Tables: blocked columnar headings in, 161; centering columns in, RG-17, 154; formatting guides, RG-17, 154; illustrated, 155; in interoffice memorandums, 179; in reports, 175; three-column, 157; three-column with columnar headings, 161; two-column on a half sheet, 155; with computations, 162; with secondary heading, 159; with source note, 161
Tabulator key, x, 21, 49; control of, 49, 82
Tabulator stops, setting, RG-2, 21, 49
Three (3), location of, 36
Title page, for leftbound report, 93
Titles: capitalization guides for, general, RG-9; in interoffice memorandums, 144; in letters, 100, 122, 125; of articles, 86, 171; of books, 27, 56, 91, 171; of magazines, 27, 91, 171; of newspapers, 27
Top margins, setting, RG-4
Topic outline, 70
Two (2), location of, 37
Two-page letter, 139
Two-page report, 89, 90, 168, 169
Typewriter: care of, RG-6

U, location of, 11
Underline key: location of, x, 45
Unbound report: formatting guides, 75; from rough draft, 80; illustrated, 76

V, location of, 17
Variables, defined, 138, A-8
Vertical alignment of paper, 104
Vertical centering, RG-11, 61

W, location of, 13
Word-division guides, RG-9, 73
Word processing, defined, A-8
Word response, 56
Word wrap, defined, A-8
Wrists, position of, RG-5, 1

X, location of, 15

Y, location of, 15

Z, location of, 19
Zero (0), location of, 34
ZIP Code abbreviations, RG-6
Zip Code numbers, spacing before, 100

INDEX TO SPECIAL DRILLS

ALPHABETIC SENTENCES
7, 9, 11, 24, 26, 28, 30, 32, 33, 35, 37, 39, 41, 43, 44, 47, 49, 51, 53, 57, 59, 61, 63, 66, 69, 71, 75, 78, 81, 82, 84, 86, 88, 94, 96, 98, 101, 102, 105, 108, 110, 113, 116, 119, 122, 126, 130, 132, 134, 136, 138, 141, 143, 146, 148, 151, 153, 156, 159, 160, 163, 166, 170, 174, 177, 178, 180, 184

COMMUNICATION/LANGUAGE ARTS SKILLS
Grammar and punctuation aids—4, 10, 17, 19, 27, 39, 41, 42, 43, 44, 45, 48, 50, 52, 56, 73, 84, 86, 91, 100, 102, 116, 122, 134, 139, 143, 149, 170, 181

Proofreading skill building—22, 51, 52, 56, 120, 130, 136, 177

Spelling aids—67, 83, 98, 109, 120, 127, 141, 157, 166

CONCENTRATION PRACTICE
146

COMPOSING AT THE KEYBOARD
28, 38, 46, 53, 64, 74, 80, 81, 95, 105, 107, 113, 117, 135, 140, 147, 149, 156, 160, 162, 188

CONTINUITY PRACTICE
Easy sentences—24, 26, 28, 30, 32, 33, 35, 37, 39, 41, 43, 49, 51, 53, 57, 59, 61, 63, 66, 69, 71, 78, 81, 82, 84, 86, 88, 94, 96, 98, 101, 102, 105, 108, 110, 113, 116, 119, 122, 126, 130, 132, 134, 136, 138, 141, 143, 146, 148, 151, 153, 156, 159, 160, 163, 166, 174, 177, 178, 184

Paragraphs—31, 35, 40, 133

DICTATION
Keystroking from—11, 12, 18, 24, 33, 35, 36, 69, 86, 101, 113, 133, 147, 160

KEY-LOCATION DRILLS
a, 4, 7, 9, 14; **b,** 15, 17; **c,** 11, 12, 13; **d,** 4, 7, 9, 14; **e,** 6, 7, 9, 11, 13; **f,** 4, 7, 9, 14; **g,** 8, 9, 11, 13; **h,** 6, 7, 9, 11, 13; **i,** 6, 7, 9, 11, 13; **j,** 4, 7, 9, 14; **k,** 4, 7, 9, 14; **l,** 4, 7, 9, 14; **m,** 15, 17; **n,** 8, 9, 11, 13, 14; **o,** 8, 9, 11, 13; **p,** 17, 19; **q,** 17, 18, 19; **r,** 6, 7, 9, 11, 13; **s,** 4, 7, 9, 14; **t,** 8, 9, 11, 13, 14; **u,** 11, 12, 13; **v,** 17, 19; **w,** 13, 14; **x,** 15, 17; **y,** 15, 17; **z,** 19, 21; **1,** 30, 31, 32; **2,** 37; **3,** 36, 37; **4,** 32, 33; **5,** 34, 35; **6,** 37; **7,** 36, 37; **8,** 30, 31, 32; **9,** 32, 33; **0,** 34, 35; **ampersand,** 42, 43; **apostrophe,** 43, 44; **asterisk,** 45; **caps lock key,** 19, 20, 21; **colon,** 19, 21, 39; **comma,** 17, 18, 19; **dash,** 41, 43; **diagonal,** 39, 40, 41; **dollar sign,** 39, 40, 41; **exclamation mark,** 48; **hyphen,** 41, 43; **number/pound symbol,** 42, 43; **parentheses,** 43, 44; **percent,** 41, 43; **period,** 10, 11, 13; **question mark,** 19, 20, 21, 30; **quotation marks,** 43, 44; **semicolon,** 4, 7, 9, 14; **underline,** 45

NUMBERS AND SYMBOLS
Number sentences—31, 33, 34, 36, 38, 39, 52, 66, 71, 78, 82, 86, 94, 96, 101, 105, 108, 113, 119, 122, 126, 130, 132, 136, 138, 151, 153, 156, 163, 166, 170, 174, 177, 178, 180, 184

Number-symbol sentences—39, 40, 41, 42, 43, 44, 45, 46, 47, 49, 50, 51, 53, 57, 59, 61, 63, 69, 75, 81, 83, 84, 86, 98, 102, 110, 116, 134, 141, 143, 146, 148, 151, 159, 160, 163, 174, 184

ROUGH DRAFT
Paragraphs—51, 52, 56, 136

Sentences—174, 178, 180

Problems—64, 69, 80, 107, 149, 185, 186

SCRIPT
Paragraphs—35, 133

Sentences—25, 29, 31, 33, 34, 36, 38, 67, 94, 166, 174, 177

Problems—60, 63, 65, 74, 158

TECHNIQUE BUILDERS
Apostrophe—81

Balanced- and one-hand words—60, 67

Balanced-hand words—49, 51, 67, 143, 151

Dash—41, 43, 105, 126, 151

Hyphen—41, 43, 69, 78, 88, 98, 134, 141, 148, 151

Keystroking—7, 9, 12, 16, 20, 22, 51, 63, 67, 75, 84, 88, 94, 110, 141, 151, 164; **adjacent keys,** 55; **difficult reaches,** 164; **double letters,** 61, 63, 84, 146, 151, 164, 170; **flowing rhythm practice,** 56, 60, 63, 110; **fourth finger,** 86, 96, 160; **left hand,** 151; **long reaches,** 102, 122, 151; **reaches, various:** ae/ea—153; **b**—24; **br**—28, 101; **ex**—136; **nu**—28; **p**—26; **pol**—110, 163; **q**—26; **x**—28; **y**—24; **z**—26; **right hand,** 151; **weak fingers,** 63, 151, 164

One-hand words—47, 57, 63, 67, 119

Quotation marks—82, 88, 113

Response patterns—**letter (stroke),** 56, 75, 84, 110; **word,** 24, 27, 28, 48, 56, 75, 84, 110; **combination,** 56, 75, 84, 110

Return/Enter key—4, 82

Rows—**first,** 51, 141; **home,** 4, 7, 9, 14, 51, 141; **third,** 24, 51, 141; **top,** 51, 141

Shift keys—9, 10, 11, 13, 14, 30, 45, 66, 71, 75, 108, 119, 132, 138, 143, 151, 159, 166, 178

Space bar control—20

Tabulator control—21, 49, 82

Underline—45, 94, 116, 130, 156

TIMED AND GUIDED WRITINGS
Straight-copy—
Sentences: 13, 16, 20, 22, 25, 26, 29, 38, 49, 58, 67, 78, 96, 110, 133
1': 13, 16, 20, 22, 23, 25, 26, 27, 29, 31, 38, 40, 46, 48, 49, 53, 57, 58, 59, 64, 67, 68, 72, 78, 83, 96, 97, 98, 109, 110, 121, 127, 130, 133, 142, 152, 153, 165, 178, 184, 187
2': 29
3': 31, 40, 46, 48, 53, 57, 68, 83
5': 97, 109, 121, 142, 152, 165, 184, 187

Script—
Sentences: 25, 29, 38, 67, 94, 166, 174
1': 25, 29, 35, 37, 38, 67, 94, 133, 166, 174
2': 37
3': 37

Rough draft—
Sentences: 174
1': 51, 52, 56, 136, 174

Statistical—
1': 47, 108, 122

PARTS OF THE ELECTRONIC TYPEWRITER

This diagram illustrates the parts of an electronic typewriter. Generally, all typewriters have similar parts. You will probably be able to locate the parts of your machine using this diagram. If you have a user's manual that accompanies your machine, you might wish to identify your machine parts from that manual.

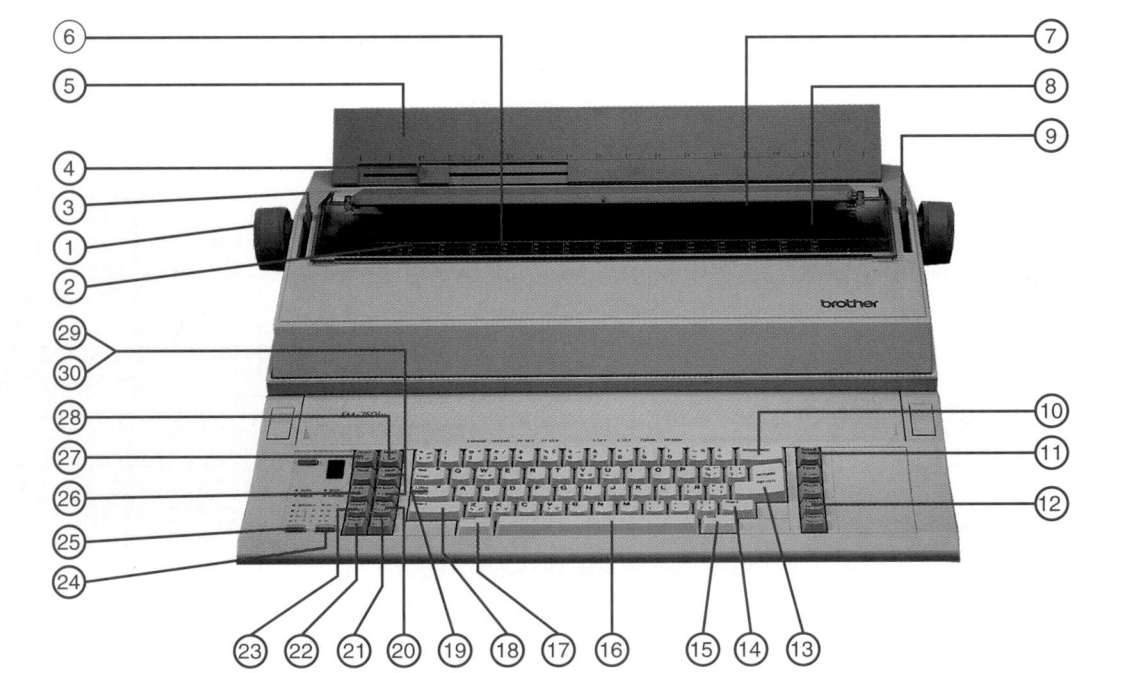

1. Left platen knob
2. Line-of-writing (margin) scale
3. Paper-bail release lever
4. Paper guide
5. Paper support
6. Print carrier
7. Paper bail
8. Platen (cylinder)
9. Paper release lever
10. Backspace key
11. Paper insert
12. Relocate (RELOC) key*
13. Return key
14. Right shift key
15. Correction key
16. Space bar

17. Code key
18. Left shift key
19. Caps lock key
20. Tab set*
21. Repeat
22. Bold key
23. Underline (UNDLN) key
24. Pitch select key
25. Line-space select key
26. Centering key
27. Auto*
28. Margin release*
29. Left margin (L MAR)
30. Right margin (R MAR)
31. Tabulator (Tab)*

*Key that performs special functions when depressed together with the CODE key

PARTS OF THE MICROCOMPUTER

All microcomputers are basically similar. However, the exact location and function of the keys illustrated may vary with your choice of both hardware (microcomputer and other physcial equipment) and software (program for the computer).

The RETURN/ENTER key performs much as the carrier return of an electric typewriter (the cursor moves to the left margin and down to the next line); however, the key is also used to save information and perform other specialized functions.

The CURSOR/HOME KEY returns the cursor to its home position.

The FUNCTION KEYS are a bank of keys for special use with various software.

The NUMERIC KEYPAD often functions as a bank of special keys or as a 10-key number pad.

The CONTROL key is one which is struck simultaneously with another key to make the latter perform a special function.

The PRINT SCREEN key is used to produce a hard or paper copy of the work on screen or in computer memory.

Other keys enumerated below are similar or identical in function to those of a typewriter.

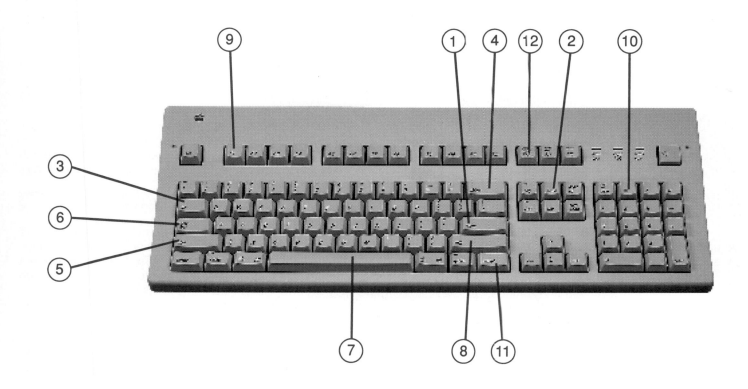

1. RETURN or RETURN/ENTER key
2. HOME key
3. TAB key
4. BACKSPACE/DELETE key
5. Right SHIFT key
6. CAPS LOCK key
7. Space bar
8. Left SHIFT key
9. Function keys
10. Numeric keypad
11. CONTROL key
12. PRINT SCREEN key

PREPARING TO KEY

Operating a computer or a typewriter involves much more than just learning to strike the keys. The information given on these pages will help you get ready to key and will help you to make the necessary machine adjustments. If you are using a computer, you will need to refer to your operator's guide or user's manual for detailed instructions regarding bringing up the system, setting the margins, and spacing with your specific type of hardware and software.

The numbers in parentheses that follow the names of machine parts are those assigned to the parts as shown on pages x and xi.

ADJUSTING THE PAPER GUIDE

The paper guide (No. 4) is used to guide the left edge of the paper into the machine. Move the guide to the left or right until it lines up with 0 on the line-of-writing scale (No. 2). Before beginning to key each day, check to see that the paper guide is on 0.

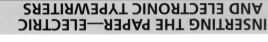

INSERTING THE PAPER—ELECTRIC AND ELECTRONIC TYPEWRITERS

1. Place the paper to the left of your machine.
2. Lift the paper bail (No. 7) or pull it forward away from the platen (No. 8).
3. Grasp the paper with your left hand. Drop the bottom edge of the paper behind the platen (No. 8) and against the paper support (No. 5). The left edge of the paper should be against the paper guide (No. 4).
4. **Electric Typewriter—With** your right hand, twirl the right platen knob with a quick move- ment of your fingers rolling the

paper into the machine. You may also strike the index key until the paper appears above the aligning scale.

Electronic Typewriter—With your right index finger (j finger), strike the paper insert key (No. 11). The paper will feed into your machine to a preset point.

5. Determine whether or not the paper needs to be straight- ened by moving the paper up until the top and bottom edges may be placed together to "square the edges." If the paper does need straightening, pull the paper release lever (No. 9) toward you (or upward on some machines), straighten the paper, and push the paper release lever back.
6. Adjust the paper bail (No. 7) so that it holds the paper against the platen (No. 8). Slide the rubber paper bail rolls into positions that divide the paper into thirds.

Computers—Follow the setup directions for your printer. Your teacher will tell you when you are to begin printing your work.

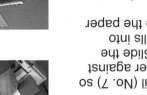
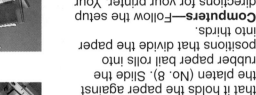
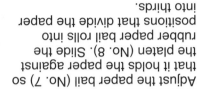
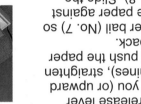
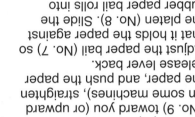
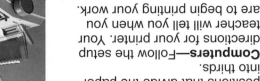

Most computer programs use automatic settings for margins, line spacing, tabs, and other machine adjustments. These automatic settings are based on common business usage, and they are referred to as "defaults." You may have a need in certain situations to change some of these defaults. If such changes are needed, consult your operator's guide or user's manual for detailed instructions for the type of equipment and software you may be using.

SETTING THE LINE-SPACE SELECTOR

Many machines offer three choices for line spacing—1, 1$\frac{1}{2}$, and 2. These choices are indicated by bars or numbers on the line-space selector (No. 25). Set the line-space selector on "1" to single-space (SS) or on "2" to double-space (DS). To quadruple-space (QS) set the line-space selector on "1" and then operate the return key four times, or set the line-space selector on "2" and operate the return key twice.

With most computers, line-spacing is automatically set for "1." This is known as a "default" setting. If you wish to change this setting, you should refer to your operator's guide or user's manual for detailed instructions on this procedure for your equipment and software.

SIZE OF TYPE—PICA OR ELITE

Some machines are equipped with pica type and some with elite. Pica is larger and has 10 spaces or characters to a horizontal inch; elite has 12 spaces or characters to a horizontal inch. When you insert a sheet of 8$\frac{1}{2}$" x 11" paper into your machine (with the paper guide on 0) and the number of the line-of-writing scale (No. 2) at the right edge of the paper is 85, your machine has pica type. If the number indicated at the right edge of your paper is 102, your machine has elite type. The spaces on the line-of-writing scale are matched to the spacing mechanism of the machine.

Pica: **kdkdkdkdkd**   (10 characters)

|←— 1 inch —→|

Elite: kdkdkdkdkdkd   (12 characters)

CENTERING POINT

If 8$\frac{1}{2}$" x 11" paper is inserted against the edge of the paper guide (No. 4), and if the paper guide is set at 0, the centering point for a pica machine will be 42 on the line-of-writing scale (No. 2), and the centering point for an elite machine will be 51. To find the center of paper that may be smaller or larger than the traditional 8$\frac{1}{2}$" x 11" size, first insert the paper into the machine; add the margin numbers at the left and right edges of the paper; and divide by 2. The resulting number is the horizontal center point of the paper.

CLEARING AND SETTING THE TABULATOR STOPS

● **Tab Clear Key**

To clear the tabulator stops, depress the TAB CLEAR key. On electronic typewriters, use the TAB key (No. 31) plus the CODE key (No. 17) and hold it down as you move the carrier the full width of your machine. To clear an individual stop without clearing others, tabulate to that stop and depress the TAB CLEAR key.

● **Tab Set Key**

To set the tabulator stops, move the carrier to the desired tab stop position; then depress the TAB SET key (No. 20).

Repeat this procedure to set as many tabulator stops as are needed.

With most computers, tabulator stops are automatically set every five spaces. This is known as a default setting. If you need to change these stops, refer to your operator's guide or user's manual for the instructions for this process.

PLANNING THE SIDE MARGIN SETTINGS

In the past, margins have been set by "spaces to a line." Current trend, however, is to use "inches in left and right margins" as the guide for setting margins. Margin stops may be set for any length of line desired such as 50, 60, or 70 spaces; or, they may be set to have side margins of $\frac{1}{2}$", 1", $1\frac{1}{2}$", or 2". Because this is a time of transition in keyboard-ing, the guides for setting margins are shown below in terms of both inches and spaces.

To have equal left and right margins when setting the margins by "inches in left and right margin," follow these two steps:

1. For the left margin, set the margin stop the correct number of inches (10 spaces to an inch for pica; 12 spaces for elite) from the left edge of the page.
2. For the right margin, set the margin stop the correct number of inches, plus 5 spaces for the end-of-line signal, from the right edge of the page.

Most computers have preset default margins of 1". Consult your operator's guide or user's manual if you wish to change these default margins.

Side Margin	Elite (12 pitch) Left Margin	Elite (12 pitch) Right Margin	Pica (10 pitch) Left Margin	Pica (10 pitch) Right Margin
$\frac{1}{2}$"	6	96 + 5 (90-space line length)	5	80 + 5 (75-space line length)
1"	12	90 + 5 (78-space line length)	10	75 + 5 (65-space line length)
$1\frac{1}{2}$"	18	84 + 5 (66-space line length)	15	70 + 5 (55-space line length)
2"	24	78 + 5 (54-space line length)	20	65 + 5 (45-space line length)

To have equal left and right margins when setting the margins by "spaces to a line," follow these two steps:

1. Subtract half the line length from the center point (42 for pica; 51 for elite). Set the left margin stop at this point.
2. Add half the line length, plus 5 spaces for the end-of-line signal, to the center point. Set the right margin at this point.

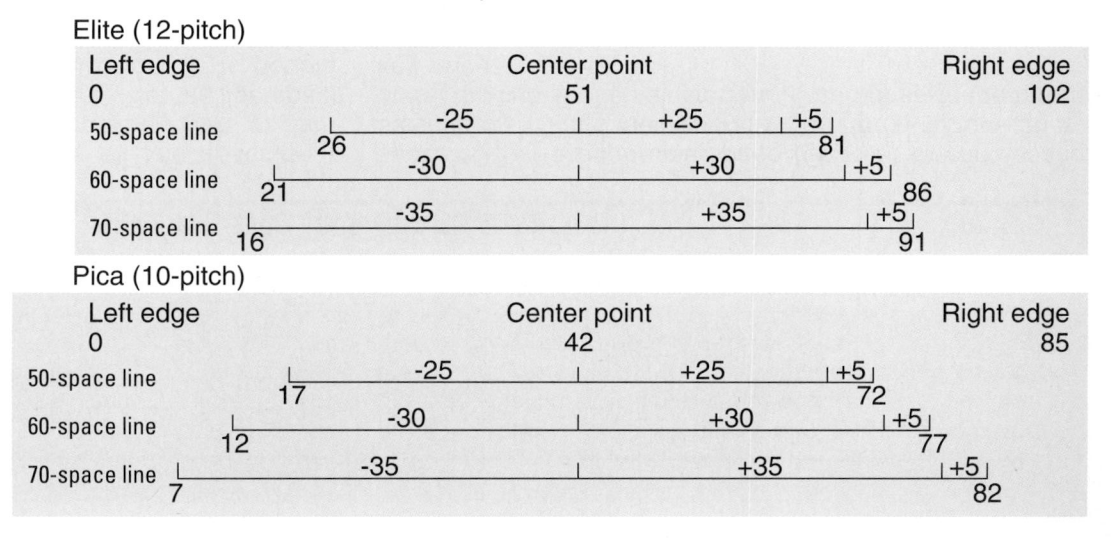

SETTING THE MARGIN STOPS

The following general information gives the steps for setting the margin stops. The procedures for your specific machine may vary, however.

● **Key-Set Margins**

1. Move the carrier to the left margin stop. Depress and hold the margin set key while moving the carrier to the desired position.
2. Release the margin set key.
3. Set the right margin in the same manner.

● **Push-Lever Margins**

1. Push in on the left margin lever and slide it to the desired position.
2. Release the left margin lever set.
3. Set the right margin in the same manner.

● **Push-Button Margins**

1. Push down on the left margin button, and slide it to the desired position.

2. Release the margin set button.
3. Set the right margin in the same manner.

● **Electronically Set Margins**

To set margins on some electronic machines, space to the desired margin position and strike the appropriate (left or right) margin key.

On other machines, space to the desired margin position and strike the CODE key and the appropriate margin key at the same time.

Computers
Most computers have automatically preset default margins. If you need to change these default margins, refer to your operator's guide or user's manual for instructions.

PLANNING THE TOP AND BOTTOM MARGINS

When you format reports, letters, memorandums, and other documents, you will need to leave appropriate top and bottom margins on your page. These margins are always determined in inches. On both pica and elite machines, there are six vertical lines to an inch. The table shown below should aid you in determining the correct number of blank lines to leave for top and bottom margins. For example, for a 1" top margin, you would leave 6 blank lines and begin keying on line 7; for a 2" margin, leave 12 blank lines and begin keying on line 13.

TOP AND BOTTOM MARGIN CONVERSION TABLE

Inches	Lines
$\frac{1}{2}$"	3 blank lines
1"	6 blank lines
$1\frac{1}{2}$"	9 blank lines
2"	12 blank lines

PROPER STROKING

Keystroking action should be centered in your fingers:
1. Keep your fingers deeply curved.
2. Use a quick, firm, sharp stroke.
3. Release the keys quickly by snapping the fingers toward the palm of the hand.

BASIC TECHNIQUES—POSITION OF HANDS

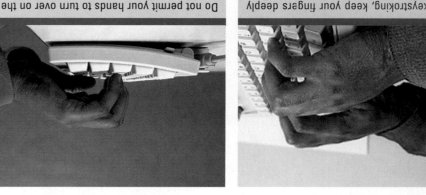

When keystroking, keep your fingers deeply curved. Your fingernails should be kept trimmed. Rest your fingers very lightly on the home keys.

Do not permit your hands to turn over on the little fingers. Hold your hands directly over the keys. Turn the hands slightly inward.

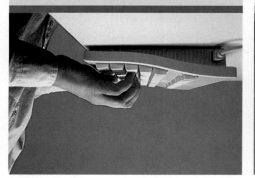

Do not buckle your wrists upward. Hold your wrists down near, but not resting on, the front frame of your machine. Keep your forearms parallel with the keyboard.

THE CORRECTING OF ERRORS

Errors that are made in documents should be corrected. The following methods may be used:

● **Computer**

Incorrect characters are removed from the screen with the backspace or delete key.

● **Electronic Typewriter**

A special key is often used to remove errors from an electronic window.

● **Typewriter**

Four methods may be used.

Automatic Correction Tape—When a special correction key is depressed, the tape will lift the error off the page.

Correction Paper—Backspace to the beginning of the error; insert the correction paper between the ribbon and the error; rekey the error exactly as it was made; remove the paper; backspace to the point where the correction began, and key the new copy.

Correction Liquid—Turn the platen up a few spaces; apply a small amount of the liquid over the entire error; allow the liquid to dry completely; turn the platen to its original position; then key the correction.

Eraser—Move the carrier to the right or left; roll the paper up; hold it firmly against the platen while erasing the error; brush eraser crumbs from the machine; roll the paper down and key the correction.

Preparing Carbon Copies

If a copy machine is not available, copies of a document may be made with carbon paper. Use the following steps to prepare such copies:

Step 1—Place the carbon paper (glossy side down) on a sheet of plain paper. The paper on which you will prepare the original is then laid on top of the carbon paper.

Step 2—Place the sheets between the cylinder and the paper support. The glossy side of the carbon should be up. Roll into the machine. The dull surface of the carbon should now be up.

CORRECTING ERRORS ON CARBON COPIES

When correcting an error on the original of a carbon pack, a 5" by 3" card should be placed in front of the first carbon sheet to avoid smudges. Even though correction tape or liquid may be used to correct the original, an eraser is often used for correcting the carbon copies. Remove the error on the copy with a soft pencil eraser. If more than one carbon copy is being made, place the card between each copy being erased and the next sheet of carbon paper as the erasure is being done. When the error has been erased on all copies, remove the card, position the carrier to the proper point, and key the correction. When you complete all erasing, brush the eraser crumbs away from the machine.

TAKING CARE OF YOUR TYPEWRITER OR COMPUTER

You can help take care of your machine in various ways. Keep your desk free of dust, and brush the dirt and dust from the keys. Cover your machine when it is not in use. Shut off the power on an electric typewriter after each use. Your teacher will tell you whether or not you should shut off your power on a computer or leave the power on for students in other classes. If your teacher tells you to do so, clean your keys and other parts of your typewriter each week. Use an approved cleaning fluid. You will want to take special care of any diskette you may be using with a computer. Do not bend or fold a disk, and do not touch exposed areas of it. Use only felt-tipped pens when writing on disk labels. Use special care when inserting a disk into and removing it from a disk drive. Store a disk in an envelope when it is not in use. Keep a disk away from direct sunlight and magnets.

COMMON PROOFREADER'S MARKS

∧ or ∨	Insert	⌐	Move right	∿	Transpose
⊙	Insert period	⌐	Move left	#	Space
∨	Insert apostrophe	Cap or =	Capitalize	¶	Paragraph
‿	Close up	ℰ	Delete	/ or lc	Lowercase

STATE ABBREVIATIONS

Alabama, AL	Illinois, IL	Nebraska,NE	Rhode Island, RI
Alaska, AK	Indiana, IN	Nevada, NV	South Carolina, SC
Arizona, AZ	Iowa, IA	New Hampshire, NH	South Dakota, SD
Arkansas, AR	Kansas, KS	New Jersey, NJ	Tennessee, TN
California, CA	Kentucky, KY	New Mexico, NM	Texas, TX
Colorado, CO	Louisiana, LA	New York, NY	Utah, UT
Connecticut, CT	Maine, ME	North Carolina, NC	Vermont, VT
Delaware, DE	Maryland, MD	North Dakota, ND	Virgin Islands, VI
District of Columbia, DC	Massachusetts, MA	Ohio, OH	Virginia, VA
Florida, FL	Michigan, MI	Oklahoma, OK	Washington, WA
Georgia, GA	Minnesota, MN	Oregon, OR	West Virginia, WV
Guam, GU	Mississippi, MS	Pennsylvania, PA	Wisconsin, WI
Hawaii, HI	Missouri, MO	Puerto Rico, PR	Wyoming, WY
Idaho, ID	Montana, MT		

ADDRESSING ENVELOPES

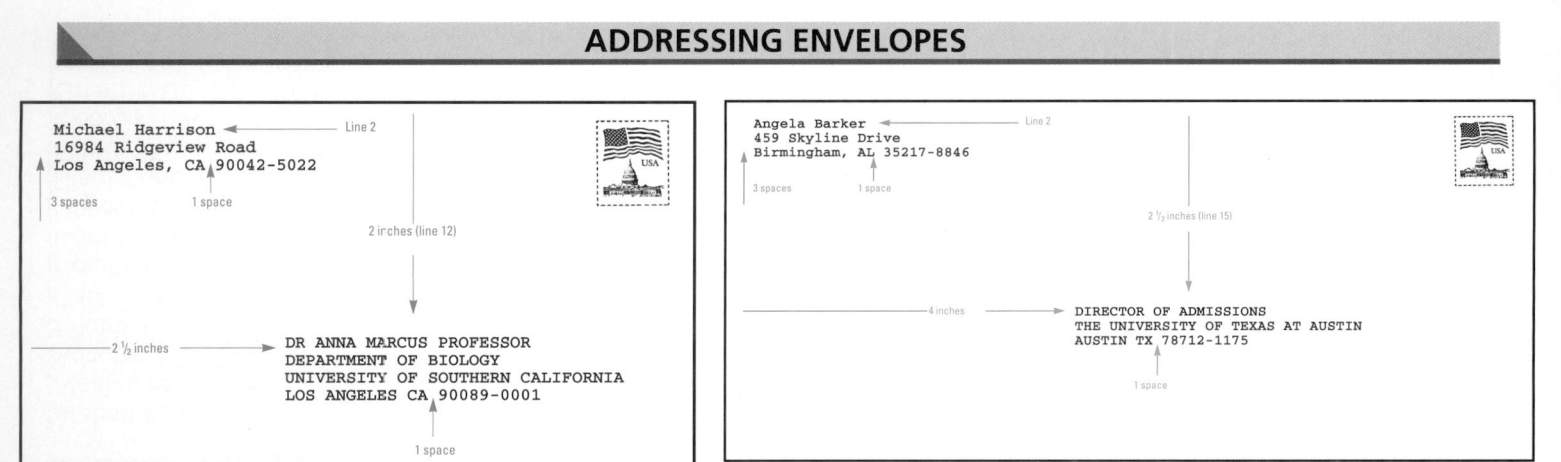

Small (No. 6³/₄) envelope (6¹/₂" x 3⁵/₈")

Large (No. 10) envelope (9 1/2" x 4 1/8")

Guidelines from the U.S. Postal Service show that every word in the address is written in all capital letters with no punctuation. This is preferred for the envelope address because optical character recognition (OCR) equipment is used to sort and process mail.

FOLDING LETTERS FOR ENVELOPES

Small Envelopes

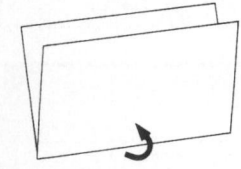 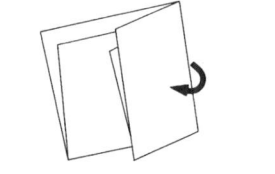 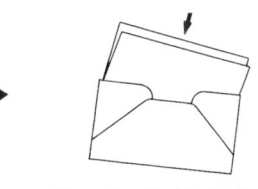

Step 1—Fold the lower edge of the letter to within half an inch of the top.

Step 2—Fold from right to left making the fold about one third the width of the sheet.

Step 3—Fold from left to right, leaving about a half-inch margin at the right in order that the letter may be opened easily.

Step 4—Insert the letter into the envelope so that the left-hand creased edge is inserted first and the last side folded is toward the backside of the envelope.

Large Envelopes

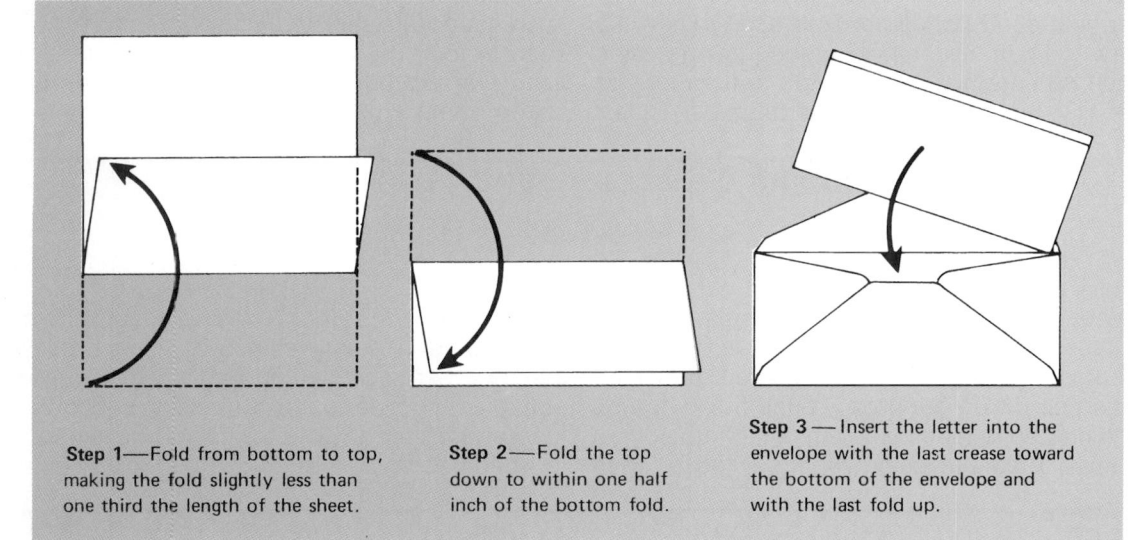

Step 1—Fold from bottom to top, making the fold slightly less than one third the length of the sheet.

Step 2—Fold the top down to within one half inch of the bottom fold.

Step 3— Insert the letter into the envelope with the last crease toward the bottom of the envelope and with the last fold up.

Personal business letter in modified block style

▼ Mixed punctuation is used in
▼ this letter. A colon follows the
▼ salutation, and a comma fol-
▼ lows the complimentary
▼ close.

Line 14

Return address ——— (Center point) ——→ 459 West Skyline Drive
Dateline ———————————————→ Birmingham, AL 35217-8846
September 16, 19--

Operate return
4 times (QS)

Letter address ——→ Director of Admissions
The University of Texas at Austin
Austin, TX 78712-1175
QS
Salutation ——→ Dear Director:
QS
SS I am interested in applying for admission to
your university for next fall. Please send
me all of the forms that I will need to com-
plete and return to you when I apply.

Body of
letter ——→ Also, please send me current information
about fees and living expenses. I am especially interested in knowing the cost of
out-of-state tuition since I am not a resi-
dent of Texas. I would also appreciate
2' information on scholarships, grants, and   2'
margin loans that are available.   margin

Your cooperation will be most appreciated.

Complimentary
close ————————→ Sincerely,

Operate return
4 times (QS)

Signature ——————→ *Angela Barker*
Typewritten
name ——————————→ Miss Angela Barker

▼ In the modified block style let-
▼ ter, the paragraphs may be
▼ blocked, or they may be
▼ indented five spaces.

Personal business letter in modified block style (Shown in pica type)

Business letter in block style

Business letter in block style
(Shown in pica type)

TAYLOR AND ASSOCIATES, INC.
1836 River Drive
Savannah, GA 31402-1836
(912) 324-4312

March 17, 19-- ◄——— Line 16

QS

Mr. Frank M. Mitchell, Manager◄—————— First line of letter address
Information Services Department   on fourth line space (QS)
Letter address ——→ Harrison Insurance Services   below the date line
8970 Harrison Road
Savannah, GA 31402-8970
QS
Salutation ——→ Dear Mr. Mitchell
QS
Thank you for your interest in our services. I believe
that I may be able to help you with the communication
functions in your company, specifically regarding the
implementation of the block letter style.
QS
I think you will be pleased with this style for your
Body of letter ——→ company correspondence. As you can see, I use it
for my own correspondence. The form has become very
popular because of its efficiency. The date line,
letter address, salutation, and closing lines are
all formatted to begin at the left margin.
Paragraphs are not indented.

1½' margin The block letter style is often combined with the   1½' margin
open punctuation style as illustrated in this let-
ter. Consequently, no mark of punctuation follows
the salutation or the complimentary close. However,
the mixed punctuation style is also acceptable to
use with the block letter format.

Please let me know if there are additional ways that
I might help you with your communication needs.
Compli-   QS
mentary ——→ Sincerely
close
(words in body 186)

Susan Monson ◄——————— Handwritten name (Signature)

Typewritten name
and title ——→ Susan Monson, Consultant ◄———— Name of writer is shown in keyed
Reference   QS   form 4 spaces (QS) below the compli-
initials ——→ xx   mentary close.

The writer's title may either follow the typewritten
name or be placed on the line below, depending on
the length of the name and the title.

First page of two-page leftbound report with internal citations

Line 13

Center title over line ——————→ THE USE OF REFERENCES IN REPORTS
of writing   QS

Indent paragraphs ——→ The basic purpose of a report is to provide detailed
information on a specific subject. Most writers are not
able to draw all the needed facts from their own minds or
their own experiences. Therefore, they must get help from
1 1/2' left margin outside sources. This help usually comes in the form of the   1" right
knowledge of others that has been published in books and   margin
magazines. If a writer uses information from others, credit
must be given to them.

Two authorities on report writing (Bovee and Thill,
Internal citation with ——→ 1992, 487) believe that "You have an ethical and a legal
short quotation
(fewer than four   obligation to give other people credit for their work."
lines)   Kuiper and Luke (1992, 200) say "An ethical researcher ac-
knowledges the sources that have contributed unique information to a research project." They also suggest that:
DS
Long quotation ——→ Report writers generally do not cite sources of in-
(four or more lines)   formation that is general knowledge among the primary
SS readers of the report; but the more specific the data
Single-spaced and   are, the greater is the need to provide source ci-
indented 5 spaces   tations.
from left margin   DS
The giving of credit to one's sources is known as citing or documenting. In addition to citing in order to avoid
the problem of plagiarism, documenting is done for other
reasons. For example, documentation supports statements.
Two other experts (Himstreet and Baity, 1990, 542) say that

At least 1"

First page of two-page leftbound report with internal citations
(Shown in pica type)

Second page of two-page leftbound report with references

Line 7   2
QS
1 1/2' left margin "If recognized authorities have said the same thing, your
work takes on credibility; and you put yourself in good
company."

What is the most effective way to cite material? A
writer has the option of using footnotes, endnotes, or any
other acceptable method of crediting the contributors who
helped provide information for the report. The simplest approach to documentation is internal citation: the last
name(s) of the author(s), the date of the publication, and
the page number(s) are given within the text material at the
point the information is cited. At the end of the report,
detailed references are listed alphabetically.   1" right
margin
The specific method used for documenting is not the
most important issue, however. The writer must maintain
ethical standards. The main point to remember is that credit
should be given where credit is due.

QS
Center over line of writing ——→ REFERENCES
DS
Bovee, Courtland L., and John V. Thill. *Business Communica-*
SS   *tion Today.* Third Edition. New York: McGraw-Hill,
Inc., 1992.
DS
Himstreet, William C., and Wayne Murlin Baty. *Business*
Communications. Ninth Edition. Boston: PWS-Kent Pub-
lishing Company, 1990.

Kuiper, Shirley, and Cheryl M. Luke. *Report Writing with*
Microcomputer Applications. Cincinnati: South-Western
Publishing Co., 1992.

At least 1"

Second page of two-page leftbound report with references
(Shown in pica type)

GUIDES FOR CAPITALIZATION, SPACING, NUMBER-EXPRESSION, WORD-DIVISION, AND PUNCTUATION

● Capitalization Guides

Capitalize:
1. The first word of a complete sentence.
2. The first word of a complete direct quotation. (Do not capitalize fragments of a quotation or a quotation resumed within a sentence.)
3. Languages and numbered school courses, but not the names of other school subjects.
4. The pronoun *I*, both alone and in contractions.
5. Titles of organizations, institutions, and buildings.
6. Days of the week, months of the year, and holidays, but not seasons
7. Names of rivers, oceans, and mountains.
8. *North, South,* etc., when they name particular parts of the country, but not when they refer to directions.
9. Names of religious groups, political parties, nations, nationalities, and races.
10. All proper names and the adjectives made from them.
11. The names of stars, planets, and constellations, except the sun, moon, and earth unless these are used with other astronomical names.
12. A title when it immediately precedes a person's name
13. First words and all other words in titles of books, articles, periodicals, headings, and plays, except words which are articles, conjunctions, and prepositions.
14. The first word, all titles, salutatory words, and proper names used in the salutation of a business letter.
15. Only the first word of the complimentary close.
16. All titles appearing in the address of a letter.
17. The title following the name of the writer in the closing lines of a letter.

● Spacing Guides

1. Space twice after a period that ends a sentence, except when the period comes at the end of a line. When it does, return the carrier/cursor without spacing.
2. Space twice after a question mark at the end of a sentence.
3. Space twice after an exclamation point at the end of a sentence.
4. Space twice after a colon except in stating time.
5. Space once after a semicolon or comma.
6. Space once after a period that ends an abbreviation but twice if that period ends a sentence. (Do not space after a period within an abbreviation.)
7. Space once between a whole number and a "made" fraction.
8. Do not space between the $ and the number which follows it.
9. Do not space before or after the diagonal.
10. Do not space between a number and a following %.

● Number-Expression Guides

1. Key even sums of money without decimals or zeros.
2. Key distance in figures.
3. Use figures to key dates. When the day comes before the month, use a figure and follow it with *th, st,* or *d.*
4. Spell a number beginning a sentence even though figures may be used later in the sentence.
5. Use figures with a.m. and p.m. Use words with o'clock.
6. Key amounts of money, either dollars or cents, in figures.
7. Key policy numbers without commas.
8. In ordinary text, numbers from one to ten are spelled out while larger numbers appear as figures. If a sentence contains a series of numbers, any of which is over ten, use all figures.

● Word-Division Guides

Divide:
1. Words only between syllables.
2. Hyphenated compounds at the point of the hyphen; for example, *self-control.*
3. Words so the *cial, tial, cion, sion,* or *tion* are retained as a unit.
4. A word that ends in double letters after the double letters when a suffix is added, such as *fill-ing.*
5. A word in which the final consonant is doubled when a suffix is added between the double letters, such as *control-ling.*

Do not:
1. Divide words of one syllable, such as *thought, friend,* or *caught.*
2. Separate a syllable of one letter at the beginning of a word, such as *across.*
3. Separate a syllable of one or two letters at the end of a word, such as *ready, greatly,* or *greeted.*
4. Divide words of five or fewer letters, such as *also, into, duty,* or *excel.*
5. Divide a word between two pages.

11. Do not space between parentheses and the material they enclose.
12. Do not space before the apostrophe or between it and the "s" which shows possession.
13. Do not space between quotation marks and the material they enclose.
14. Do not space before or after a dash.
15. Do not space before or after the hyphen in a hyphenated word.

● **Apostrophe**

1. Use an apostrophe in writing contractions.
2. *It's* means it is. *Its*, the possessive pronoun, does not use an apostrophe.
3. Use the contraction *o'clock* (of the clock) in writing time.
4. Add 's to form the possessive of any singular noun.
5. Add 's to plural nouns that do not end in s.
6. If a plural noun does end in s, add only an apostrophe after the s.
7. The apostrophe denotes possession. Do not use it merely to form the plural of a noun.
8. Use 's to form the plural of figures, letters, and signs.

● **Colon**

1. Use a colon to introduce a list of items or expressions.
2. Use a colon to separate the hours and minutes when they are expressed in figures.
3. Use a colon to introduce a long quotation (four lines or more).

● **Comma**

1. Use a comma after each item in a series, except the last.
2. Use a comma to separate consecutive adjectives when the *and* has seemingly been omitted. Do not use the comma when the adjectives do not apply equally to the noun they modify.
3. Use a comma to separate a dependent clause that precedes the main clause.
4. Use a comma to separate the independent parts of a compound sentence joined by *and, but, for, or, neither, nor*.
5. Use a comma to set off a restrictive phrase at the beginning of a sentence or to separate identical words.
6. Use a comma to set off a direct and complete quotation from the rest of the sentence.
7. Do not set off an indirect quotation from the rest of the sentence.
8. Use commas to set off parenthetic expressions that break the flow of a sentence. If the parenthetic expression begins or ends a sentence, use one comma.
9. Use a comma after an interjection, such as *yes, no, well, now*.
10. Use commas to set off the name of the person addressed.
11. Use commas to set off appositives that are not restrictive of the noun to which they are in apposition. For example: My wife, Edna, is home. My son John is not.
12. Use commas to separate a date from the year and the name of a city from the name of the state.

● **Dash and Parentheses**

1. Use a dash to show a sudden break in thought.
2. Use a dash before the name of an author when it immediately follows a direct quotation.
3. Use parentheses to enclose an explanation.

● **Period, Question Mark, Exclamation Point**

1. Use a period after a sentence making a statement or giving a command.
2. Use a period after each initial.
3. Use a period after most abbreviations. (Nicknames are not followed by periods.)
4. Use a question mark after a question.
5. Use an exclamation point to express strong or sudden feeling.

● **Quotation Marks**

1. Place quotation marks around the exact works of a speaker.
2. When the quotation is broken to identify the speaker, put quotation marks around each part. If the second part of the quotation is a new sentence, use a capital letter.
3. Use no quotation marks with an indirect quotation.
4. Use quotation marks around the titles of articles, songs, poems, themes, short stories, and other items which are parts of the whole or would not be bound on their own.
5. Always place the period or comma within the quotation marks.

● **Semicolon**

1. Use a semicolon between the clauses of a compound sentence when no conjunction is used. (If a conjunction is used to join the clauses, but there is a comma contained in one or both clauses, use a semicolon before the conjunction.)
2. Use a semicolon between the clauses of a compound sentence that are joined by such words as *also, however, therefore,* and *consequently*. (The semicolon precedes the connecting word, and a comma follows the word.)
3. Use a semicolon between a series of phrases or clauses that are dependent upon a main clause.

FREQUENTLY REFERENCED GUIDELINES

The following formatting guidelines appear throughout the book. They are also placed here for the convenience of students who may need to make frequent references to them.

Horizontal Centering Steps

Centering material so that there will be equal left and right margins is called horizontal centering.

In order to center lines on odd-size paper, you must first learn how to find the center point.

1. Insert the paper into the machine.
2. Add the margin numbers at the left and right edges of the paper, and divide the total by 2. The resulting number is the horizontal center point of the paper. Begin your backspacing from that point for all centering.

Step 1—Check the placement of the paper guide to see that is set on 0. Turn to page 5 and read the directions for adjusting the paper guide.

Step 2—Move to the center point. When using 8 $\frac{1}{2}$" x 11" standard size paper, use 51 as the center point for elite and 42 as the center point for pica type.

Step 3—Backspace once for every two letters or spaces in the line to be centered. If there is one letter left over, do not backspace for it. Begin to key.

If you are using a computer or an electronic typewriter, your teacher may give you different instructions for horizontal centering. With word processing software, centering may be accomplished automatically.

Vertical Centering Steps

Centering copy on a page so that there are equal top and bottom margins is called vertical centering.

Step 1—Count the lines in the copy to be centered. Be sure to count all blank lines in double spacing.

Step 2—Subtract the total lines from the lines available on the paper you are using. There are 6 lines to a vertical inch; therefore, when using standard size paper, 8 1/2" by 11", a half sheet with the long side up has 33 lines and a full sheet 66 lines.

Step 3—After subtracting, you will know exactly how many blank lines you will have on the paper. Divide these remaining lines by 2. Disregard any fraction. The answer is the number of blank lines in the top and bottom margins.

If you are directed to center the problem in reading position, subtract 2 lines from the normal top margin attained in Step 3; then move on to Step 4. Reading position is used only when formatting on a full sheet of paper.

Step 4—Insert your paper so that the top edge is exactly even with the alignment scale. Roll the paper up the proper number of lines (the answer from Step 3). Begin to key on the next line so that you retain the correct number of blank lines in the top margin.

 If you are using a computer, your teacher may give you different instructions for vertical centering. With word processing software, vertical centering may be done automatically.

Step 1—Set the line spacing for single spacing.

Step 2—Set the side margins. These will vary according to the length of the letter. Use 2" margins for short letters (up to 100 five-stroke words in the body); $1\frac{1}{2}$" for average letters (101-200 words); 1" for long letters (201-300 words) and for two-page letters (more than 300 words). The Letter Placement Guide shown below will help you with margin settings.

Step 3—Space down to line 14 to begin the writer's return address. This is a standard placement suggested for use with personal business letters in this book. However, the number of lines to space down can vary according to the length of the letter. This point can be raised for longer letters or lowered for shorter letters. For a block style letter (see the illustration on page 100), start the return address at the left margin. For a modified block style letter (see the illustration on page 103), start the return address at the center point of the paper.

Step 4—Place the date (month, day, year) a single space (SS) below the last line of the return address.

Step 5—Place the letter address on the fourth (QS) line space below the date.

Step 6—Begin the salutation (greeting) a double space (DS) below the letter address.

Step 7—Start the body of the letter (message) a double space (DS) below the salutation. In the block style, the paragraphs are always blocked at the left margin. In the modified block style, paragraphs may be blocked or they may be indented. Single-space the paragraphs and double space between them.

Step 8—Begin the complimentary close (farewell) a double space below the last line of the body. For block style, start at the left margin. For modified block style, start at the center point of the page.

Step 9—Key the name of the writer on the fourth line space (QS) below the complimentary close. The writer's handwritten name (signature) should be placed between the complimentary close and the typewritten name.

Step 10—If something is being enclosed within the letter (check, order form, etc.) key the word Enclosure or Enclosures a double space below the writer's name.

LETTER PLACEMENT GUIDE

Letter Classification	5-Stroke Words in Letter Body	Side Margins	Margin Settings	
			Elite	Pica
Short	Up to 100	2"	24–78"	20–65"
Average	101–200	$1\frac{1}{2}$"	18–84"	15–70"
Long	201–300	1"	12–90"	10–75"
Two-Page	More than 300	1"	12–90"	10–75"

*plus 5 spaces for end-of-line signal

Punctuation Styles for Letters—Letters may be formatted in *open* or *mixed* punctuation.

Open Punctuation—In this style there is no colon following the salutation and no comma following the complimentary close.

Mixed Punctuation—In this style a colon is placed after the salutation and a comma is placed after the complimentary close.

Formatting Guides for Business Letters

Letter Styles—The two most widely used letter styles are the block and the modified block. They are illustrated on pages 125 and 128.

Punctuation Styles—The two most commonly used punctuation styles are open and mixed. In open, no punctuation marks are used after the salutation or the complimentary close. In mixed, a colon is placed after the salutation and a comma after the complimentary close.

Stationery—Most business letters are prepared on standard-size ($8\frac{1}{2}$" by 11") letterhead paper with the company name, address, and telephone number printed at the top.

Envelopes—Most firms use large envelopes (No. 10) for one-page letters, although small envelopes (No. 6 3/4) may be used. A large envelope should be used, however, for two-page letters and when items are enclosed. Company envelopes usually have the return address printed in the upper left corner.

Copies—One or more copies are usually made of business letters. They are usually made by a photocopier, but may be done with carbon paper.

Margins—Many business firms use standard margin defaults set on computers for all letters. To make the letter appear more balanced on the page, however, margins which vary according to the length of the letter should be used. Use the following chart for letters in this unit.

> 🖥 **Computer:** Use standard default unless your teacher directs you to change margins.

Length 5-Stroke Words		Side Margin Setting	Margins in Letter Body		Dateline
			Pica	Elite	in Letter Body
Short	Up to 100	2"	24-78*	20-65*	18
Avg.	101-200	1½"	18-84	15-70*	16
Long	201-300	1"	12-90*	10-75*	14
2-page	More than 300	1"	12-90*	10-75*	14

* Add 5 spaces for end-of-line signal.

Basic Letter Parts—The various parts of a business letter are described in order of their occurrence.

Heading—This part is printed as a letterhead at the top of the paper and includes the name, address, and telephone number of the company.

Date—Vertical placement of the dateline varies according to the letter length. If a deep letterhead prevents placing the date on the line indicated in the table, place it a DS below letterhead.

> 🖥 If you use default margins on your computer, you will need to place the dateline further down on the page when formatting short and average length letters.

Letter Address—This address should begin on the fourth line space (QS) below the date. A title (Mr., Mrs., Miss, Dr., etc.) should be used as a courtesy to the person to whom a letter is addressed. When a woman's preferred title is not known, use Ms. as her personal title. Use the standard two-letter state abbreviations as shown on page RG-6.

Salutation—The salutation (greeting) should be placed a double space (DS) below the letter address. If the letter is addressed to a company rather than an individual, the salutation Ladies and Gentlemen should be used.

Body—The body (message) of the letter begins a double space (DS) below the salutation. Paragraphs are single-spaced (SS) with a double space between them. They are most frequently blocked, but they may be indented in the modified block style letter.

Complimentary Close—The complimentary close (farewell) should be placed a double space below the body.

Name of the Writer—The name of the writer should be keyed on the fourth line space (QS) below the complimentary close. The title of the writer may be keyed on the same line as the writer's name, or the title may be keyed on the line below the writer's name. The name of the writer is signed between the complimentary close and the typewritten name.

Reference Initials—The initials of the keyboard operator are keyed a double space (DS) below the writer's name.

Enclosure Notation—The word Enclosure, which indicates that something is included with the letter, is placed a double space below the reference initials. Use the plural Enclosures if more than one item is enclosed.

Special Letter Parts—A letter may also contain one or more of certain special parts such as an attention line, a subject line, or a postscript. The correct placement of these parts is illustrated in the various lessons of Unit 11.

Formatting Guides For Interoffice Memorandums

The interoffice memorandum (memo) is used to send messages within a company or an organization. Its major advantages are that it is less structured and can be formatted quickly. Two styles of memorandums are commonly used: **formal** and **simplified**.

Form—Formatting guides for interoffice memorandums are listed below.
1. Use either a full or half sheet of paper.
2. Use block style.
3. Use 1" side margins.
4. Begin on line 7 (1" top margin) for half-page memorandums; begin on line 10 (1½" top margin) for full-page memorandums.
5. Omit personal titles (Mr., Ms., etc.) on the memo, but do include them on the company envelope. Use the person's business title for clarity.
6. SS the body, but DS between paragraphs.
7. Key reference initials a DS below the message. Other notations (such as Enclosure) are placed in the same position as in letters.

Formal Memorandums—Heading words, **TO, FROM, DATE,** and **SUBJECT** are keyed at the left margin followed by a colon and two spaces. Key the information following these guide words by aligning words one under the other. See the illustration on page 145. Begin on line 7 for a half sheet and line 10 for a full sheet.

Simplified Memorandums—Begin the date on line 7 for a half sheet and line 10 for a full sheet. DS between all parts of the simplified memorandum except after the date and after the last paragraph of the body. Quadruple space (QS) after the date and after the last paragraph of the body. Key the writer's name and business title a QS below the body. (See the model below for an example of this style.)

Envelopes—If a company interoffice envelope is not used, use a plain envelope and key COMPANY MAIL in the stamp position. On the envelope, include the receiver's personal title, name, and business title. Key the receiver's department a DS below the name.

	1"
Date	November 15, 19-- ◄——— line 7
	QS
Addressee	Carole Kim, Student Council President
	DS
Subject	All-school Assembly on December 5
	DS
Body	Mr. Daniel Petlin of the Office of Public Relations, Los Angeles Department of Water and Power, called me today to confirm his presentation at our all-school assembly on December 5. He will speak on the topic of "Water Conservation," and he will show a videotape on the subject. This should be a very interesting topic for all of us because of the severe shortage of water in our area.
	DS
1" ——►	Thank you for planning this assembly and for inviting Mr. Petlin ◄—— 1" to be the speaker.
	QS
Writer	Gary Packler, Principal

Simplified Memorandum, Block Format (Shown in pica type)

Formatting Leftbound Reports

Many reports are placed in ring binders or heavy paper covers with clasps. These are referred to as "leftbound" reports and an extra half inch of space is needed in the left margin for the "binding." Follow the directions shown below in preparing leftbound reports.

Margins—Set the margin stops for a 1½" left margin (pica, 15 spaces; elite, 18 spaces) and a 1" right margin (pica, 10 spaces; elite, 12 spaces).

Leave a top margin of 2" on the first page. A good standard placement for the title on both pica and elite machines is on line 13 from the top edge. Pages after the first should have a top margin of 1". Leave a bottom margin of at least 1" on all pages.

Spacing—The body of the report should be double-spaced, and paragraphs should be indented 5 spaces throughout the report.

Title—The title of the report should be centered in all capitals over the line of writing. To find the horizontal center for a leftbound report, add the numbers at the left and right margins and divide by 2. (This procedure places center 3 spaces to the right of the point normally used.) Quadruple-space (QS) after the title.

Quotations—Short quotations (fewer than four lines) should be placed within the text material and enclosed by quotation marks.

Long quotations (four or more lines) should be single-spaced and indented five spaces from the left margin. Double-space above and below the quotation.

Paging—The first page of the report is not numbered. On the second and following pages, the number is placed 1" from the top (line 7) at the right margin. Double-space below the number before keying the first line of the body of the report on that page.

When formatting a report that contains several pages, at least 2 lines of a paragraph should appear on the bottom of a page, and at least 2 lines should be carried over to the new page.

References—Reference notations to give credit to others for material taken from various sources may be accomplished by the use of internal citations, footnotes, or endnotes. The internal citation method is becoming very popular because it is more efficient to format. Internal citations should include the name(s) of the author(s), the date of the referenced publication, and the page number(s) of the material cited.

All references cited are listed alphabetically by author surname at the end of the report. These references may appear on a separate page or on the final page of the body of the report if enough lines are available.

If a separate reference page is used, the same margins should be employed as on the first page of the report. If the references appear at the bottom of the final page, a quadruple space (QS) should be placed after the last line of the report before centering the heading REFERENCES. A QS should follow this heading. Each reference is single-spaced with a double space between references. The first line of a reference begins at the left margin. All other lines are indented 5 spaces.

Directions for formatting footnotes and endnotes are given in Unit 14 and on page RG-16.

Formatting Footnotes, Endnotes, And Internal Citations

Several methods of acknowledging sources of quoted or closely paraphrased material are footnotes, endnotes, or internal citations. Follow the directions to format sources used in reports.

Footnotes—Number footnotes consecutively throughout a report. The number of the footnote reference should be keyed a half space above the line of writing immediately after the quoted material and a correspondingly numbered footnote at the bottom of the page. To determine vertical line space for copy to end and to place footnotes, follow these steps.

1. Allow 3 lines for divider rule and the blank line space above and below it, 3 lines for each note, and 6 lines for the bottom margin.
2. Subtract the sum of these figures from 66 (the number of lines on a full sheet). This will give you the last line on which text should be keyed.
3. After keying the last line of text, DS and key a 1 1/2" line (15, pica and 18, elite). DS and indent 5 spaces; key a superscript (raised 1/2 line space) number for the first note; follow with the reference material. DS and continue in the same manner for footnote 2.
4. Leave at least a 1" margin at bottom.

Computer: Many word processing software packages have a footnote and endnote function. If your teacher directs, use the procedure given in your software instructions to key footnotes and endnotes.

For equipment that does not permit half spacing, the reference figure may be keyed on the line of writing immediately preceded and followed by a diagonal:

```
...as reported." /1/ Other writers. . .
```

Endnotes—References to quoted or closely paraphrased material may be placed at the end of the report on a separate page. To format endnotes, follow these steps.

1. Use consecutively numbered superscripts to cite quoted material within the body of a report.
2. Use the same margins and center point as for the report and begin endnotes on a separate page.
3. Key the page number on line 7 at the right margin and center the heading, ENDNOTES on line 13.
4. Key the first superscript followed by the reference. The second line of the endnote begins at the margin. DS after the endnote.
5. Key the second and succeeding endnotes in the same manner.

Internal Citations—This citation method is rapidly replacing the footnote method because it is easier and quicker. Follow these steps to use internal citations in reports.

1. Immediately following the quoted material, key in parentheses: the name of the author(s), the year of publication, and the page number(s) cited.
2. Complete reference citations are keyed on a separate page or on the last page of the report if adequate room exists.
3. The reference page uses the same top and side margins as the first page of the report. The word REFERENCES is centered.

A Resume, A Letter Of Application, And An Interview Follow-Up Letter

A resume, which is also known as a personal data sheet, and a letter of application are very important papers for anyone who may be looking for a job. These documents should be designed to help a person get an interview. The follow-up letter is important to write after an interview has been completed.

Resume: The resume should be prepared first and should include any information that may be of value in getting an interview. The resume should include the complete name, address, and telephone number of the applicant as well as the educational background and work experience. It may also include references and other personal data that may be of interest to the potential employer. A one-page resume is usually preferable, although it may be longer if necessary.

Letter of Application: A one-page letter should accompany the resume. The letter should be addressed to the person who may be responsible for arranging an interview. The letter should emphasize the major points from the resume.

Interview Follow-up Letter: A letter should be written immediately following the interview. This letter should express appreciation for the interview and show continued interest in the job and in the company. This letter should be concise.

Format: An appropriate format should be followed for both of these letters and for the resume. Also, they should be proofread very carefully for correct spelling, grammar, and punctuation.

Steps in Formatting a Table

Horizontal Centering of Columns

1. Set the paper guide at 0 and insert paper into the machine.
2. Move the left and right margin stops to the ends of the scale. Clear all tab stops.
3. If the spacing between columns is not specified, decide how many spaces to leave between columns (preferably an even number such as 4, 6, or 8.)
4. Move the carrier to the center of the machine (51 elite; 42 pica).
5. Note the longest line in each column.
6. Backspace once for each 2 characters and spaces in the longest line in each column and once for each two spaces left between columns. If the longest line in one column has an extra character, combine that character with the first character in the next column for calculating purposes. A character left over after backspacing all columns is dropped.
7. Set the left margin stop at the point at which you stop backspacing. This is the point at which you will begin to key the first column.
8. From the left margin, space forward once for each character and space in the longest line in the first column and once for each space to be left between Columns 1 and 2. Set a tab stop at this point for the second column. Continue in this manner until stops have been set for all columns of the table.
9. Return the carrier. Operate the tab key to determine whether or not all the tab stops have been set.
10. Your right margin stop will remain at the end of the scale as you will not use it when formatting a table.

> With computers, tables may be formatted automatically. Your teacher may give you instructions and tell you if you are to use the automatic functions on your computer to format the tables in the problems of Unit 13.

Vertical centering and spacing directions are given on page RG-11. Review the directions again.

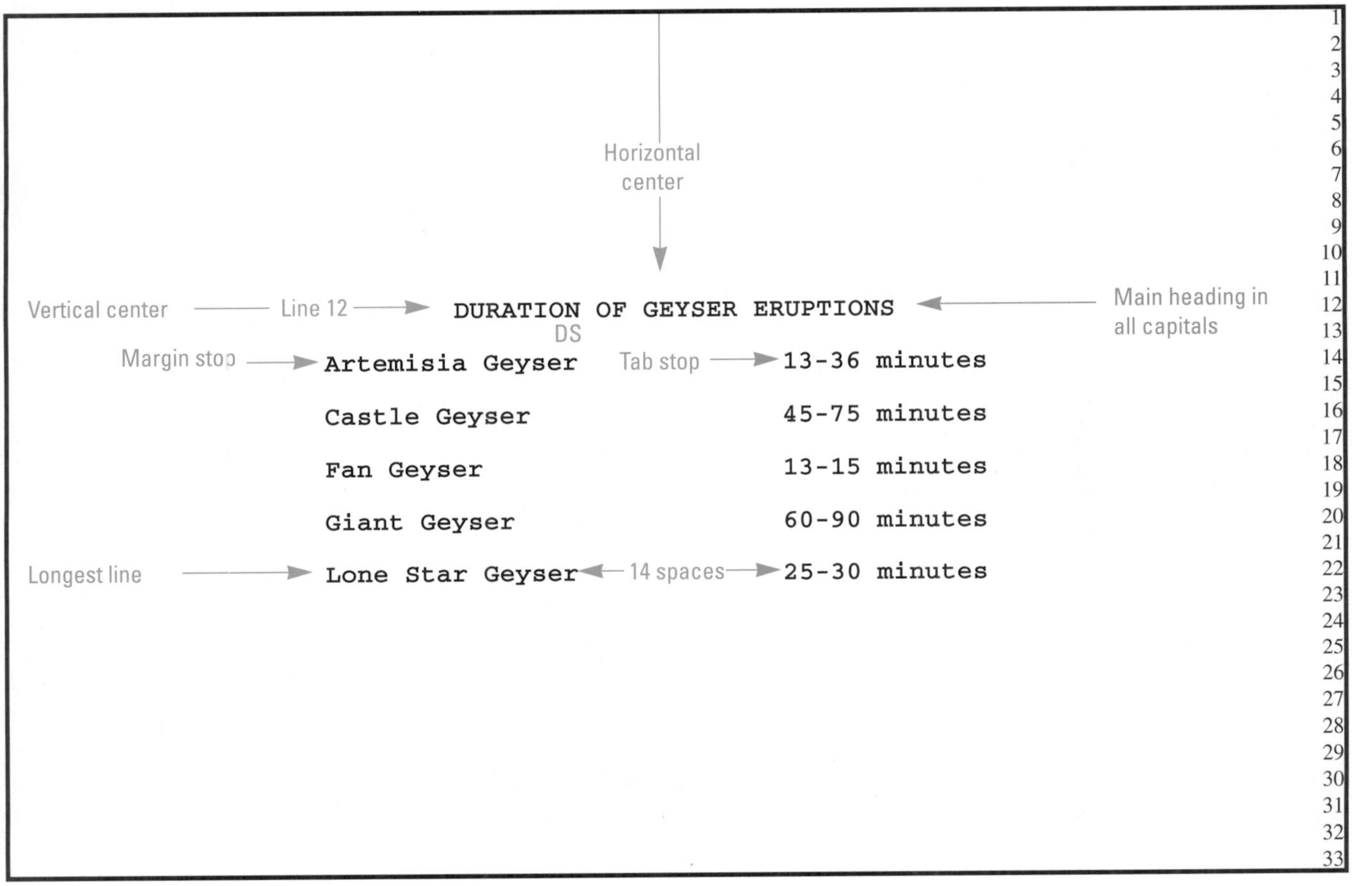

Scale (1–33) with table layout:

← Vertical center	Line 12 →	Main heading in all capitals → **DURATION OF GEYSER ERUPTIONS**	DS
← Margin stop	Artemisia Geyser ← Tab stop →	13-36 minutes	
	Castle Geyser	45-75 minutes	
	Fan Geyser	13-15 minutes	
	Giant Geyser	60-90 minutes	
← Longest line →	Lone Star Geyser → 14 spaces →	25-30 minutes	

Horizontal center

• PART 1 •
DEVELOPING KEYING SKILLS

Lessons 1-25

The goal of Part One is to help you develop basic keying skills by touch. You will learn the letter keys, the punctuation keys, the number keys, and the basic symbol keys. You will learn to use the basic service keys: SPACE BAR, RETURN/ENTER key, SHIFT keys, CAPS LOCK, and TABULATOR. You will build continuity in your keying of words, sentences, and paragraphs. You will also begin composing at the keyboard, improving communication skills, and developing critical thinking skills.

CORRECT POSTURE AND POSITION

Good posture and proper position are vital in learning to key effectively, and they are the same for the typewriter and the computer. Study the following guidelines for good form as illustrated in the photographs below. Observe them whenever you work at your machine.

1. Put your book at the right of your machine on a bookholder or with something under the top hinge. Slant it for easier reading.
2. Keep the table free of unneeded books and papers.
3. Place the front frame of the machine even with the edge of the desk.
4. Have your body centered opposite the **h** key, 6 to 8" from the front frame of the machine.
5. Sit back in the chair. Hold your shoulders erect with your body leaning forward slightly from the waist.
6. Hold your elbows near your body.
7. Hold your wrists low with your forearms parallel to the slant of the keyboard. Do not rest your lower hand on the frame of the machine or keyboard.
8. Place your feet on the floor, one just ahead of the other for good balance.
9. Keep your head turned toward the book and keep your eyes on the copy.
10. Keep your fingers well-curved and hold them over the second row of keys. This row is known as the home keys.

Correct posture and position at typewriter

Correct posture and position at computer

- **Problem 1 -** Format the following letter in modified block style with indented paragraphs. Use mixed punctuation, appropriate margins, correct date placement, and proper spacing throughout the letter. Address a large envelope. The letter contains 210 words.

> May 12, 19--/ Mr. and Mrs. Bryan Carlson / 11680 Roxbury Road / Corvallis, OR 97331-2602 / Dear Mr. and Mrs. Carlson:
>
> (¶) I was pleased to discuss with you the plans for your new house. Based on the information you gave me, I have been able to estimate the cost for the type of construction you desire. I do not believe, however, that you should consider building a one-story house with so much square footage on the property you currently own. I would suggest that you either secure a larger lot or that you consider building a two-story house on the land you have.
>
> (¶) If you are interested in seeing about a larger lot, there are several excellent real estate salespeople to whom I can refer you. Any one of these people could show you lots that would be acceptable for a one-story house of your size specifications.
>
> (¶) Please call my office so that we can schedule an appointment for you to come in again to discuss your building plans in more detail. I feel certain that I can stay within your cost specifications.
>
> Sincerely, / Lorina Kimble, Architect / xx

- **Problem 2 -** Format the following interoffice memorandum on a full sheet of plain paper. Use appropriate margins, placement, and spacing. Center the names of the real estate salespeople.

> TO: Susan Ray / FROM: Lorina Kimble / DATE: May 12, 19-- / SUBJECT: Appointment for Mr. and Mrs. Bryan Carlson
>
> (¶) Please expect a call from Mr. or Mrs. Bryan Carlson for an appointment to discuss the plans for their new house. I should like to see them very soon; therefore, schedule the appointment for any day except during the week of May 25-29. I shall be in Cincinnati for a conference that week.
>
> (¶) Also, please get in contact with the following real estate salespeople and find out what lots are still available (size and price) in the Highland Hills subdivision:
>
> Alan Chase, Murphy Realty, Inc.
> Karen Davis, The Lockwood Real Estate Agency
> Sharon Hill, Hill and Winston Associates
>
> (¶) I wish to have some potential lots to suggest to Mr. and Mrs. Carlson. They may be interested in purchasing a larger one for their new house.

- **Problem 3 -** Compose and format a memo to the Associate Dean. Invite her to attend the Senior Reception which will be held on Thursday, May 3, 19—, form 4:00 until 6:00 p.m. in the College Career Center. Be sure to tell her that the Information Systems Department Advisory Board Members have been invited. Prepare your document in draft form; proofread, make corrections, and reformat if necessary.

- **Problem 4 -** Compose and format a news release concerning some event that will be happening in you school.

- **Problem 5 -** Compose and format an itinerary for a trip that you or a member of your family is planning.

PRELIMINARY INSTRUCTIONS

1. Clear all unneeded papers and books from the table.
2. Turn on the equipment (ON/OFF control of typewriter or computer/monitor).
3. Make needed machine adjustments (see page x for typewriter and page xi for computer).
4. Typewriter: Adjust paper guide and insert paper into your typewriter as explained on page RG-1.
   Computer: Use the appropriate power-up procedure for the type of equipment you are using. If you are using a printer, turn the printer on and check paper supply and paper feed. Your teacher will tell you when you are to use the printer.
5. Typewriter: Follow the directions for setting margins as explained on page

RG-4. Use 1" side margins throughout Part One.
Computer: You have margins already set with the software you are using. These are called default margins. Use these unless your teacher tells you otherwise.

6. As parts of your machine are introduced to you throughout the lessons, find the parts for the typewriter on page x and for the computer on page xi. Learn the names of the parts as they will be used throughout the book.
7. Key every line once and then repeat as many times as your teacher suggests or as time may permit. Follow all directions, both oral and written, very carefully.
8. Review the guidelines for correct posture and position, and be sure that you are following them.

If you are using a computer for this course, your teacher may need to give you additional directions regarding your specific type of equipment (hardware) as well as your specific program (software). You should also become familiar with the user's manual or operator's guide for your specific hardware and software.

PROPER STROKING

1. Use a quick, firm, sharp stroke.

2. Release the keys quickly by snapping the fingers toward the palm of the hand.

UNIT 1
LEARNING THE LETTER KEYS   Lessons 1-10

Use 1" side margins for all lessons in Unit 1.

Use default margins for the computer.

In Unit 1 you will develop efficient key-stroking of all letters of the alphabet and all punctuation marks. You will also learn the proper use of the SPACE BAR, RETURN/ENTER key, SHIFT KEYS, CAPS LOCK, and tabulator (TAB). By the end of this unit, you will be keying complete sentences and paragraphs. You will also learn how to proofread your work for errors.

Placement Guide

side margins	margin settings	
	Elite	Pica
1"	12–90*	10–75*

*Plus 5 spaces for end-of-line signal

Follow the directions on page 184. Key the first 5′ writing. Circle errors and determine the *gwam*. Key a second 5′ writing over all the paragraphs. Circle errors and determine *gwam*. Compare the two 5′ writings and submit the better one to your teacher.

All letters

gwam

	1′	5′

We are now in an information age. During the past few years our | 13 | 3 | 55 |
economy has evolved from manufacturing to information. This means | 26 | 5 | 57 |
that more people now work in office jobs than work in factory jobs. | 40 | 8 | 60 |
With the change from the factory to the office, many positive aspects | 54 | 11 | 63 |
have emerged, but there have also been negative ones. | 65 | 13 | 65 |

In this new age, many of the positive factors are tied to the | 12 | 15 | 67 |
computer. This new form of technology has helped to meet many human | 26 | 18 | 70 |
needs. For example, computers help to grow food, to improve health | 40 | 21 | 73 |
care, and to provide entertainment. The computer was developed over | 54 | 24 | 76 |
many years to meet the growing needs of a modern society. | 65 | 26 | 78 |

Some people think that a computer does have some negative | 12 | 28 | 80 |
features. They say it has decreased the human element in our new age. | 26 | 31 | 83 |
There are also some interested in the possible problems of radiation | 40 | 34 | 86 |
from display terminals. Many more people are fearful of the | 52 | 36 | 88 |
potential for the electronic theft of data found in a computer. | 65 | 39 | 91 |

Regardless of what we may think about the computer, it is a | 12 | 41 | 93 |
unique part of an information age. The total number of computers | 25 | 44 | 96 |
is now into the millions, and this number will continue to grow | 38 | 47 | 99 |
as new applications keep evolving. We must each learn to maximize the | 52 | 50 | 102 |
positive and to minimize the negative aspects of this machine. | 65 | 52 | 104 |

1.5 si
5.7 awl
80% hfw

```
1'|  1  |  2  |  3  |  4  |  5  |  6  |  7  |  8  |  9  | 10  | 11  | 12  | 13  | 14  |
5'|          1          |          2          |          3          |
```

LESSON 1

1a Home Keys and Space Bar

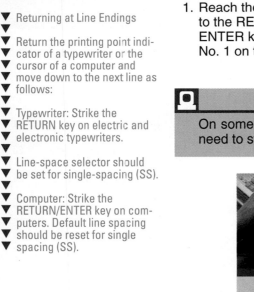

1. Place the fingers of your left hand on **a s d f**.
2. Place the fingers of your right hand on **j k l ;**.
3. Take your fingers off the home keys. Replace them and say the keys of each hand as you touch them. Repeat several times to get the feel of these keys.

4. Hold your right thumb over the middle of the SPACE BAR; strike it with a quick, inward motion. Keep your left thumb out of the way.
5. Curve your fingers. Hold them very lightly over the home keys. Key the line below. Say and think each letter and space as you strike it.

Space once

ff▼jj▼dd▼kk▼ss▼ll▼aa▼;;▼fdsa▼jkl;▼fdsa▼jkl;▼fj▼fj

1b RETURN/ENTER Key—Typewriter and Computer Keyboard

▼ Returning at Line Endings
▼
▼ Return the printing point indi-
▼ cator of a typewriter or the
▼ cursor of a computer and
▼ move down to the next line as
▼ follows:
▼
▼ Typewriter: Strike the
▼ RETURN key on electric and
▼ electronic typewriters.
▼
▼ Line-space selector should
▼ be set for single-spacing (SS).
▼
▼ Computer: Strike the
▼ RETURN/ENTER key on com-
▼ puters. Default line spacing
▼ should be reset for single
▼ spacing (SS).

1. Reach the little finger of your right hand to the RETURN key or the RETURN/ENTER key (No. 13 on the typewriter; No. 1 on the computer keyboard)

2. Tap the RETURN or RETURN/ENTER key quickly and return the finger to its home-key position. Try to keep from moving your other fingers.

On some computer keyboards, the reach will be longer than on a typewriter. You may need to stretch your little finger.

Typewriter
RETURN

Computer
RETURN/ENTER

▼ Check ahead to align colons
▼ in times given.
▼
▼ Review the illustration on
▼ page 183.

• **Problem 2 -** Itinerary in Rough Draft

Directions: On a full sheet of plain paper format the itinerary for Davida Lipscomb for May 8-9, 19--. Correct the rough draft below.

words

Charlotte

Monday, May 8	~~Gastonia~~, NC, to Washington, DC	9/27
7:15 a.m.	Leave Douglas Airport, AB Air Flight No. 7650.	38
8:53 a.m.	Arrive Dalles International Airport, Washington, DC. Take airport limousine to smith Electronics.	50 / 60
10:00 a.m.	Meeting with Johnston Smith, Tayloe Segon, and Sue Flaherty to discuss equipment needs.	73 / 80
2:00 p.m.	Lunch with Sales Representatives for Charlotte district.	92 / 94
Tuesday, May 9	Washington to Charlotte	109
9:00 a.m.	Seminar on "Electronics for the Office of the Future."	120 / 122
12:00 noon	Lunch with management staff.	130
4:00 p.m.	Leave Dulles Airport, AB Air Flight No. 6913.	141
4:30 p.m.	Arrive Douglas Airport.	148

• **Problem 3 -** Table—Rough Draft

Directions: Format the table below in reading position on a full sheet. Make all necessary decisions concerning correct placement and spacing. Correct all errors as indicated.

▼ For a review of formatting
▼ tables, refer to page 154.

words

all caps Motion Picture Academy Awards for *Best* Actor and Actress — 11

1985-1990 — 13

Year	Actor	Actress	
1985	William Hurt	Geraldine page	28
1968	Paul Newman	Marlee Matlin	34
1988	Dustin Hoffman	Jodie Foster	39
1989	Daniel Day Lewis	Jessica Tandy	46
1990	Jeremy Irons	Cathy Bates	53
1987	Michael Douglas	cher	59

1c Home-Key and Space Bar Practice

▼ Drill lines are numbered for
▼ easy reference. Do not key
▼ these numbers.

Directions: Key each line once; repeat.
Technique Goal: Think and say each letter and space as you strike it.

SS

1 ff jj ff jj fj fj fj fj dd kk dd kk dk dk dk dk dk

2 ss ll ss ll sl sl sl sl aa ;; aa ;; a; a; a; a; a;

3 Home Keys ffjf ddkd ssls aa;a fj dk sla; fdsa jkl; fdsa jkl;

4 fj dk sl a; fj dk sl a; asdf ;lkj aa ;; a; sl dksl

5 asdf ;lkj fj; dk; as; a; s; d; f; j; k; l; fj; dk;

Refer to the illustrations on page 2 to see if you are striking the keys properly.

1d Return Practice

Directions: Key each line once; repeat.
Technique Goal: Reach with your little finger; do not move your hand.

SS

1 ff jj dd kk ss ll aa ;; asdf ;lkj fj dk sl a; asdf

2 fdsajkl; a; sl dk fj ff jj dd kk ss ll aa ;; asdf;

3 a; sl dk fj asdf ;lkj aa ;; ss ll dd kk ff jj asdf

4 asdf;lkj jf kd ls ;a fdsa jkl; a; sl dk fj asdf a;

5 af ad as ;j lj kj asdf ;lkj fj dk sl a; fj dk; sl;

*Refer to the illustrations on page 3 to see if you are operating the
RETURN/ENTER key properly. Use a quick, firm stroke; release key quickly.*

1e Word and Phrase Practice

Directions: Key each line once; repeat.
Technique Goal: Keep your eyes on your copy as you key words and phrases.

▼ Spacing Guide: Space
▼ once after a semicolon (;)
▼ used as punctuation within
▼ a line.

SS

1 a as ask ask ad ad fad fad lad lad sad sad all all

2 dad dad add add ask fad lads sad all dads ads fads

3 fall fall lass lass adds dads fads falls lass lads

4 a fad; a lad; a lass; a fall; all ads; ask a lass;

5 ask a lad; a dad; a sad lass; ask all dads; a fad;

75c Critical Thinking Skill Development—Formatting Business Documents

25 minutes

- **Problem 1 -** Business Letter in Block Style—Rough Draft

▼ In this final lesson, the problems are designed to help you review the types of documents you learned to format in Part Three.

Directions: Format the letter shown below. Use block style with mixed punctuation, appropriate margins, correct date placement, and correct spacing throughout the letter. Address a large envelope. Make all indicated corrections.

words

May 5, 19-- 2

3995 Oak st 6

Tulsa, OK 74101-6713 9

Dear Mr. Lane, 14

I am pleased thatyou have re tained us to represent you you in con- 17

nection with your recnet accident. information regarding the mishap 29

including the name ofyour Doctor, is confidential, and should remain 43

so Refer any curious third par ties to me for any infromation. All 57

aspects of the accident will be invetsigated carefully. I shall keep 69

you in formed of developements inyour case. Pleasecall me at any 85

time if you have any questions or con cerns. 98

sincerely Yours, 106

Lisa Johnson Attorney 109

xx 114

Mr. Kenneth C. Lnae 114/125

1f Ending the Lesson

Typewriter:

1. Raise paper bail (No. 7) or pull it forward.
2. Depress paper release lever (No. 3).
3. Remove paper with left hand, and return paper release lever to original position.

4. Turn power switch to OFF.
5. Clear desk of books and papers.

Computer:

1. Exit your program as directed by your teacher.
2. Remove diskette from disk drive and store it.
3. If directed to do so by your teacher, turn power switch to OFF.
4. Clear desk of books and papers.

Electronic Typewriter:

1. Press the PAPER UP or EJECT key to remove paper.
2. Turn power switch to OFF.
3. Clear desk of books and papers.

LESSON 2

2a Machine Adjustments

▼ Your teacher will give you
▼ additional directions regard-
▼ ing the operations of your
▼ computer. You should also
▼ become familiar with the
▼ user's guide or the operator's
▼ manual for your computer.
▼ Your teacher will also give
▼ you instructions on how and
▼ when to operate your printer.

Typewriter:

1. Find your machine parts as shown on page x.
2. Check placement of the paper guide. It should line up with 0.
3. Insert your paper.
4. Check to see that the line-space selector is set for single-spacing.
5. Set margin for 1".
6. Check for correct posture and position (see page 1).

Computer:

1. Check to see that your equipment is properly plugged in.
2. Power up your computer according to the correct procedures.
3. Make sure you have the appropriate diskette.
4. Use the default settings for margins and for single line-spacing.
5. Check for correct posture and position (see page 1).

2b Keyboard Review

Directions: Key each line once; repeat. **Technique Goal:** Think each key as you strike it.

1   SS   ff jj dd kk ss ll aa ;; ff jj dd kk ss ll aa ;; fj

2   fj dk sl a; fj dk sl a; fj dk sl a; fj dk sl a; fj

3 Home keys   asdf ;lkj a; sl dk fj fdsa jkl; a; sl dk fj a; sl;

Review the instructions and illustrations for proper keystroking that are found on page 2.

LESSON 75

75a Keyboard Review

5 minutes

Directions: Key each sentence three times.

1	All letters	Jo, a valiant explorer, found quality zinc by making that wide search.
2	All numbers	That international club had 14,750 British and 23,689 Spanish members.
3	Number-symbol	I received a 10% discount ($82.73) for paying the bill within 15 days.
4	Easy	We should make some plans now for the best ways to use our new skills.

| 1 | 2 | 3 | 4 | 5 | 6 | 7 | 8 | 9 | 10 | 11 | 12 | 13 | 14 |

75b Timed Writings

15 minutes

Directions: Key two 5′ timed writings on the paragraphs below. Circle your errors and determine your *gwam*. Submit the better of the writings to your teacher.

	gwam	
	1′	5′

Travel to nearby or distant locations is a way to broaden your — 12 | 2 | 31

travel experiences. Whether your travel is for business or pleasure, you — 27 | 5 | 34

need to make arrangements for places to stay, modes of travel, and any — 41 | 8 | 37

special events. — 44 | 9 | 38

Your visit may include national and state parks. The first national — 14 | 12 | 40

park was begun more than a century ago. Since then, many parks have been — 29 | 15 | 43

established in all parts of the country. Various parks feature mines, — 43 | 17 | 46

rocks, seashore, or trees. — 48 | 18 | 47

If you have seen many of the parks, perhaps you will want to try — 13 | 21 | 50

a cruise. This floating hotel includes rooms, entertainment, meals, and — 28 | 24 | 53

even classes. One price is charged for the cruise. Some cruises are — 42 | 27 | 56

for three or four days while others may take a year. — 52 | 29 | 58

| 1 | 2 | 3 | 4 | 5 | 6 | 7 | 8 | 9 | 10 | 11 | 12 | 13 | 14 |

● Learning New Keys

1. Find the new key on the chart.
2. Locate the key on your machine.
3. Place your fingers over home keys; keep them curved.
4. Know which finger strikes each key.
5. Watch your finger make the reach without striking the key.

6. Key the drill line once slowly as shown to learn the new reach; repeat it a second time at a faster rate.
7. Keep your eyes on the book when keying.
8. Be sure to use the correct finger.
9. Use a quick, firm, sharp stroke.
10. Release the keys quickly by snapping the fingers toward the palm of the hand.

2c Learning to Keystroke H and E

Reach to H
1. Find **h:** on chart.
2. Find **h** on keyboard.
3. Place fingers over home keys.
4. Strike **h** with **j** finger.
5. Watch finger as you touch **hj** lightly.
6. Hold other fingers in position over home keys.
7. Key line 1 below.

Reach to E
1. Find **e** on chart.
2. Find **e** on keyboard.
3. Place fingers over home keys.
4. Strike **e** with **d** finger.
5. Watch finger as you touch **ed** lightly.
6. Hold other fingers in position; move **d** finger upward without moving hand.
7. Key line 2 below.

```
1   hj jhj jhj had hall hall jhj jhj jhj had hall hall

2   ed ded ed ed led led led ded ded ed ed led led led
```

2d Location Drills—H and E

> **Directions:** Key each line once; repeat. **Technique Goal:** Use quick, sharp strokes.

▼ Strike **h** with the **j** finger.   1   h
▼ ▼ Strike **e** with the **d** finger.   2   SS
                                               e

```
jjhj jjhj hj hj hj jhj jhj has has had had has had

ded ed ded ed ded led led sled sled fled fled fled
```

2e Learning to Keystroke I and R

Reach to I
1. Strike **i** with **k** finger.
2. Touch **ik** lightly.
3. Hold other fingers in position; move **k** finger upward without moving hand.
4. Key line 1 below.

Reach to R
1. Strike **r** with **f** finger.
2. Touch **rf** lightly without moving hand.
3. Move only **f** finger as you reach to **r**.
4. Key line 2 below.

```
1   ik kik kik ik ik kid kid kid ik ik kik kik kid kid

2   rf frf frf rf rf her her her rf rf frf her her her
```

Before starting to key a column of numbers, check ahead to see if you will need to indent the first item to align with one farther down the column.

Heading on Line 13

ITINERARY FOR KARL H. BAECHTOLD   6
                        DS
6 spaces   July 15-17, 19--   10
                        DS
Monday, July 15   San Francisco to Salt Lake City   29
                        DS
   7:30 p.m.   SS   Leave San Francisco International Airport,   40
                       Flightway Airlines, Flight No. 321.   47

   9:48 p.m.   Arrive Salt Lake City. Take airport limousine to   59
                       Hotel Utah. Reservations confirmed for July 15 and 69
                       16.   DS   70

Tuesday, July 16   Salt Lake City   83

   8:30 a.m.   Janis Esmay of the Salt Lake City office will meet   95
                       you at the hotel.   99

  10:00 a.m.   Meeting to discuss merger plans.   108

   1:00 p.m.   Tour of Salt Lake City facilities.   117

Wednesday, July 17   Salt Lake City to Denver to San Francisco   142

1" margin   9:00 a.m. Leave Salt Lake City Airport, Global Airlines,   1" margin   153
                       Flight No. 78.   156

  10:10 a.m.   Arrive Denver Airport. Robert Shenson of the   168
                       Denver office will meet you for a tour of the   177
                       Denver facilities.   181

   6:00 p.m.   Dinner with management personnel. Present speech   193
                       on merger plans.   197

   9:00 p.m.   Leave Denver Airport, ISA, Flight No. 71.   207

  10:05 p.m.   Arrive San Francisco International Airport.   218

Itinerary (Shown in elite type)

2f Location Drills—I and R

Directions: Key each line once. **Technique Goal:** Hold your wrists low and steady.

▼ Strike **i** with the **k** finger.　1　　i　　`kik ik kik ik kik kid kid if if is is his his dish`

▼　　　　　　　　　　　　　　2　　SS　`dish dish fill fill lid lid kid kid; a kid; a lid;`

▼ Strike **r** with the **f** finger.　3　　r　　`frf rf frf rf frf fir fir her her jar jar ear hear`

　　　　　　　　　　　　　　　4　　　　`hear hear far far hair hair fear; her hair; a jar;`

2g Technique Builder—Keystroking

▼ Spacing Guide: To double-space (DS) between groups of lines, operate the RETURN or RETURN/ENTER key twice.

▼ When ending the lesson, review the directions on page 5.

Directions: The line-space selector or default spacing should be set on "1" for single spacing (SS). Key each line twice as shown below and then double-space (DS).

1　SS　`he had she had ash hash led fled ale sale eel feel`

2　DS　`he had she had ash hash led fled ale sale eel feel`

3　　　`if is if is kid lid did hid fir fire air fair hair`

4　　　`if is if is kid lid did hid fir fire air fair hair`

LESSON 3

3a General Directions

▼ Spacing: Single

▼ Margins: 1" (Refer to page 2)

1. Adjust your machine as explained at the beginning of Lesson 2, page 5.
2. Check your posture and position at the machine with each point illustrated on page 1.
3. Double-space (DS) after repeating a line. Quadruple-space (QS) between parts of a lesson by striking the RETURN/ENTER key four times.

3b Keyboard Review

Directions: Key each line once; repeat. **Technique Goal:** Keep fingers curved.

1　Home row　`fdsa jkl; asdf ;lkj fj jf all fall as ask dad lad;`

2　h, e　`hj hj has had halls ed ed led fed fell he she held`

3　i, r　`ik ik kid aid aide rf rf fir sir fire ire rid fill`

4　All letters learned　`ad all far ask fire shell; half a shelf; a red jar`

Line 13

Center point

words

NEWS RELEASE   FOR RELEASE: Upon receipt   8
                                    CONTACT: Lois Ullmer Davidson   14
                                             803-555-2619   17
                                          QS

CHARLESTON, SC, December 1, 19--. Historic Charleston Consortium, a   31
DS
society dedicated to preserving America's heritage, announces the Annual   45

Winter Concert Series. The first concert is scheduled for December 10, 19--,   61

at 7:30 p.m. Guest pianist Matthew Pinckney Sholes will accompany the   75

Charleston Symphony Orchestra. New compositions will be performed as well   90

1" side   as seasonal favorites.   95
margin

Additional concerts are scheduled for December 17 and December 30, 19--.   110

Tickets are $32 in advance and may be ordered through the Historic Charleston   125

Consortium office at 1001 Central Row, Charleston, SC 29402-1001.   139

Winter Concerts will be held at historic Toomb Hall Plantation. Dating   153

from 1681, this plantation was a grant from the Lords Proprietors to Major   168

John Toomb, a member of Charles Towne's first fleet of settlers. Primarily   183

a cotton plantation, Toomb Hall once comprised 17,000 acres. It has one of   198

the most beautiful entrances in the South. Ancient live oak trees lead the   214

way for three quarters of a mile into the plantation complex. Join with your   229

friends to celebrate the winter season and preserve a part of this nation's   244

heritage.   246
           DS
                              ###   247

1" side
margin

▼ The symbols ### are centered
▼ a double-space below the
▼ last line to indicate the end of
▼ the release.

News release (Shown in elite type)

3c Learning to Keystroke O and T

Reach to O
1. Strike **o** with **l** finger.
2. Touch **ol** lightly.
3. Keep **j** and **;** fingers over home keys.
4. Key line 1 below.

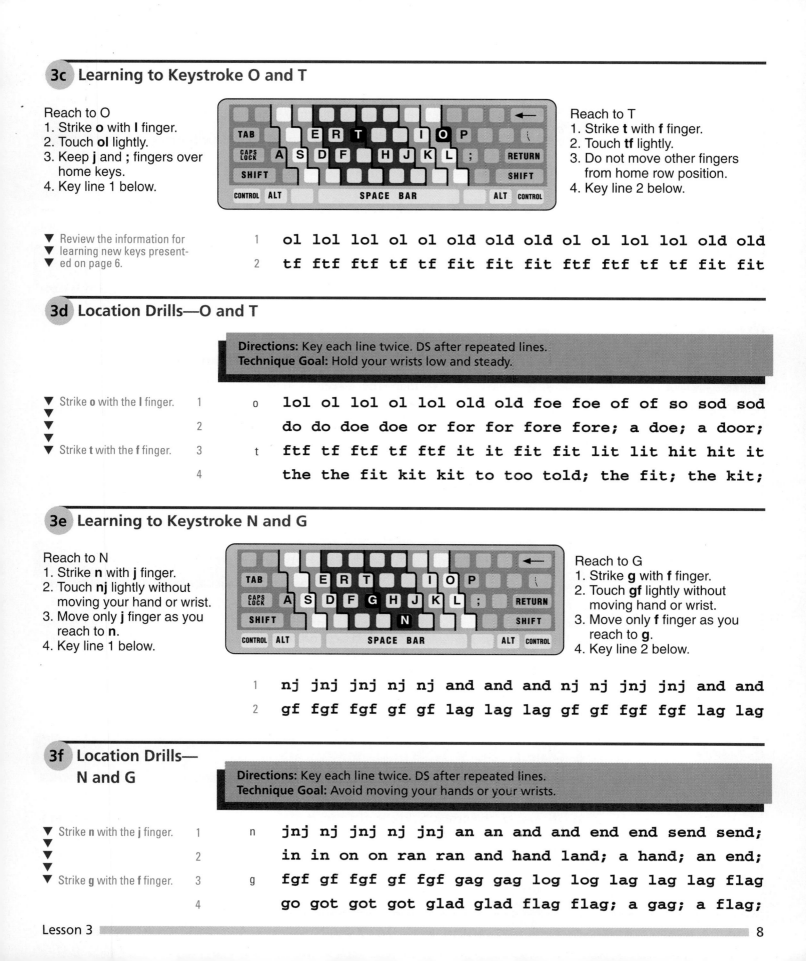

Reach to T
1. Strike **t** with **f** finger.
2. Touch **tf** lightly.
3. Do not move other fingers from home row position.
4. Key line 2 below.

▼ Review the information for
▼ learning new keys present-
▼ ed on page 6.

1 ol lol lol ol ol old old old ol ol lol lol old old

2 tf ftf ftf tf tf fit fit fit ftf ftf tf tf fit fit

3d Location Drills—O and T

Directions: Key each line twice. DS after repeated lines.
Technique Goal: Hold your wrists low and steady.

▼ Strike **o** with the **l** finger.
▼
▼
▼
▼ Strike **t** with the **f** finger.

1 o lol ol lol ol lol old old foe foe of of so sod sod

2   do do doe doe or for for fore fore; a doe; a door;

3 t ftf tf ftf tf ftf it it fit fit lit lit hit hit it

4   the the fit kit kit to too told; the fit; the kit;

3e Learning to Keystroke N and G

Reach to N
1. Strike **n** with **j** finger.
2. Touch **nj** lightly without moving your hand or wrist.
3. Move only **j** finger as you reach to **n**.
4. Key line 1 below.

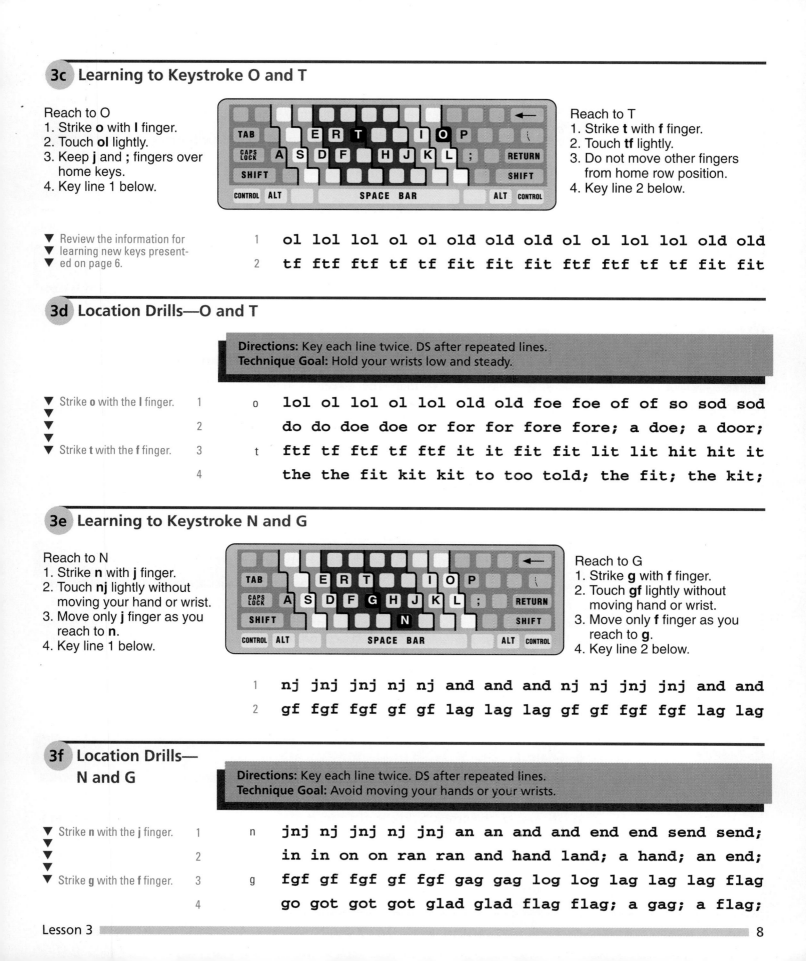

Reach to G
1. Strike **g** with **f** finger.
2. Touch **gf** lightly without moving hand or wrist.
3. Move only **f** finger as you reach to **g**.
4. Key line 2 below.

1 nj jnj jnj nj nj and and and nj nj jnj jnj and and

2 gf fgf fgf gf gf lag lag lag gf gf fgf fgf lag lag

3f Location Drills— N and G

Directions: Key each line twice. DS after repeated lines.
Technique Goal: Avoid moving your hands or your wrists.

▼ Strike **n** with the **j** finger.
▼
▼
▼
▼ Strike **g** with the **f** finger.

1 n jnj nj jnj nj jnj an an and and end end send send;

2   in in on on ran ran and hand land; a hand; an end;

3 g fgf gf fgf gf fgf gag gag log log lag lag lag flag

4   go got got got glad glad flag flag; a gag; a flag;

74b Skill Comparison

5 minutes

Directions: Key a 1' writing on each sentence in 74a on page 180. Compare your *gwam* on each writing.

74c Communication Skill—Review of Punctuation

5 minutes

▼ For review, see the
▼ following pages:
▼
▼ ; 56c, page 134
▼
▼ ! 58c, page 139
▼
▼ : 60c, page 143
▼
▼ () 66c page 159
▼
▼ '70c, page 169

Directions: Key each sentence twice; punctuate and capitalize correctly. The rules have been given in the communication skill drills in Part Three.

1   plan to attend the next meeting it should be of great benefit to you

2   hurry you will be late you may not be able to find any good seats

3   she will need to buy some items dress earrings purse and sweater

4   i have a new map the street is hard to find to the football stadium

5   ellen s essay received a much higher grade than mike s research paper.

74d Problem Formatting

30 minutes

- **Problem 1 -** News Release

Directions: Format on a full sheet of plain paper the news release shown on page 182. Follow the directions given on the illustration.

News releases announce items of special interest to newspapers and other news media. Top and side margins are 1" and paragraphs are double-spaced. Letterhead or plain paper may be used.

- **Problem 2 -** Itinerary

▼ Although there are many
▼ acceptable formats for an
▼ itinerary, the one shown on
▼ page 183 is frequently used.

Directions: Format on a full sheet of plain paper the itinerary shown on page 183. Follow the directions given on the illustration.

An itinerary is the proposed route of a trip. It is often referred to as a travel schedule and usually includes departure and arrival times, mode of travel, and scheduled activities.

3g Technique Builder—Keystroking

Directions: Key each line twice; DS after repeated lines.
Technique Goal: Keep fingers deeply curved; use quick, direct strokes.

▼ Review the keystroking
▼ illustrations on page 2. Be
▼ sure you are stroking
▼ properly.

1		fdsa jkl; fdsa jkl; hj ed ik rf ol tf nj gf to too
2		do doe does or for fore oar door soar soars floors
3		it its its its the the their fit sit kit fits sits
4		in in an an and and hand hands land lands end send
5		go go gold log logs got got dig digs lag lags glad
6	All keys learned	to go; he is; of all; go right; an oak; a red jar;

LESSON 4

4a Keyboard Review

Directions: Key each line once; repeat.
Technique Goal: Return quickly; begin a new line without pausing.

▼ Spacing: Single
▼
▼ Margins: 1"
▼
▼ Technique Goals are given
▼ for all drills. Keep these
▼ goals in mind and be guid-
▼ ed by them. Your practice
▼ should have a clear, definite
▼ purpose if it is to be helpful.

1	Home keys	fdsa jkl; a; sl dk fj as ask; all; fall; lad; sad;
2	h and e	jhj jhj has had hall ash hash ded ded led led fled
3	i and r	kik kik kid kid his is if frf frf fir fir her hear
4	o and t	lol lol old old of of ftf ftf fit fit hit kit kite
5	n and g	jnj jnj an an and end sends fgf fgf gag lags flags
6	All keys learned	he did it; she said; go for a long jog; the desks;

4b Shifting for Capital Letters—Left SHIFT Key

1. The left SHIFT key (No. 18) is used when keystroking capital letters with the right hand.
2. Use a one-two count.

One: Depress the SHIFT key with the **a** finger. Hold it down.
Two: Strike the capital letter; then quickly release the SHIFT key and return the **a** finger to its home-key position.

Directions: Key each line twice. DS after repeated lines.
Technique Goal: Use a quick, firm reach to the SHIFT key.

1	jJ jJ hH Hal Hal Lee Lee Hal Lee Jane Jane Jo Joan
2	Lee ran; Joe fell; Hal hid; Joan does; Jan did it;

• **Problem 2 -** Report in Memorandum Form with Table

Directions: 1. Format a memorandum report from the information which follows. Use a full sheet of paper. **2.** Center the table a double space below the last line of text. Center the main heading and block the columnar headings. Leave 10 spaces between columns. **3.** Proofread and correct any errors.

	words
TO: Thomas Coleman, Branch Manager / FROM: Clyde S. Thompkins / DATE:	14
June 10, 19-- / SUBJECT: Stugart Employee Information /	24
(¶) Ms. Candace Stugart from the corporate headquarters office has asked all	39
human resource managers to submit data which will be used to evaluate pro-	54
ductivity, need for new employees, and cost of personnel benefits.	67
(¶) The table below shows the number of regular and temporary employees as	82
of June 1, 19--. We believe the figures for the production department verify	99
our need to add additional full-time employees in that department.	111

STUGART EMPLOYEES — 114

Department	Regular	Temporary	words
			125
Accounting	42	8	129
Human Resources	13	1	133
Information Services	31	6	138
Maintenance	18	1	141
Production	446	34	145
Shipping	85	3	148

▼ Remember to align figures on
▼ the right.

LESSON 74

5 minutes

Directions: Key each sentence three times.

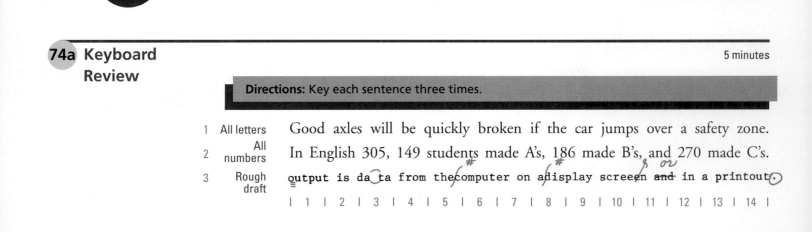

1 All letters   Good axles will be quickly broken if the car jumps over a safety zone.

2 All numbers   In English 305, 149 students made A's, 186 made B's, and 270 made C's.

3 Rough draft   output is da ta from the computer on a display screen and in a printout

| 1 | 2 | 3 | 4 | 5 | 6 | 7 | 8 | 9 | 10 | 11 | 12 | 13 | 14 |

4c Learning to Keystroke . (Period)

Reach to . (Period)
1. Strike . with I finger.
2. Touch .I lightly.
3. Lift little finger only enough to give freer movement.

Directions: Key each line twice. DS after repeated lines.
Technique Goal: Keep your wrists and arms from moving.

1   1.1 .1 1.1 .1 1.1 all. all. fill. fill. sell. all.
2   all. ail. fail. fail. rail. rail. tell. tell. ail.

4d Location Drills—Left Shift Key and . (Period)

▼ Spacing Guide: Space twice
▼ after a period that ends a
▼ sentence, except when the
▼ period comes at the end of a
▼ line. When it does, return
▼ without spacing. Space
▼ only once after a period
▼ following an initial or an
▼ abbreviation.

Directions: Key each line twice. DS after repeated lines.
Technique Goal: Keep your eyes on your copy.

1   Lea did.   Kara had it.   He did.   Jane does.   I do.
2   I hit it.   Joan hit it higher.   Jo hit it highest.
3   Hale did it.   H. J. shall do it.   Kent has a sled.
4   Lt. Keller took that train.   O. L. Hanes did also.

4e Technique Builder—Left Shift Key Control

Directions: Key each line twice. **Technique Goal:** Hold the SHIFT key down until you strike the capital letter, then release it quickly.

1   I see it.   He sees it.   Joan sees it.   Oki had it.
2   Lori Lee asked to go.   K. L. got the jar.   He did.
3   L. H. Hall sold it to her.   Lisa Lei shall see it.
4   He lost a ski at the lodge.   I had it at the lake.
5   Kent Hall shall go to Long Lake.   He shall go too.
6   Lee and I led the girls in a song in Langlee Hall.

• **Problem 1 -** Report in Memorandum Form with a Table

Directions: 1. Format a memorandum report from the information given below. Use a full sheet of paper. **2.** Center the table a double space below the last line of text. Center the main heading and block the columnar headings. Leave an even number of spaces between columns. **3.** Proofread and correct any errors.

words

TO: Ann Linden, Personnel Manager / FROM: Lee Keyes, Training Director /   14
DATE: January 8, 19-- / SUBJECT: Annual Report on Training Programs   28
(¶) Our instructional programs were very successful last year. We trained   42
all new employees, and retrained many other employees to help them move   57
into more demanding jobs. Our efforts were directed toward management as   72
well as nonmanagement personnel. Almost seventy-five percent of all em-   86
ployees in the company participated in some type of training activity.   100
(¶) We used four approaches to training: a mentor system whereby an   113
experienced employee trained a new employee; a corporate training staff   128
for instruction in areas of new technology; outside consultants for spe-   142
cialized seminars; and fee reimbursement for employees who took job-   156
related courses in a community college, college, or university.   169
(¶) A summary of last year's programs is shown in the following table: 182

SUMMARY OF TRAINING PROGRAMS, 19--   189

Type of Program	Number of Employees Participating
Microcomputer Applications	573
Word Processing Operations	482
Written Communication Seminars	416
Oral Communication Seminars	301
Telecommunications	265
Mentor Training	174
College or University Courses	93

  193
  205
  211
  217
  224
  231
  235
  239
  246

▼ Within a company or an orga-
▼ nization, an informal report
▼ which does not contain refer-
▼ ences is frequently formatted
▼ as a memorandum.

▼ Review the guides given on
▼ page 144 for formatting
▼ interoffice memorandums.

▼ You may also wish to review
▼ the steps given on page 154
▼ for formatting a table.

4f Keystroking from Dictation

Directions: Key the words as your teacher dictates them. **Technique Goal:** Think the whole word as you stroke it. Say the word to yourself as you keystroke.

SS

1 if if if is is is he he he if he if he is if he is

2 she she she is is is she is she is did did she did

3 had had she had he had or of of or or for or go go

4 for as for as if he is go for as she had as he did

LESSON 5

5a Keyboard Review

Directions: Key each line once; repeat.
Technique Goal: Keep your eyes on the copy in your book; avoid pauses.

▼ Spacing: Single
▼
▼ Margins: 1"

1 h, e hj ed hj ed has had ash shall led sled fled he she

2 i, r ik rf ik rf kid if is his lid fir her jar ear fear

3 o, t ol tf ol tf old for foe so for fit lit hit it that

4 n, g nj gf nj gf an and end send in go lag gag log flag

5 Shift jJ jJ jJ Joan rode. Hal led. Lee ran. Kent hit.

6 . (period) l.l .l l.l .l Lt. Hall did it. J. H. Lee had one.

7 All letters learned Fran and Joe will take sleds to the old ski lodge.

5b Learning to Keystroke U and C

Reach to U
1. Strike **u** with **j** finger.
2. Touch **uj** lightly.
3. Hold other fingers in position.
4. Key line 1 below.

Reach to C
1. Strike **c** with **d** finger.
2. Touch **cd** lightly.
3. Hold the **a** finger in position; let other fingers move slightly with the stroke.
4. Key line 2 below.

▼ Review the information for
▼ learning new keys present-
▼ ed on page 6.

1 uj juj juj uj uj dud dud dud uj uj juj juj dud dud

2 cd dcd dcd cd cd cod cod cod cd cd dcd dcd cod cod

LESSON 73

73a Keyboard Review

Directions: Key each sentence three times.

1	All letters	Sharp, young executives quickly amazed overjoyed bankers from Wichita.
2	All numbers	Order 486-957 was mailed on May 20, but I didn't get it until July 31.
3	Shift	The article, "How to Write Letters," appeared in the <u>Writer's Journal</u>.
4	Easy	Our taxes this year may be much more than I had thought they would be.

| 1 | 2 | 3 | 4 | 5 | 6 | 7 | 8 | 9 | 10 | 11 | 12 | 13 | 14 |

73b Paragraph Guided Writings

5 minutes

Directions: 1. Set goals of 40, 50, and 60 words a minute. Key a 1' writing at each rate. Try to key your word goal as time is called. Your teacher may call the quarter or half minutes to guide you. **2.** Key one additional writing at the 60-word rate.

60 words
1.5 si

People gain success in a variety of ways. Some people feel that they are successful if they are rich. Others feel that fame indicates success. The truly successful people, however, may be those who have found contentment and happiness in what they do. They may be rich or poor, famous or obscure.

73c Sentence Skill Builder—Rough Draft

5 minutes

Directions: Key each sentence three times.
Technique Goal: Proofread carefully and correct all errors.

1 it is predictde for computor costs to increase in the nest rive years?

2 the hotels owner wanted to loacte a cite for tow new high rise hotels?

3 Jane dais, you never get a secodn change to maek a first impresion."

5c Location Drills— U and C

Directions: Key each line twice. DS after repeated lines.
Technique Goal: Use quick, direct strokes.

▼ Strike **u** with the **j** finger.
▼
▼ Strike **c** with the **d** finger.

1 u `juj uj juj uj juj us us fuss fuss dud dud; a fuss;`

2 c `dcd cd dcd cd dcd cod cod cold cold sick sick such`

3 `such such lick lick luck luck; her luck; his cold;`

5d Technique Builder— Keystroking

Directions: Key each line twice. DS after repeated lines. **Technique Goal:** Keep your eyes on your book; avoid looking at your fingers when keystroking.

1 `us fuss dud full dusk husk due sue fur jug lug use`

2 `cute cues duck clue cure luck; her luck; his clue;`

3 `He can get the ice for the jug.  I can cut a cake.`

4 `Lou found ducks on June Lake.  I can use the dock.`

5e Review of Correct Posture and Position

1. Review the photograph and guides shown on page 1 for correct posture and position.

2. Notice the photographs below and make sure that you are using straight, direct stroking.

▼ Proper techniques are critical
▼ in helping you achieve key-
▼ stroking success.
▼
▼ Use straight, direct key-
▼ stroking.

Do not turn
hands sideways

Hold hands upright,
directly over keys

5f Keystroking from Dictation

Directions: Key the words as your teacher dictates them.
Technique Goal: Think the words as you are keystroking them.

▼ Review the information on
▼ page 5 for ending a lesson.

1 `he he the the she she the the an an and and an and`

SS

2 `is is his has go go got got it it fit fit it is it`

3 `an and he her go got it fit is fit go got do go so`

4 `to to to do if if if it did and is and she and the`

LESSON 72

72a Keyboard Review

Directions: Key each sentence three times.

1	All letters	Keep extra frozen jam in quaint cafe bowls or gift dishes for my view.
2	All numbers	Complete items 4, 6, and 8 before you place order #1792 by 5:30 today.
3	Script	*Paris is a large cosmopolitan city with fine restaurants and theaters.*
4	Easy	Tom will call early if he plans to come for a visit to our home today.

| 1 | 2 | 3 | 4 | 5 | 6 | 7 | 8 | 9 | 10 | 11 | 12 | 13 | 14 |

72b Proofreading Skill Builder—Correct Spelling of Names

5 minutes

Directions: Key the following paragraph and correct the errors in the spelling of names. The correct spelling for each name is Manuel Del Otro, Suzanne Peeples, Carmelo Delgado, Renae Julien, Sasha Donotev, Rudolph Vassar, and Ruriko Munemitsu. Repeat the paragraph as many times as possible. Work for accuracy.

DS   The concert features artists Manual del Orto, Susanne Peebles, Carmela Delcado, and Renee Julian. The actors in the play include Sashe Denotev, Rudolff Vesser, and Ruriko Mumemitso. I hope to attend both the concert series and the plays. Ms. Sashe Denotev will sign autographs on August 9 and 10.

72c Sentence Skill Builder

5 minutes

Directions: Key a 1' writing on each sentence in 72a. Try to increase your rate of speed on each sentence.

72d Problem Formatting

30 minutes

- **Problem 1 -** Formatting a Report

Directions: Continue formatting the report you started in Lesson 71. Follow all of the directions given with that report.

- **Problem 2 -** Reformat the references for the report on entrepreneurship. This time, however, format them on a separate page. Remember to use the same top and side margins as the first page of the report. Format the page number on line 7 at the right margin.

6a Keyboard Review

Directions: Key each line once; repeat. **Technique Goal:** Keep fingers curved.

1	h, e, i	`hj ed ik has had hall led he shed is his dish fill`
2	r, o, t	`rf ol tf her ear hair of so sod old it fit to told`
3	n, g	`nj gf an and in ran send lag log gag got glad flag`
4	u, c	`uj cd dud us full husk cod cold sick lick can such`
5	. (period) Left shift	`.l l.l .l jJ hH Hal led.  Jo ran.  Lee has.  I do.`

6b Learning to Keystroke W

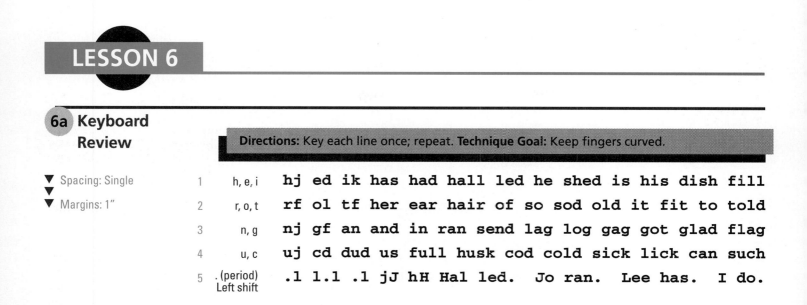

Reach to W
1. Strike **w** with **s** finger.
2. Touch **ws** lightly.
3. Lift the **a** finger slightly to give freer movement.
4. Key line below.

`ws sws sws ws ws wish who ws sws sws sws wish wish`

6c Location Drills—W

Directions: Key line twice. Repeat.
Technique Goal: Keep fingers positioned properly when making this new reach.

▼ Strike **w** with the **s** finger.

`w sws ws sws ws sws won won will will work work`

6d Shifting for Capital Letters—Right Shift Key

1. The right SHIFT key (No. 14) is used when keystroking capital letters with the left hand.
2. Use a one-two count.

One: Depress the SHIFT key with the ; finger. Hold it down.
Two: Strike the capital letter; then quickly release the SHIFT key and return the ; finger to its home-key position.

Directions: Key line twice. **Technique Goal:** Hold the SHIFT key down and release it quickly.

`Dot hid.  Sue fell.  Gus does.  Al said.  Flo did.`

SELECTED NATIONAL FRANCHISES

▼ DS before and after a table in
▼ a report, and single space the
▼ table.

Franchise	Rank	Business
McDonald's	1	Fast Food Restaurant
H & R Block	6	Tax Preparation
Jiffy Lube	37	Auto Maintenance
RE/MAX	24	Real Estate Broker
Jazzercise	7	Dance Fitness Center

Source: The Universal Almanac, 1990

Future Growth

    Small businesses lead the way in the creation of new jobs in the American economy. Between 1987 and 1988 over two million new jobs were generated in small-business dominated industries. The fastest-growing entrepreneurships appear to be amusement and recreation, eating and drinking establishments, trucking firms, medical offices, and computer and data services.

    While large multi-national corporations have a significant impact on consumers, the small entrepreneurship may be most familiar to the average citizen. Small business, too, contributes substantially to the economic health of our nation.

REFERENCES

Hunt, Roger W. Entrepreneurship Starting Your Own Business. 2d ed. Cincinnati: South-Western Publishing Co., 1988.

Wright, John W. The Universal Almanac. ed. Kansas City: Andrews and McMeel, 1990.

Yakal, Kathy. "With a Portable, You Can Take It With You." The Office, February 1992, 38-39.

Column word counts: 424, 431, 437, 443, 449, 456, 459, 471, 477, 490, 504, 518, 533, 548, 550, 564, 579, 595, 598, 600, 623, 633, 652, 655, 671, 675

6e Technique Builder—Shift Key Control

Directions: Key each pair of lines as shown. DS between 2-line groups. Repeat if time permits.
Technique Goal: Hold the SHIFT key down and release it quickly.

▼ Spacing Guide: Remember
▼ to space only once after a
▼ period following an initial
▼ or an abbreviation.

1   `Al has a car.  She has it.  Don can go.  Fran did.`

SS

2   `Will told Gus and Al who won.  Sue and Flo won it.`

DS

3   `Lt. Kirk and Sgt. Dale will go.  She will go also.`

4   `Dr. D. K. Eng and Dr. Sue Gee can win.  I can win.`

6f Sentence Skill Builder

▼ Your teacher will explain
▼ the procedure to be followed
▼ for timed writings.

Directions: Key two 1' writings on each sentence. Compute your gross words a minute (*gwam*). Double-space these timings.
Technique Goal: Eliminate wasted motions in the arms and wrists. Return quickly; key steadily.

Computing Gross Words a Minute (*gwam*)

In keyboarding, 5 strokes are counted as one word. Each line below has 50 strokes, or 10 words. Each complete line keyed gives you a score of 10 words. For a partial-ly keyed line, note the scale. Add the figure nearest the last word or letter keyed to your complete sentence score. This is your gross words a minute (*gwam*).

1   `Joan will work hard and win the race she will run.`

2   DS   `Ken said that he saw the two girls go to the gate.`

3   `I will go and find the sign that is near the lake.`

    | 1 | 2 | 3 | 4 | 5 | 6 | 7 | 8 | 9 | 10 |

LESSON 7

7a Keyboard Review

Directions: Key each line once; repeat. **Technique Goal:** Sit back in your chair, body erect.

▼ Spacing: Single
▼
▼ Margin: 1"

1 Home row   `fdsa jkl; fdsa jkl; gf hj gf hj lad glad shad half`

2   w   `sws sws ws ws wish win wind well will low slow how`

3   t, n   `tf nj tf nj tide lift fit end lend an and tan than`

4   Shift   `Dr. J. F. Lee saw Dr. Rose and his wife on a tour.`

- **Problem 2** - Leftbound Report with Internal Citations and Table

Directions: 1. Study the information on page 167 for formatting internal citations in a report. **2.** Review the steps for arranging a table horizontally on the page. **3.** On plain paper, format the following report that includes a table. **4.** On the last page of your report, QS after the last line of the report text and format the references.

words

ENTREPRENEURSHIP

3

In the United States, small businesses account for about 99 percent of the nonfarm businesses. Many Americans get their first employment experience through small firms. Many small business firms begin as entrepreneurships.

17
31
45
49

<u>Entrepreneurships</u>

56

"Entrepreneurship refers to the act or process of getting into and managing a business enterprise" (Hunt, 1988, 3). People who begin these businesses are known as entrepreneurs. The businesspeople usually begin a business because they have an idea--a way of better serving consumers with a product or service.

69
83
97
111
118

Entrepreneurships exist in all phases of American business from manufacturing to wholesaling and even to a myriad of service industries. One style of service which has shown growth in the past few years is the research service. These entrepreneurs are trained to gather and analyze data and make projections for companies or individuals. These "number crunchers" make use of computers to process their information. Many researchers use laptops or portables. "There is a growing trend toward making portable computers do double duty, working on the road and in the office" (Yakal, 1992, 39).

131
146
161
175
189
203
218
231
238

An important retail industry which most Americans use often is the restaurant business. These may be local or national. Some restaurants are franchises.

251
264
268

<u>Franchising</u>

273

Franchising, a century-old tradition, has gained wide popularity in the United States. "Franchises accounted for more than one-third of all consumer purchases in 1989" (Wright, 1990, 231). The franchiser can expand a business without borrowing great amounts of capital; franchisers receive fees from franchisees and a steady flow of income from each franchised unit. The franchise fee is usually about five percent of the franchisee's gross income.

286
301
315
328
342
356
363

In return for the fee paid, the franchisee receives training, financial assistance, other business expertise, and the benefits of a national reputation. Following are some of the national franchises most Americans recognize.

376
389
403
409

▼ You may not be able to finish
▼ the entire report in this les-
▼ son. Complete as much as
▼ you can. You will be given
▼ extra time in Lesson 72 for
▼ completing it.

▼ Remember to listen for and
▼ key by your line end signal.

▼ continued on the next page

7b Learning to Keystroke B and Y

Reach to B
1. Strike **b** with **f** finger.
2. Touch **bf** lightly.
3. Allow **d** and **s** fingers to move slightly to give freer movement.
4. Key line 1 below.

Reach to Y
1. Stroke **y** with **j** finger.
2. Touch **yj** lightly.
3. Do not move other fingers from home-key position.
4. Key line 2 below.

1   bf fbf fbf bf bf bf buf buff fbf fbf fbf buff buff

2   yj jyj jyj jyj yj yj jay jay yj yj jyj jyj jay jay

7c Location Drills—B and Y

Directions: Key each line twice. DS after repeated lines. **Technique Goal:** Curve your fingers deeply to make the long reaches to **b** and **y** without moving your hand.

▼ Strike **b** with the **f** finger.
▼
▼ Strike **y** with the **j** finger.

1   b   fbf bf fbf bf fbf buff buff bluff bluff buy buy by

2   y   jyj yj jyj yj jyj jay jay fly fly way way ray rays

7d Learning to Keystroke M and X

Reach to M
1. Strike **m** with **j** finger.
2. Touch **mj** lightly.
3. Do not twist hand or move other fingers from home-key position.
4. Key line 1 below.

Reach to X
1. Strike **x** with the **s** finger.
2. Touch **xs** lightly.
3. Lift the **a** finger slightly to give freer movement.
4. Key line 2 below.

1   mj jmj jmj mj mj jam jam ham ham mj mj jmj jam ham

2   xs sxs sxs xs xs six six fix fix xs xs sxs six fix

7e Location Drills—M and X

Directions: Key each line twice. DS after repeated lines. **Technique Goal:** Keep your hands and wrists positioned properly when making these new reaches.

▼ Strike **m** with the **j** finger.
▼
▼ Strike **x** with the **s** finger.

1   m   jmj mj jmj mj jmj jam jam mar mar mad mad make mad

2   x   sxs xs sxs xs xsx six six mix mix fox fox fix next

3   made smash fixed mixed mixed tax tax lax lax taxed

LESSON 71

71a Keyboard Review

5 minutes

Directions: Key each sentence three times.

1	All letters	A young bank executive in High Falls was amazed at Joan's quick reply.
2	All numbers	There were 185 people from Idaho, 396 from Maine, and 2,470 from Iowa.
3	Script	*A menu is a list of options from which a keyboard operator may choose.*
4	Easy	We must work hard for our success, but we can also hope for some luck.

| 1 | 2 | 3 | 4 | 5 | 6 | 7 | 8 | 9 | 10 | 11 | 12 | 13 | 14 |

71b Paragraph Skill Builder

10 minutes

Directions: Key two 1' writings on each paragraph in 63d, page 152. Work for control. Try to maintain speed with accuracy.

71c Skill Comparison

5 minutes

Directions: Key a 1-minute writing on each sentence. Try to key all sentences at the rate set on the first one.

1	Easy	The very best way to build a high level of skill is through hard work.
2	Number-Symbol	Order 14 dozen (Style 3729) headphones for our new stereo--Model 5680.
3	Script	*Learn to control your errors by learning to control the rate of speed.*
4	Rough draft	your new skill may prove to be quite useful top you in a job or career

| 1 | 2 | 3 | 4 | 5 | 6 | 7 | 8 | 9 | 10 | 11 | 12 | 13 | 14 |

71d Problem Formatting

25 minutes

- **Problem 1 -** Completing a Report

Directions: Continue formatting the report that you started in Lesson 70. Follow all of the directions given with that report.

7f Technique Builder—Keystroking

▼ Let your fingers do all the
▼ work.

● **FINGER-ACTION STROKING**

When you reach from home position to strike another key, keep the other fingers on or near their home keys. Make the reach with the finger without twisting the wrist or moving the arm or elbow.

Directions: Key each line twice. DS after repeated lines.
Technique Goal: Make reaches without twisting the wrist or moving the arm.

1   win won word work works will with how show row low

2   am same aim lame flame come dome mad made mar mark

3   big rob fib but bout about bold both buff bluff by

4   jay try yes year they gray slay tray yell buy byte

5   hoax sixth sixty text coax fix fax fox lox flax ax

6   Walt will go for six weeks. Max may go for sixty.

7   Robb and Marie Young were taxed on their new boat.

8   Bobby and Judy may win gold medals in their races.

| 1 | 2 | 3 | 4 | 5 | 6 | 7 | 8 | 9 | 10 |

7g Sentence Skill Builder

Directions: Key two 1' writings on each sentence. Compute your gross words a minute (*gwam*). **Technique Goal:** Hold the hands directly over the keys. Strike the keys with straight, direct strokes.

1   We will try to work hard and win at all the games.

2   Jo can win if she does not need to meet that girl.

3   Maxie saw your team win that game by a high score.

| 1 | 2 | 3 | 4 | 5 | 6 | 7 | 8 | 9 | 10 |

7h Ending a Lesson

Refer to page 5 to review the proper procedures to follow when you end a lesson. Always remember to turn your power switch to OFF.

▼ Continued from the previous
▼ page

Being ethical means more than being honest. Honesty does not just mean
not lying and not stealing.   "Honesty needs to be affirmative--giving a
full day's work for a day's pay . . . and not deliberately being
nonproductive."[3]   An example of deliberate nonproductivity would be
taking longer to complete tasks than required, refusing to use the
most up-to-date equipment and techniques for processing work, and
using the company phone for excessive personal calls.

Employees should take responsibility for their ethical behavior.
They need to be good at the jobs they perform, and they should request
additional training if necessary to perform the best they can. One way
to increase productivity and set good examples is to arrive for work on
time each day and work until the designated hour. Return from lunch
and other breaks on time. Don't be a "time thief."

Corporate and Personal Ethics

▼ Remember to key by your line
▼ end signal.

Ethical conduct applies to corporations, organizations, and businesses
as well as to individuals. Ethical issues are in the news and have become a public concern. "Ethical companies do not trade on inside information or give bribes to business people or government officials--they
do not conspire to fix prices."[4]

Businesses that maintain ethical standards demonstrate a sincere
dedication to health, safety, and productivity in the workplace.
Ethical companies and employees share this goal.

ENDNOTES

[1]Phyllis Ohlemacher, "Integrating Ethics in High School Accounting," Business Education Forum, January 1990, p. 15.

▼ Remember to format the END-
▼ NOTES on a separate page.

[2]Steven Bavaria, "Corporate Ethics Should Start in the Boardroom,"
Business Horizons, January-February 1991, p. 12.

[3]Ivan Hill, "Everyday Ethics for the Secretary," The Secretary,
August-September 1978, p. 7.

[4]Andres T. Nappi, "Teaching Business Ethics--A Conceptual Approach,"
Journal of Education for Business, January 1990, p. 177.

words
410
424
437
451
464
477
488
501
516
530
545
559
569
581
595
609
623
637
644
657
670
680
682
695
711
724
738
754
760
774
792

LESSON 8

8a Keyboard Review

Directions: Key each line once; repeat. **Posture Goal:** Sit erect with both feet on the floor.

▼ Spacing: Single
▼
▼ Margins: 1"

1	b	fbf fbf bf bf bug but both bold rob rub buff bluff
2	y	jyj jyj yj yj yet yell year sly they lay flay gray
3	m	jmj jmj mj mj jam fame same lame mar mad made make
4	x	sxs sxs xs xs six fix next mixed lax flax box hoax

8b Learning to Keystroke P and V

Reach to P
1. Strike **p** with ; finger.
2. Touch **p;** lightly.
3. Keep elbows still.
4. Keep right wrist low and steady.
5. Key line 1 below.

Reach to V
1. Strike **v** with the **f** finger.
2. Touch **vf** lightly without moving hand.
3. Keep other fingers over home keys.
4. Key line 2 below.

| 1 | p; ;p; ;p; p; p; p; lap flap ;p; ;p; lap flap flap |
| 2 | vf fvf fvf vf five five dive fvf fvf fvf five dive |

8c Location Drills— P and V

Directions: Key each line twice. DS after repeated lines.
Technique Goal: Key with wrists and arms in position.

▼ Strike **p** with the ; finger.
▼
▼ Strike **v** with the **f** finger.

1	p	;p; p; ;p; p; ;p; rap rap map map lap lap rip rips
2	v	fvf vf fvf vf fvf five five give gives lives lives
3		trip trap plan play slip view void void move moves

8d Learning to Keystroke Q and , (Comma)

Reach to Q
1. Strike **q** with the **a** finger.
2. Touch **qa** lightly.
3. Do not move wrist and elbow in or out.
4. Key line 1 below.

Reach to , (Comma)
1. Strike **,** with **k** finger.
2. Touch **,k** lightly.
3. Lift **j** finger slightly to give freer movement.
4. Space once after , used as punctuation.
5. Key line 2 below.

| 1 | qa aqa aqa qa aqa quit quite qa qaq qaq quit quite |
| 2 | ,k k,k k,k ,k ,k work, work, ,k k,k ,k work, work, |

• **Problem 3 -** Leftbound Report with Side Headings and Endnotes

▼ You will not be able to finish
▼ the entire report in this les-
▼ son. Complete as much as
▼ you can. You will be given
▼ extra time in Lesson 71 for
▼ completing it.

Directions: 1. Format the material shown below and on the following page in leftbound report form. **2.** When formatting side headings in a report, double-space above and below them. Key the headings even with the left margin and underline them. **3.** In the problem you will find the references at the end of the report. Format them on a separate sheet to be used as the last page. When references are placed at the end of a report instead of foot-notes, they are called *endnotes.* Key the page number on line 7 at the right margin and cen-ter the heading, ENDNOTES, on line 13. Next, quadruple-space (QS). Indent the first line of each note 5 spaces. Single-space (SS) the notes but double-space between. Key them consec-utively. **4.** Format a title page and use your name on it. **5.** Assemble your report in the appro-priate sequence and bind it at the left.

	words
ETHICS IN THE WORKPLACE	5

Each person in a business environment is faced with decisions involving ethical choices. These choices may not occur on a daily basis, but they do affect the manner in which work is performed and the atmosphere in the business office. Many educators today feel that interactive ethics education should be a viable part of all business education curricula. "Developing an atmosphere that rewards and re-inforces ethical conduct should be of paramount importance."[1]

	17
	31
	44
	58
	72
	86
	98

Basis for Ethics — 105

Each culture develops what is considered to be appropriate ways of behaving in various situations. Beliefs about these behaviors are handed down from generation to generation. When individuals change, eventually society reflects these changes in business and other areas of society. Some theories of ethics can be traced to Aristotle and Plato, ancient philosophers.

	118
	132
	146
	160
	173
	179

▼ Whether you are using pica
▼ or elite type, do not key this
▼ material line for line as shown
▼ here. Set your margins for a
▼ leftbound report and key by
▼ your line end signal.

▼ Use the word wrap feature if
▼ you are using a computer.

Simply defined, ethics deals with right and wrong and what is fair and just. Reports of illegal and unethical activities by some business executives in recent years have caused a drop in public con-fidence. Some business executives, however, have become more aware of a need to demonstrate ethical conduct in all aspects of business. "Enlightened members . . . must begin to stand up, publicly and pri-vately, for ethical principles."[2]

	192
	205
	219
	232
	246
	266
	267

Employee Ethics — 273

As high school and college graduates begin job searching, they may encounter new dimensions to the pre-employment tests. While most prospective employees expect to be asked for a resume and application, they may now be expected to complete integrity testing. Along with routine reference and prior employment checks, paper and pencil honesty tests are being used by some institutions to judge job candidates.

	286
	300
	314
	328
	342
	356

Honesty tests usually cost about $6 to $15 each. Customers may buy packets of these questionnaires that call for "yes" or "no" answers. Once they are completed, the forms are scored by computers.

	368
	383
	395

▼ continued on the next page

8e Location Drills—Q and , (Comma)

Directions: Key each line twice. DS after repeated lines.
Technique Goal: Keep your eyes on your copy.

▼ Strike **q** with the **a** finger.
▼
▼ Strike **,** with the **k** finger.

1   q   aqa qa aqa qa aqa quit quit quite quite quote quip

2   quip quick quick quays quays quack quack quad quad

3   , (comma)   k,k ,k k,k ,k k,k mark, fork, lark, dark, the ark,

4   if it, and the, had gone, can do, will see, I did,

8f Technique Builder—Control of , (Comma)

Directions: Key each line twice. DS after repeated lines.
Technique Goal: Be sure that you are using the correct fingering techniques.

Spacing Guide: Remember to space once after a , (comma) used as punctuation.

▼ Spacing Reminder: Space
▼ twice after a period that
▼ ends a sentence; space
▼ only once after a period
▼ following an initial or an
▼ abbreviation. Space once
▼ after a comma.

1   to try, and they, to have, if they, and yet, if my

2   the view, to live, can move, will try, if they try

3   if I, if he, and move, a view, to quote, the quiet

4   Pat, Vern, and Quig will quit the team quite soon.

5   Paul will quit, too. Vickie and I may quit, also.

6   Vic P. lost two books, one pen, and seven pencils.

7   Anne Kane owns one farm, one ranch, and two boats.

8   Lt. Quincy, Sgt. Raye, and Dr. Vance met in Cairo.

8g Keying from Dictation

Directions: Key these words as your teacher dictates them.
Technique Goal: Think the word; key it; space quickly after each word.

1   to to do do to do to do it if he he if he if he if

2   SS   she she the the they they then then them them they

3   an and and she and she and she and she and she and

4   go go got got if it got if it got if they got they

• **Problem 1 -** Title Page

> **Directions:** Format a title page for the report that you completed in Lesson 69. Use the form shown in the illustration of a title page on page 93, and follow the directions given on that page. On your title page, however, use your own name as the writer.

▼ Be sure that you key the bibli-
▼ ography by your end-of-line
▼ signal.
▼
▼ Assemble the report in the
▼ proper sequence and bind it
▼ at the left.

• **Problem 2 -** Bibliography

> **Directions:** Format the bibliography illustrated below for the report that you completed in Lesson 69. Use the same margins that you would use in a leftbound report. Center the heading BIBLIOGRAPHY on line 13. Page number on line 7.

A bibliography is a list of all references cited by the writer in preparing a report. This list is placed at the end of the report. The items in a bibliography are listed in alphabetical sequence by the author's last name.

	words
BIBLIOGRAPHY	3

QS

One author; Magazine article — Chester, Jeffrey A. "Artificial Intelligence: Is MIS Ready for the | 16
Indent ⟶ Explosion?" <u>Infosystems</u>, April 1985, pp. 74-78. SS | 28
DS

Two Authors; Book — Clark, James F., and Kathy Brittain White. <u>Computer Confidence: A</u> | 45
<u>Challenge for Today</u>. Cincinnati: South-Western Publishing Co., | 62
1986. | 63

Henderson, Albert. "Have Your Questions Ready When Shopping for | 76
Software." <u>Office Systems '85</u>, April 1985, pp. 42-46. | 91

Three Authors; Book — Smith, Allen N., Wilma Jean Alexander, and Donald B. Medley. <u>Advanced</u> | 106
<u>Office Systems</u>. Cincinnati: South-Western Publishing Co., 1986. | 123

Will, Mimi, and Donnette Dake. <u>Concepts in Information Processing</u>. | 143
2nd ed. Boston: Allyn and Bacon, 1985. | 151

LESSON 9

9a Keyboard Review

Directions: Key each line once; repeat. **Technique Goal:** Eyes on copy.

1   p   ;p; p; ;p; p; rap map lap rip trip help plan plain

2   v   fvf vf fvf vf van via vim five give live love have

3   q   aqa qa aqa qa quit quip quo aqua quad quite quotes

4   ,   k,k ,k k,k ,k mark, a mark, fork, a fork, the ark,

9b Learning to Keystroke Z and : (Colon)

Reach to Z
1. Strike **z** with the **a** finger.
2. Touch **za** lightly.
3. Keep other fingers in home-key position.
4. Key line 1 below.

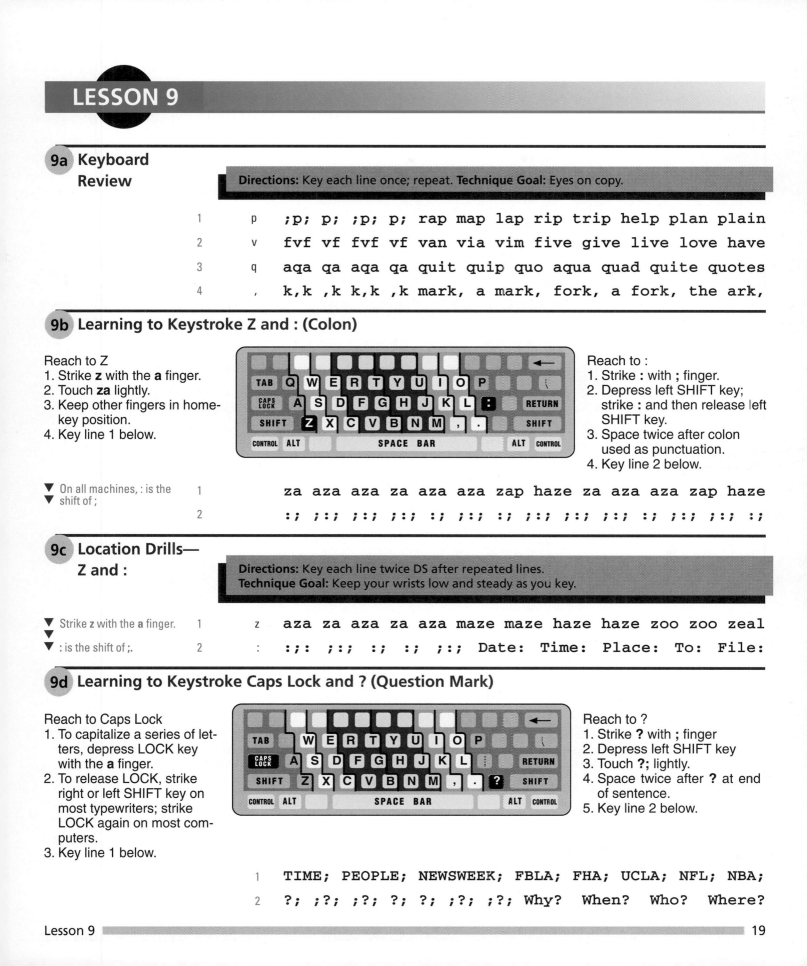

Reach to :
1. Strike : with ; finger.
2. Depress left SHIFT key; strike : and then release left SHIFT key.
3. Space twice after colon used as punctuation.
4. Key line 2 below.

▼ On all machines, : is the
▼ shift of ;

1   za aza aza za aza aza zap haze za aza aza zap haze

2   :; ;:; ;:; ;:; :; ;:; :; ;:; ;:; ;:; :; ;:; ;:; :;

9c Location Drills— Z and :

Directions: Key each line twice DS after repeated lines.
Technique Goal: Keep your wrists low and steady as you key.

▼ Strike **z** with the **a** finger.
▼
▼ : is the shift of ;.

1   z   aza za aza za aza maze maze haze haze zoo zoo zeal

2   :   :;: ;:; :; :; ;:; Date: Time: Place: To: File:

9d Learning to Keystroke Caps Lock and ? (Question Mark)

Reach to Caps Lock
1. To capitalize a series of letters, depress LOCK key with the **a** finger.
2. To release LOCK, strike right or left SHIFT key on most typewriters; strike LOCK again on most computers.
3. Key line 1 below.

Reach to ?
1. Strike ? with ; finger
2. Depress left SHIFT key
3. Touch ?; lightly.
4. Space twice after ? at end of sentence.
5. Key line 2 below.

1   TIME; PEOPLE; NEWSWEEK; FBLA; FHA; UCLA; NFL; NBA;

2   ?; ;?; ;?; ?; ?; ;?; ;?; Why? When? Who? Where?

DS

stores.   Custom software is written exclusively for the job   12

to be done and is usually much more expensive than canned.   24
DS

Henderson has estimated that "20,000 to 34,000 software pack-   36

ages are available for microcomputers."³   Some experts think   48

that custom software plays only a minor role: 58

DS

      Relatively little custom application programming is   67
      done for business microcomputers.   Rather, the market is   77
      delineated principally by the availability of applica-   88
      tion programs that prospective users can understand and   98
      use profitably. . . .   Thus, off-the-shelf application   108
      packages have become major factors in the sale and use   119
      of microcomputers in business.⁴   130

DS

As the new artificial intelligence generation of comput-   141

ers grows, software is becoming very different because of the   153

ability of these units to communicate in simple English.   One   166

authority in this field believes that a selling point for   177

artificial intelligence is "easier communication between hu-   189

mans and machines."⁵   In the new era, software is predicted   201

to reduce costs and improve productivity as computers become   213

more useful than ever before.   219

On the last page of a report the dividing line and footnotes may begin a DS below the last line of text or be placed at the bottom of the page with at least 1" of white space in the bottom margin.

223

_____
DS
SS   ³Albert Henderson, "Have Your Questions Ready When Shop-   234
ping for Software," Office Systems '85, January 1985, p. 42.   250
      DS
      ⁴Allen N. Smith, Wilma Jean Alexander, and Donald B.   261
Medley, Advanced Office Systems. (Cincinnati: South-Western   277
Publishing Co., 1986), pp. 226-227.   284

      ⁵Jeffrey A. Chester, "Artificial Intelligence: Is MIS   295
Ready for the Explosion?" Infosystems, April 1985, p. 75.   309

1 1/2" left margin

1" right margin

Long quotation (four lines or more): single-spaced and indented 5 spaces from left margin.

At least 1"   Second page of two-page leftbound report with footnotes
(Shown in pica type)

9e Location Drills—Caps Lock and ? (Question Mark)

Directions: Key each line twice. DS after repeated lines.
Technique Goal: Release SHIFT key quickly.

▼ Strike LOCK key with the **a** finger.
▼ Strike **?** with ; finger.

1	Caps Lock	I gave reports on LOST HORIZON and DOCTOR ZHIVAGO.
2		Katie read NEWSWEEK and TIME in the library today.
3	Question mark	;?; ?; ;?; ?; ;?; Why? When? How? Will they go?
4		Did he pass the quiz? Did they pass? Did I pass?

9f Technique Builder—Keystroking and Space Bar Control

Directions: Review your space bar control with the illustration at the side. Key each line once. **Technique Goal:** Curve your thumb over the space bar and strike with quick motion.

Curve right thumb over space bar.

Strike with quick down, up, and in motion.

1 qa quit quite quiet quote quotes quest queen quire
2 xs ox oxen lax flax mix mixed fix fox next book six
3 quite sure, and quit, will quote, your quiet quest
4 and mix, can fix, my next, his box, our tax, an ox
5 the prize, my size, any zone, with zeal, and seize
6 Will she go? Who else will go? What is the time?
7 May I use the car? Will he fix it? Can I fix it?
8 Did Zoe write the article for the CHICAGO TRIBUNE?

| 1 | 2 | 3 | 4 | 5 | 6 | 7 | 8 | 9 | 10 |

9g Sentence Guided Writings

Directions: 1. Key each line twice for practice. **2.** Key each line for 1' with the call of the guide. Try to complete each line as the guide is called. **3.** Key 1' writings on the last sentence without the call of the guide.

▼ On guided writing drills, your teacher will explain how the guide will be called.

			words	gwam
1	All letters	Sit up straight while you key.	6	12
2		You must think right to work right.	7	14
3		Fix your eyes on the book as you stroke.	8	16
4		As you tap the keys, do not move your wrists.	9	18
5		Just put some zip in your work; use quick strokes.	10	20

| 1 | 2 | 3 | 4 | 5 | 6 | 7 | 8 | 9 | 10 |

• **Problem 2** - Second Page of a Two-Page Leftbound Report with Footnotes

▼ In the next lesson, you will
▼ format a title page and a bibli-
▼ ography to attach to this
▼ report.

Directions: Format the second page of the report you began in Problem 1. This second page is shown on page 170. If you are using elite type, continue page 2 where you left off in Problem 1, page 166. Refer to page 87 for information on formatting the second page of a leftbound report.

LESSON 70

70a Keyboard Review

5 minutes

Directions: Key each sentence three times.

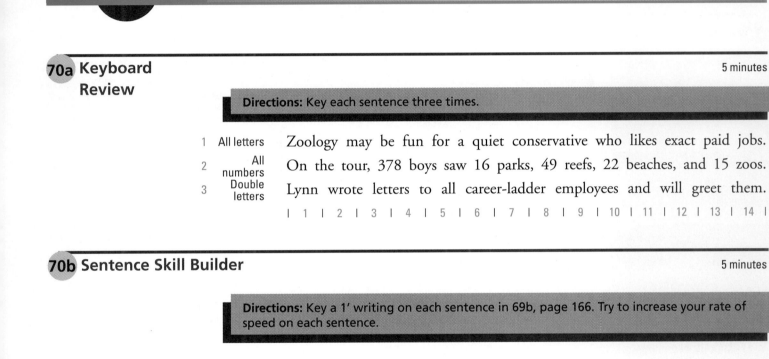

1 All letters   Zoology may be fun for a quiet conservative who likes exact paid jobs.
2 All numbers   On the tour, 378 boys saw 16 parks, 49 reefs, 22 beaches, and 15 zoos.
3 Double letters   Lynn wrote letters to all career-ladder employees and will greet them.

| 1 | 2 | 3 | 4 | 5 | 6 | 7 | 8 | 9 | 10 | 11 | 12 | 13 | 14 |

70b Sentence Skill Builder

5 minutes

Directions: Key a 1' writing on each sentence in 69b, page 166. Try to increase your rate of speed on each sentence.

70c Communication Skill—Use of the Apostrophe

5 minutes

Directions: Key each sentence three times. The first line gives the rule; the remaining lines apply it. Capitalize and punctuate the last sentence correctly.

1   To show possession, use the apostrophe plus "s" after a singular noun.
2   The student's term paper was written about Australia's big Ayers Rock.
3   Coach Wang's trophy had each team member's name engraved on the front.
4   ted s computer and jo s recorder were used for the group s experiment

LESSON 10

10a Keyboard Review

Directions: Key each line twice; repeat if time permits.
Technique Goal: Be sure that you are using a correct keystroking pattern.

▼ Spacing: Single
▼
▼ Margins: 1"

1	z	aza za aza za zone zones zeal size maze doze dozed
2	:	To: From: Date: Subject: Dear Sue: Dear Rick:
3	Caps Lock	She visited these states: CA, TX, NV, MI, MD, OH.
4	?	May she go to the game? Which one? When? Where?

10b Learning to Use the Tab Key for Indenting Paragraphs

TYPEWRITERS
Clearing Tab Stops—Electric
 1. Move the carrier so that the point of key-ing is at the right margin of the paper.
 2. Depress the TAB CLEAR key (same as TAB key on some models) and hold it down as you return the carrier so that the point of keying is at the left margin of the paper. You have now cleared all tab stops.

Clearing Tab Stops—Electronic
 1. Strike TAB Key (No. 31) to move carrier to tab stop you wish to clear.
 2. Depress the TAB CLEAR key to remove the stop.
 3. To remove all stops, depress TAB CLEAR key, then REPEAT key (No. 21)

Setting Tab Stop: Electric/Electronic
 1. Space in five spaces from the left margin.
 2. Depress the TAB SET key (No. 20). You now have a tab stop set for your para-graphs.

COMPUTERS
Your computer has a preset (default) tab for a paragraph indention.

Operating the Tab Key
 1. Depress the RETURN/ENTER key on your typewriter or computer.
 2. Find the TAB key (No. 3) on your machine.
 3. Touch the TAB key lightly using your nearest little finger.
 4. You are now at the point to begin your paragraph.

Other applications of the TAB key will be explained in future lessons.

words

COMPUTER SOFTWARE   4

QS

When working with a computer, one should understand all   15

DS

aspects of the software that must be used. In computer ter-   27

minology, software refers to all the instructions or programs   38

that tell the computer what to do. The two basic types of   50

software are systems and applications.   58

Systems software consists of programs that are designed   69

to keep the computer running and performing tasks related to   82

the system. This software performs general operations and is   94

not designed to solve specific problems. According to Clark   106

and White, several of the more popular operating systems that   119

are used with microcomputers are UNIX, XENIX, MS-DOS, PC-DOS,   131

CP/M, Apple DOS, and TRS-DOS.[1]   137

Applications software consists of programs designed to   148

solve specific problems for the user or to do specific work.   161

Will and Dake say, "Today the most typical microcomputer ap-   173

plications software is electronic spreadsheets, word process-   185

ing, data base, graphics, and communication."[2]   195

Applications software may be either canned or custom.   206

Canned software is a prefabricated program and is purchased in   218

DS

_____   222

DS

SS [1]James P. Clark and Kathy Brittain White, Computer Confi-   236
dence: A Challenge for Today. (Cincinnati: South-Western Pub-   254
lishing Co., 1986), pp. 170-171.   261

DS

[2]Mimi Will and Donnette Dake, Concepts in Information   276
Processing, 2nd ed. (Boston: Allyn and Bacon, Inc., 1985),   290
p. 45.   291

First page of two-page leftbound report with footnotes
(Shown in pica type)

10c Paragraph Keying

To figure *gwam,* note the number at the end of the last complete line keyed in the column at the right. For part of a line completed, note the last stroke according to the scale below the paragraph. Add the two numbers together to find your total *gwam.*

Directions: Set the machine for a 5-space paragraph indention. DS between lines. Complete the paragraph twice. Repeat if time permits. If you are using an electronic typewriter with automatic return or a computer with word wrap, your teacher will give instructions on how to handle the right margin.

	words
Tab → When you key these words, make sure that you	9
DS keep your eyes on your book. Do not look up when	19
you end a line or hit the tab.	25

| 1 | 2 | 3 | 4 | 5 | 6 | 7 | 8 | 9 | 10 |

10d Skill Builder—Keystroking

Directions: Take several 1' timings on each sentence.
Technique Goal: Work alternately for speed and for accuracy.

1   We won the big game when I hit the ball with ease.

2   I do hope that she can play on our team this year.

| 1 | 2 | 3 | 4 | 5 | 6 | 7 | 8 | 9 | 10 |

10e Proofreading Your Work

Directions: You must learn to find and mark your keying errors. Some common errors are shown below. 1. Read the error description below. 2. Refer to the examples circled. Always circle the entire word containing any error.

1. Count only one error per word.

2. Failure to space between words is an error.

3. An omitted letter or an extra letter is an error.

4. The wrong letter or a strikeover is an error.

5. An omitted or an added word is an error.

6. A missed or wrong punctuation mark is an error.

7. An extra space is an error.

8. A transposed letter is an error.

One of the points to (hhavve) in mi
must (thinkwell) to write well; a clear
the (prim) (neeed.)
    We (mush) know, too, how to (usy) the
for ^the right job. Words are (are) tools us
who write Learn to use them (,)
    We (sh ould) all learn to write we
skill high on the (lits) of things

Several methods of acknowledging sources of quoted or closely paraphrased material are footnotes, endnotes, or internal citations. Follow the directions to format sources used in reports.

Footnotes—Number footnotes consecutively throughout a report. The number of the footnote reference should be keyed a half space above the line of writing immediately after the quoted material and a correspondingly numbered footnote at the bottom of the page. To determine vertical line space for copy to end and to place footnotes, follow these steps.

1. Allow 3 lines for divider rule and the blank line space above and below it, 3 lines for each note, and 6 lines for the bottom margin.

2. Subtract the sum of these figures from 66 (the number of lines on a full sheet). This will give you the last line on which text should be keyed.

3. After keying the last line of text, DS and key a 1 1/2-inch line (15, pica and 18, elite). DS and indent 5 spaces; key a superscript (raised 1/2 line space) number for the first note; follow with the reference material. DS and continue in the same manner for footnote 2.

4. Leave at least a 1" margin at bottom.

Computer: Many word processing software packages have a footnote and endnote function. If your teacher directs, use the procedure given in your software instructions to key footnotes and endnotes.

For equipment that does not permit half spacing, the reference figure may be keyed on the line of writing immediately preceded and followed by a diagonal:

```
...as reported." /1/ Other
writers. . .
```

Endnotes—References to quoted or closely paraphrased material may be placed at the end of the report on a separate page. To format endnotes, follow these steps.

1. Use consecutively numbered superscripts to cite quoted material within the body of a report.

2. Use the same margins and center point as for the report and begin endnotes on a separate page.

3. Key the page number on line 7 at the right margin and center the heading, ENDNOTES.

4. Key the first superscript followed by the reference. The second line of the endnote begins at the margin. DS after the endnote.

5. Key the second and succeeding endnotes in the same manner.

Internal Citations—This citation method is rapidly replacing the footnote method because it is easier and quicker. Follow these steps to use internal citations in reports.

1. Immediately following the quoted material, key in parentheses: the name of the author(s), the year of publication, and the page number(s) cited.

2. Complete reference citations are keyed on a separate page or on the last page of the report if adequate room exists.

3. The reference page uses the same top and side margins as the first page of the report. The word REFERENCES is centered.

10f Paragraph Keying

Directions: 1. Set the machine for a 5-space paragraph indention. DS between lines. **2.** Key the paragraphs below one time, and circle any errors. **3.** Key a 1' writing on each paragraph. Try to make fewer errors and try to increase your *gwam* on each paragraph.

▼ The syllable intensity (*si*) is
▼ given for the paragraphs. It is
▼ a guide to the difficulty of the
▼ material. Copy of average dif-
▼ ficulty is said to have an si of
▼ 1.5. Thus, this material is con-
▼ sidered quite easy.

¶ 1
22 words
1.0 si

¶ 2
25 words
1.0 si

¶ 3
28 words
1.0 si

All letters are used

	words in ¶	total words
DS One of the points to have in mind is that we	9	9
must think well to write well; a clear thought is	19	19
the prime need.	22	22
We must know, too, how to use the right word	9	31
for the right job. Words are tools used by those	19	41
who write. Learn to use them.	25	47
We should all learn to write well. Fix this	9	56
skill high on the list of the things that we need	19	66
to do; we may go on a quest for it with zeal.	28	75

| 1 | 2 | 3 | 4 | 5 | 6 | 7 | 8 | 9 | 10 |

LESSON 69

69a Keyboard Review

5 minutes

Directions: Key each sentence three times.

1	All letters	Philip Jackson wanted Norma Z. Gorman to move to Quebec next February.
2	Shift	Zack attended LSU; Juan, Ohio State; Keiko, USC; and Anne, Ball State.
3	Numbers	If you add 15, 23, 64, 90, 124, and 78, you will get an answer of 394.
4	Easy	You may think that money is easy to spend but usually hard to save.

| 1 | 2 | 3 | 4 | 5 | 6 | 7 | 8 | 9 | 10 | 11 | 12 | 13 | 14 |

69b Sentence Skill Builder—Script

5 minutes

Directions: Key each sentence three times.

1 *You should work to attain both speed and accuracy in your keyboarding.*

2 *Speed and accuracy are reached only through your hard work and effort.*

3 *Your teacher will help, but you must have the desire to be successful.*

69c Communication Skill—Spelling

5 minutes

Directions: Key each sentence twice.
Technique Goal: Study the spelling of each word shown in italics.

1 English classes *adopted* the use of that *reference style* to *cite* works.
2 Mr. Umeki used *alphabetic*, *numeric*, and *geographic illustrations* well.
3 *Further* research will be done with *publications* and *technical manuals*.

69d Problem Formatting

30 minutes

- **Problem 1** - First Page of a Two-Page Leftbound Report with Footnotes

Directions: Format the first page of the report illustrated on page 168. Study the directions given on the illustration. Refer to page 167 for directions on formatting footnotes. Also, review the directions that were given on page 87 for formatting leftbound reports. The illustration on page 168 is shown in pica type. If you are using elite type, do not remove your paper when you finish formatting the first page. Continue with content for Problem 2 until your first page is filled to the divider line.

In Unit 2 you will begin to develop a higher level of keying skill, and you will attempt to increase your speed and accuracy. You will also begin to apply keying to communication skills, and you will begin to compose at your typewriter or computer.

General Directions: Single-space (SS) sentences and drill lines. Double-space (DS) between groups of repeated lines. Double-space paragraph copy. Set your machine for a 5-space paragraph indention. Use 1" side margins or default margins for all lessons in this unit.

Time Schedule: Beginning with this unit, practice time is given for each section of a lesson. If varying this time schedule seems best, do so with the approval of your teacher.

Technique Goals: Good techniques are critical in the development of high-level keyboarding skill. Read and follow all technique goals. Review the guides for good form given on page 1.

LESSON 11

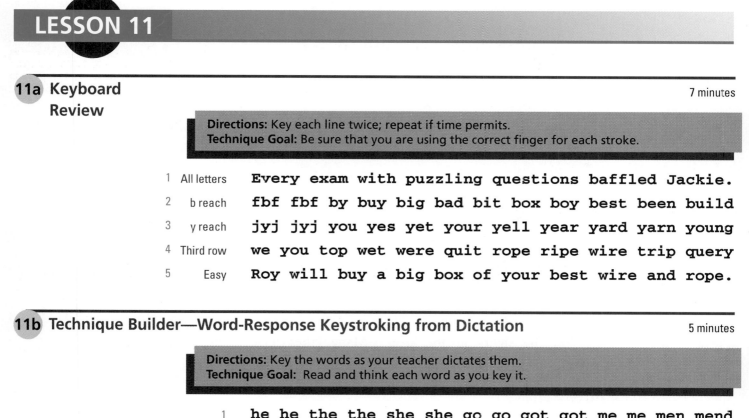

11a Keyboard Review
7 minutes

Directions: Key each line twice; repeat if time permits.
Technique Goal: Be sure that you are using the correct finger for each stroke.

1 All letters   Every exam with puzzling questions baffled Jackie.

2 b reach   fbf fbf by buy big bad bit box boy best been build

3 y reach   jyj jyj you yes yet your yell year yard yarn young

4 Third row   we you top wet were quit rope ripe wire trip query

5 Easy   Roy will buy a big box of your best wire and rope.

11b Technique Builder—Word-Response Keystroking from Dictation
5 minutes

Directions: Key the words as your teacher dictates them.
Technique Goal: Read and think each word as you key it.

1   he he the the she she go go got got me me men mend

2   an an and and all all air air but but box box book

3   and then and that and this and he and she and they

4   this is this was this will can go can do we can go

5   he will go she will go for them for they for it is

Directions: 1. Key a 5' writing on the paragraphs below. Circle errors and determine *gwam*. **2.** Key a 1' writing on each paragraph. Push for speed; try to reach the end of the paragraph within the minute. **3.** Key another 5' writing over all paragraphs combined. Circle errors and determine *gwam*. Submit the better of the writings to your teacher.

All letters

Copy difficulty level: Average

	gwam	
	1'	5'

Travel to nearby or distant locations is a way to broaden your travel experiences. Whether your travel is for business or pleasure, you need to make arrangements for places to stay, modes of travel, and any special events.

Your visit may include national and state parks. The first national park was begun more than a century ago. Since then, many parks have been established in all parts of the country. Various parks feature mines, rocks, seashore, or trees.

1.5 si
5.7 awl
80% hfw

If you have seen many of the parks, perhaps you will want to try a cruise. This floating hotel includes rooms, entertainment, meals, and even classes. One price is charged for the cruise. Some cruises are for three or four days while others may take a year.

Flying is a popular mode of travel. It is a quick way to reach your destination, and many flights are nonstop from one city to another. The added bonus of air travel is earning points toward free flights. The points are based on the number of miles one flies with each airline.

Once you reach your destination, you may wish to get information on the sights in the area. Many cities have a visitor's guide which lists places of interest, historic tours, museums, zoos, and special events. Some guides include places to dine as well as useful phone numbers. Enjoy a nice visit!

gwam values by line:

1'	5'
13	3 / 55
27	5 / 57
41	8 / 60
44	9 / 61
14	12 / 63
29	14 / 68
43	17 / 70
48	18 / 71
13	21 / 73
28	25 / 76
42	27 / 78
52	29 / 81
13	31 / 83
27	34 / 86
41	37 / 89
56	40 / 92
13	42 / 94
27	45 / 97
41	48 / 100
54	51 / 102
60	52 / 104

1' | 1 | 2 | 3 | 4 | 5 | 6 | 7 | 8 | 9 | 10 | 11 | 12 | 13 | 14 |
5' | 1 | 2 | 3 |

11c Sentence Guided Writings

Directions: 1. Key each line twice for practice. **2.** Key each line for 1' with the call of the guide. Try to complete each line as the guide is called. **3.** Key 1' timings on the 5th sentence without the call of the guide.

	All letters are used	words	gwam 30'
1	Do keep your eyes on the book.	6	12
2	The big goal is to key as you view.	7	14
3	Skill is the right mix of mind and zeal.	8	16
4	Words are fine tools used by those who write.	9	18
5	We should plan ways to use these tools quite well.	10	20
6	*Your job here is to key each line by a time guide.*	10	20

| 1 | 2 | 3 | 4 | 5 | 6 | 7 | 8 | 9 | 10 |

11d Paragraph Keying

Directions: 1. Set the machine for a 5-space paragraph indention and for double spacing. **2.** Key the paragraphs once. Circle any errors. **3.** Key a 1' writing on each paragraph.

		words in ¶	total words
¶1 24 words 1.0 si	A skill is not easy to build. It takes much	9	9
	hard work. As you learn to stroke, try to keep a	19	19
	clear view of your goals.	24	24
¶2 28 words 1.0 si	One goal is to keep your eyes on the book as	9	33
	your stroke. This goal will help you to push your	19	43
	skill to a high rate of speed with more ease.	28	52
¶3 32 words 1.0 si	One more goal is to strike each key with the	9	61
	best reach. This goal will aid you in all you do	19	71
	in this course. Your skill will grow as you meet	29	81
	all your goals.	32	84

| 1 | 2 | 3 | 4 | 5 | 6 | 7 | 8 | 9 | 10 |

68c Skill Comparison

Directions: Key a 1' writing on each sentence in 68a, page 163. Compare *gwam* on each sentence.

68d Technique Builder—Keystroking

5 minutes

Directions: Key each line three times.

1	Difficult reach	Many informed scientists were unanimously united to fight the unknown.
2	Weak fingers	Polite political opponents shouldn't publicly oppose popular opinions.
3	Weak fingers	We were unaware that the puzzled quorum wouldn't quickly award prizes.
4	Double letters	That bookkeeper had an occasion to correct the errors in the accounts.

| 1 | 2 | 3 | 4 | 5 | 6 | 7 | 8 | 9 | 10 | 11 | 12 | 13 | 14 |

68e Skill Comparison

5 minutes

Directions: Key a 1' writing on the lines in 68d above. Compare your *gwam* on the varied types of keystroking.

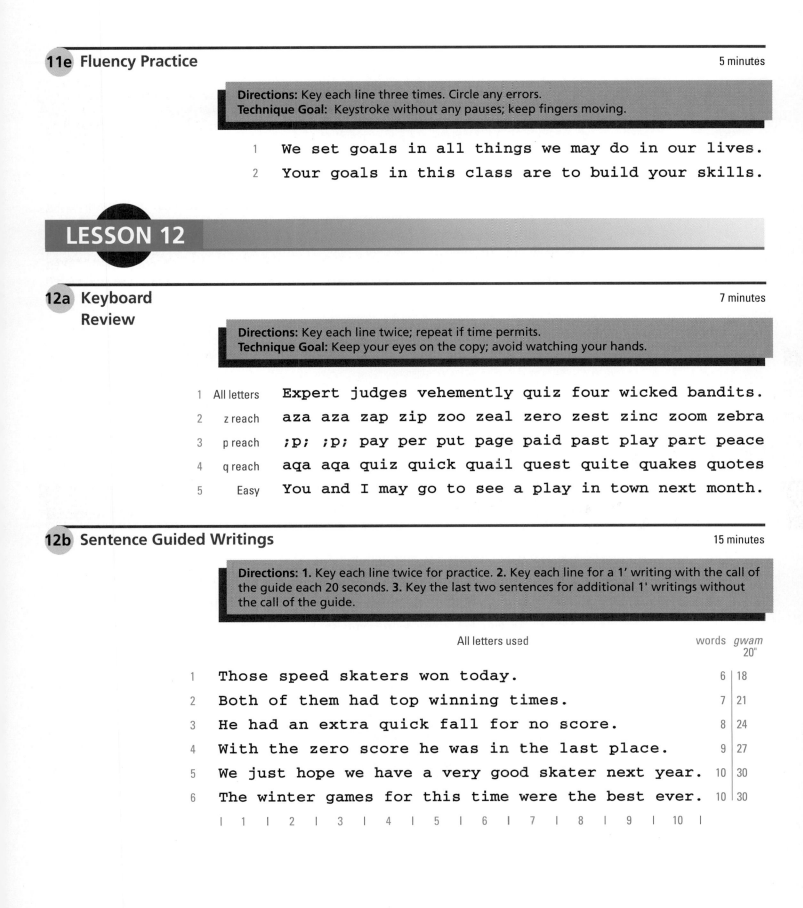

11e Fluency Practice

5 minutes

Directions: Key each line three times. Circle any errors.
Technique Goal: Keystroke without any pauses; keep fingers moving.

1   We set goals in all things we may do in our lives.
2   Your goals in this class are to build your skills.

LESSON 12

12a Keyboard Review

7 minutes

Directions: Key each line twice; repeat if time permits.
Technique Goal: Keep your eyes on the copy; avoid watching your hands.

1	All letters	Expert judges vehemently quiz four wicked bandits.
2	z reach	aza aza zap zip zoo zeal zero zest zinc zoom zebra
3	p reach	;p; ;p; pay per put page paid past play part peace
4	q reach	aqa aqa quiz quick quail quest quite quakes quotes
5	Easy	You and I may go to see a play in town next month.

12b Sentence Guided Writings

15 minutes

Directions: 1. Key each line twice for practice. **2.** Key each line for a 1' writing with the call of the guide each 20 seconds. **3.** Key the last two sentences for additional 1' writings without the call of the guide.

	All letters used	words	*gwam* 20"
1	Those speed skaters won today.	6	18
2	Both of them had top winning times.	7	21
3	He had an extra quick fall for no score.	8	24
4	With the zero score he was in the last place.	9	27
5	We just hope we have a very good skater next year.	10	30
6	The winter games for this time were the best ever.	10	30

| 1 | 2 | 3 | 4 | 5 | 6 | 7 | 8 | 9 | 10 |

UNIT 14 FORMATTING PROFESSIONAL REPORTS AND DOCUMENTS

Lessons 68-75

In this unit, you will learn how to format reports that have footnotes, endnotes, and internal citations. You will also format a title page, bibliography, and a memorandum report as well as other professional documents. You will continue to build skills in keying, communicating, composing, and proofreading.

General Directions: For drills and timed writings in this unit, use side margins of 1" for elite, 1/2" for pica, and standard defaults if you are using a computer. For problems, set margins as directed. SS sentences and drill lines and DS paragraph copy. DS between groups of repeated lines. Space problem copy as directed in each lesson.

LESSON 68

68a Keyboard Review

5 minutes

Directions: Key each sentence three times; repeat if time permits.

1	All letters	Rex jumped up and ran quickly over the hills away from a grizzly bear.
2	All numbers	Insurance claim number A780452C6 was paid in full on January 31, 1992.
3	pol	A policy that police favor is not always popular with all politicians.
4	Easy	As you key these words you should not ever need to look at your hands.

| 1 | 2 | 3 | 4 | 5 | 6 | 7 | 8 | 9 | 10 | 11 | 12 | 13 | 14 |

68b Building Skill on Numbers and Symbols

5 minutes

Directions: Key each line three times.
Technique Goal: Work for control.

1 Zeb owed $431. 92 on invoice #57680; he paid 10% of the bill on May 25.

2 "Who," Drake asked, "is the new officer selected to command the ship?"

3 State-of-the-art technology is often used in modern-day legal offices.

4 The new payment policy (2/10, n/30) will start next week (February 1).

| 1 | 2 | 3 | 4 | 5 | 6 | 7 | 8 | 9 | 10 | 11 | 12 | 13 | 14 |

12c Paragraph Keying

Directions: 1. Use a 5-space paragraph indention and double spacing. **2.** Key the paragraphs once. Circle any errors. **3.** Key a 1' writing on each paragraph.

All letters used

	words in ¶	total words

¶1
28 words
1.0 si

Do not let a pause slow you down if you want — 9 | 9
to stroke fast. In great part, your speed may be — 19 | 19
based on a way you have made your time count. — 28 | 28

¶2
28 words
1.0 si

Size up the way that you strike all of your — 9 | 37
keys. Your strokes should be quick, crisp, and — 19 | 47
sharp. Just know that lost time can tax speed. — 28 | 56

| 1 | 2 | 3 | 4 | 5 | 6 | 7 | 8 | 9 | 10 |

12d Communication Skill—Keying in All Capital Letters

Directions: Key each line twice; repeat if time permits.
Technique Goal: Depress the lock key with the a finger.

▼ The complete names of
▼ books, magazines and
▼ newspapers may be under-
▼ lined or capitalized. On
▼ some computers they may
▼ be italicized.

1 A most recent book by Alvin Toffler is POWERSHIFT.

2 I can see a new issue of SEVENTEEN in our library.

3 Kerry wrote those articles for the NEW YORK TIMES.

12e Technique Builder—Word Response Keystroking

Directions: Key each line twice; repeat if time permits.
Technique Goal: Think each word as you key it.

▼ Begin to think in groups of
▼ words as shown by the
▼ vertical lines. Do not key
▼ the lines between the
▼ words.

1 he | he | did | he did | she did | she did | she did the

2 an | and he | and she | and she | and if she | and she

3 do | go | do go | and do | and do go | and go | to go to

4 for | for | it | for it | for it is | is the | it is the

▼ For these problems, use your
▼ judgment on spacing
▼ between columns. Key a
▼ rough draft; edit; key a final
▼ copy.

• **Problem 1 -** Three-Column Table with Main and Secondary Headings

Directions: Compose and format a table which includes the following information. The main heading will be MY TWENTY MOST-USED ZIP CODES. The secondary heading will be Compiled by (Your Name). Three columns will have blocked headings for City, State, Zip Code. Center the table vertically and horizontally on a full sheet of paper. Be sure to include locations which you key frequently.

• **Problem 2 -** Table With Computations

Directions: Format a table which lists total cost for the quantity and price of bicycles on hand. Use the current date as secondary heading and an appropriate main heading. You will need to compute the total cost for the third column. Center vertically and horizontally on a half sheet.

Quantity	Price	Total Cost
6	$ 564.39	$
3	321.00	
1	2,000.00	
2	195.99	
5	68.75	
8	219.99	

• **Problem 3 -** Compose and Format a Two-Column Table

Directions: Format a table with the names of ten people who are prominent in the entertainment world. Indicate the medium in which each is best known. Use main, secondary, and blocked columnar headings. Format the table on a half sheet of paper.

• **Problem 4 -** Table With Source Note

Directions: Format a table using the information shown below of the population of the largest U.S. cities according to the 1990 census. Use main, secondary, and blocked columnar headings. Use a source note: The World Almanac and Book of Facts, 1993 (New York: Pharos Books, 1992), p. 392. Center the table vertically and horizontally on a full sheet of paper.

New York, NY - 7,322,564; Los Angeles, CA - 3,485,398; Chicago, IL - 2,783,726; Houston, TX - 1,630,553; Philadelphia, PA - 1,585,577; San Diego, CA - 1,110,549; Detroit, MI - 1,027,974; Dallas, TX - 1,006,877; Phoenix, AZ - 983,403; San Antonio, TX - 935,933

LESSON 13

13a Keyboard Review

7 minutes

Directions: Key each line twice; repeat if time permits.
Technique Goal: Key without pauses; keep your fingers moving.

1	All letters	Knox Duque saw my large zebra jump over his craft.
2	br reach	brown brake broke bright bronze brain brief brands
3	nu reach	nut null nun nudge number nurse nugget nutty nudge
4	x reach	sxs sxs six fix mix fox next text hoax sixty taxed
5	Easy	Keep your eyes on the book when you key this line.

13b Composing at the Keyboard

7 minutes

Directions: With this drill, you will begin to start building your skill at composing directly at your keyboard without using a pen or pencil. This valuable skill will save you time and energy. Watch your paper or your screen, not your hands, as you compose.

▼ When composing, do not
▼ worry about accuracy on
▼ your first copy, the rough
▼ draft. Later you will learn how
▼ to edit and prepare a final
▼ copy.

1. Key all the words you recall beginning with the letter **r**.

2. Key all the words you recall beginning with the letter **u**.

3. Key all the words you recall ending with the letters **ing**.

4. Key all the words you recall ending with the letters **ed**.

13c Technique Builder—Word Response Keystroking

5 minutes

Directions: Key each line twice; repeat if time permits.
Technique Goal: Think each word as you key it.

▼ Try to think in groups of
▼ words
▼
▼ Do not key the lines
▼ between the words.

1	my | and | my | and may | and may | and it may | and may
2	now | now | it | now it | now it is | now it| now it is
3	we | we | had | we had | she had | she had | she had the
4	not | not | us | not us | not us or | not us | not us or
5	let | let | me | let me | let me go | let me | let me go

- **Problem 1 -** Three-Column Table with Blocked Columnar Headings

Directions: 1. Format the table shown below. **2.** Center it in reading position on a full sheet of paper. **3.** Double-space all parts. **4.** Leave 6 spaces between columns. **5.** Block and underline the columnar headings at the left edge of each column.

words

NOTED PERSONALITIES			4
(Firsts by American Women)			9
Year	Woman	Achievement	19
1916	Jeanette Rankin	U.S. Congress, Representative	29
1921	Edith Wharton	Pulitzer Recipient (in fiction)	39
1924	Nellie Tayloe Ross	Governor	46
1981	Jeane J. Kirkpatrick	United Nations, U.S. Representative	58
1981	Sandra Day O'Connor	U.S. Supreme Court Justice	68

- **Problem 2 -** Table With Blocked Columnar Headings and Source Note

Directions: 1. Format the table below. **2.** Center the table in exact vertical and horizontal center on a full sheet of paper. **3.** Double-space all parts. **4.** Leave 4 spaces between columns. **5.** Block (flush) and underline the columnar headings at the left edge of each column. **6.** Format the source note using the directions given to the left of the problem.

▼ Reference notes or sources are placed directly below the table even though the table may fill only a partial page. After the last line of the table, double-space and key a line (use the underline) 1 1/2" long. Double-space after this line, and key the reference note or source.

▼ The * (asterisk) may be used to refer the reader to a reference note.

▼ The word "source" may be used to refer to the source of the information for the table.

▼ A two-line note or source is keyed the width of the table.

▼ Notes or sources should be single-spaced with a double space between them if more than one is given.

words

TOP CABLE NETWORKS			4
Compiled by National Cable Television Association			14
Network	Started	Content	23
ESPN	1979	Business, Sports Events	30
CNN	1980	News, Special Interest	36
TBS	1976	Movies, Sports	41
USA Network	1980	Sports, Family	50
Entertainment			58
Nickelodeon	1979	Children, Young Adult	65
MTV	1981	Music Videos, Concerts	70
TNN	1983	Country Music, Talk	76
C-SPAN	1979	Public Affairs	86
The Family Channel	1977	Movies, Family, Religious	97
The Discovery Channel	1985	Nonfiction, Nature, Science	101
			118

Source: The Universal Almanac, 1991 (Kansas City: Andrews and McMeel, 1990), p. 241.

119

13d Sentence Guided Writings

15 minutes

> **Directions: 1.** Key each line twice for practice. **2.** Key each line for a 1' writing with the call of the guide each 20 seconds. **3.** Key the last two sentences for additional 1' timings as time permits without the call of the guide.

All letters used

		words in line	gwam 20' guide
1	Set a high goal for your work.	6	18
2	Work hard and reach your high goal.	7	21
3	Use a quick stroke for each of the keys.	8	24
4	Just fix your eyes on the copy as you stroke.	9	27
5	Do your best to key a line as the guide is called.	10	30
6	*If you add zip to the work, you can have some fun.*	10	30

| 1 | 2 | 3 | 4 | 5 | 6 | 7 | 8 | 9 | 10 |

13e Timed Writings

10 minutes

> **Directions: 1.** Key the paragraphs once for practice, then complete a 1' writing on each. **2.** Take a 2' writing on both paragraphs combined. Circle errors. Determine *gwam* on all writings. In figuring your *gwam* for the writings on the paragraphs, use the 1' column at the right and the 1' scale underneath the paragraphs to figure your 1' rate. Use the 2' column and scale to figure your 2' rate.

		gwam	
		1'	2'

¶1
34 words
1.0 si

That first time when one gets a new car is a — 9 | 5
great day. That car will look new; it will feel — 19 | 10
new; and it will smell new. But it will get old — 29 | 15
much too soon if we let it. — 34 | 17

¶2
38 words
1.0 si

We can try to keep a car new. We can change — 9 | 22
the oil. We can check the tires. We can tune it. — 19 | 27
We can wash and shine it. We can try our best to — 29 | 32
keep it new, but a car will still grow old. — 38 | 36

| 1' | 1 | 2 | 3 | 4 | 5 | 6 | 7 | 8 | 9 | 10 |
| 2' | | 1 | | 2 | | 3 | | 4 | | 5 | |

- **Problem 2 -** Three-Column Table with Main and Secondary Headings

Directions: Format the three-column table shown below. Center it in reading position on a full sheet of paper. Double-space all parts. Leave 6 spaces between columns.

			words
SHUSTER TECHNICAL INSTITUTE			6
Spring President's List			10
Eva Manuel	High Honors	Business	17
Ada Wilfredo	Honors	Chemistry	23
Susan Thompson	High Honors	Drafting	30
Joseph Weiss	Honors	Electronics	36
Mary Polk	Distinction	Geology	42
Fumiko Masami	Honors	Horticulture	49
Leighton Holland	High Honors	Mathematics	57

- **Problem 3 -** Critical Thinking Skill Development—Compose a Three-Column Table

Directions: On a half-sheet, format a three-column table with the following main and secondary headings: UNITED STATES / Tourist Attractions. List five or more of your favorite tourist attractions, such as Disney World. After the name of the attraction, list the city and state in which it is located. Decide on appropriate spacing between the columns.

LESSON 67

67a Keyboard Review

5 minutes

Directions: Key each sentence three times.

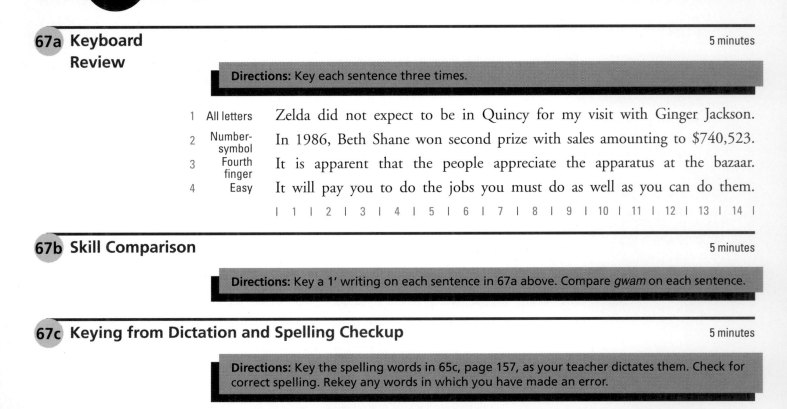

1	All letters	Zelda did not expect to be in Quincy for my visit with Ginger Jackson.
2	Number-symbol	In 1986, Beth Shane won second prize with sales amounting to $740,523.
3	Fourth finger	It is apparent that the people appreciate the apparatus at the bazaar.
4	Easy	It will pay you to do the jobs you must do as well as you can do them.

| 1 | 2 | 3 | 4 | 5 | 6 | 7 | 8 | 9 | 10 | 11 | 12 | 13 | 14 |

67b Skill Comparison

5 minutes

Directions: Key a 1' writing on each sentence in 67a above. Compare *gwam* on each sentence.

67c Keying from Dictation and Spelling Checkup

5 minutes

Directions: Key the spelling words in 65c, page 157, as your teacher dictates them. Check for correct spelling. Rekey any words in which you have made an error.

UNIT 3 LEARNING THE NUMBER KEYS Lessons 14-18

In Unit 3 you will develop efficient key-stroking of all the numbers on the keyboard. You will continue to build continuity as well as develop greater speed and accuracy.

General Directions: Use 1" side margins or default margins for all lessons in this unit. SS sentence and drill lines and DS paragraph copy. DS between groups of repeated lines. Set a tab stop for a 5-space paragraph indention.

If you are using a computer with a numeric keypad, directions and drills for its use are found in the Appendix of this book. Your teacher will give you instructions and tell you if and when you will work with the keypad in this course.

LESSON 14

14a Keyboard Review
5 minutes

Directions: Key each line twice; repeat if time permits.
Technique Goal: Keep your keys on your copy as you strike the keys.

1	All letters	Haze just blocked my sixth quest to view Fern Gap.
2	Shift keys	Ray, Luis, Sue and Oki will go to Seattle in July.
3	?	May Carol go? Can Haru go now? Why will Lisa go?
4	Easy	That old key will not fit the lock on my new door.

14b Learning to Keystroke 8 and 1
7 minutes

Learning new keys: Follow the instructions given in Lesson 2, page 6, as you learn the number keys.

Reach to 8
1. Strike **8** with **k** finger.
2. Touch **k8k** lightly several times.
3. Make reaches to top row by extending fingers.
4. Key line 1 below.

Reach to 1
1. Strike **1** with **a** finger.
2. Touch **a1a** lightly several times.
3. Keep other fingers in home position.
4. Key line 2 below.

| 1 | k8k k8k k8k 8k 8k 8k k8k k8k k8k k8k 8k 8k k8k |
| 2 | a1a a1a a1a 1a 1a 1a a1a a1a a1a a1a a1 a1 a1a |

LESSON 66

66a Keyboard Review

5 minutes

> **Directions:** Key each sentence three times.

1	All letters	Mickey Peck will attempt to squeeze five or six juicy oranges by hand.
2	Number-symbol	We took 1/2 (50%) from the cost of invoice 367 and 1/4 (25%) from 368.
3	Shift	Kara Wilson and Cris Waler were UCLA fans, but Carl Perry favored USC.
4	Easy	We bought the land by the lake to build a cabin for our fishing trips.

| 1 | 2 | 3 | 4 | 5 | 6 | 7 | 8 | 9 | 10 | 11 | 12 | 13 | 14 |

66b Paragraph Skill Builder

5 minutes

> **Directions:** Key two 1' writings on each paragraph in 64b, page 153. Try to increase your rate on each writing by 2 to 4 words.

66c Communication Skill—Use of Parentheses

5 minutes

> **Directions:** Key each sentence three times. The first line gives the rule; the remaining lines apply it. Capitalize and punctuate the last sentence correctly.

1. Parentheses should be used to enclose nonessential explanatory matter.
2. Fifteen (15) girls, twelve (12) boys, and two (2) teachers were there.
3. Two players (Jon Zemp and Tracy Green) were asked to present an award.
4. tuition costs $2000 and fees $100 were given to the winner jody

66d Problem Formatting

30 minutes

- **Problem 1** - Two-Column Table with Main and Secondary Heading

> **Directions: 1.** Format the table shown below. **2.** Position it in exact vertical and horizontal center on a half sheet of paper with long side up. **3.** Leave 6 spaces between columns. Double-space all parts of the table.

		words
FASTEST GROWING OCCUPATIONS		6
Civilian Employment		10
Medical Assistants	Home Health Aides	17
Radiology Technicians	Medical Secretaries	25
Financial Service Workers	Travel Agents	33
Computer Systems Analysts	Computer Programmers	43
Human Services Workers	Corrections Officers	51
Electronics Engineers	Information Clerks	59

14c Location Drills—8, 1

7 minutes

Directions: Key each line twice; repeat.
Technique Goal: Use the correct finger on each of the number keys.

▼ Strike **8** with the **k** finger.
▼
▼ Strike **1** with the **a** finger.

```
1    8    k8k 8k k8k 8k 8k 8k 8k 8 kids, 88 kites, 888 kilos
2    1    a1a a1a a1a 1a 1a 1a 11 apes, 11 apples, 11 actors
3         I had 8 keys.  He has 88 kegs.  I own 1,111 acres.
```

14d Key-Location Practice

10 minutes

Directions: Key each line twice; repeat.
Technique Goal: Keep your eyes on your book as you are keystroking.

```
1    Now read pages 18 to 81 and 88 to 111 in the book.
2    Al worked 18 hours last week and sold 818 tickets.
3    All 88 of the students made higher than 81 points.
4    She read 81 pages in 81 minutes. I read 88 pages.
5    We own 8,181 acres in Texas and 11,818 in Arizona.
```

14e Continuity Practice

16 minutes

Directions: Key once; circle errors; repeat.
Technique Goal: Keystroke steadily and try to maintain accuracy.

All letters

		gwam	
	1'	3'	

```
          We now live in a new age.  Science is moving     9    3   28
at such a dizzy pace that we can get out of touch          19    6   31
so quickly.  Just to expose ourselves to life is          29   10   35
not enough.  We should know why things change.            38   13   38
          If we look around us, we will find the key       47   16   41
to the change in this new age.  That key is the           56   19   44
computer.  Our world is now built around this new         66   22   47
machine, and we must all understand how it works.         76   25   50
```

¶1
38 words
1.2 si

¶2
38 words
1.2 si

```
1'|  1  |  2  |  3  |  4  |  5  |  6  |  7  |  8  |  9  |  10  |
3'|     1     |       2       |       3       |      4      |
```

- **Problem 2 -** Three-Column Table in Script

Directions: 1. Format a table with the information shown below. **2.** Center it in exact vertical and horizontal center on a full sheet of paper. **3.** Center the main heading. **4.** Double-space all parts. **5.** Leave 8 spaces between columns.

▼ Option: Your teacher may
▼ direct you to center the prob-
▼ lem in reading position. For
▼ reading position, subtract 2
▼ lines from the normal top
▼ margin.
▼
▼ SS a two-line entry; DS fol-
▼ lowing the second line of the
▼ column

			words
SELECTED NOBEL PEACE PRIZE RECIPIENTS			8
1990	Mikhail S. Gorbachev	U. S. S. R.	15
1989	Dalai Lama	Tibet	19
1988	United Nations		23
	Peacekeeping Forces	----	28
1987	Oscar Arias Sanchez	Costa Rica	35
1986	Elie Wiesel	U. S.	40
1985	Intl. Physicians for the		47
	Prevention of Nuclear War	U. S.	53
1984	Bishop Desmond Tutu	South Africa	61
1983	Lech Walesa	Poland	66
1982	Alva Myrdal	Sweden	71
	Alphonso Garcia Robles	Mexico	77
1981	Office of the United Nations		83
	High Commissioner for Refugees	----	90
1980	Adolfo Perez Esquivel	Argentina	98
1979	Mother Teresa of Calcutta	India	105
1978	Menachem Begin	Israel	110
	Anwar Sadat	Egypt	114
1977	Amnesty International	----	120

LESSON 15

15a Keyboard Review

5 minutes

Directions: Key each line twice; repeat.
Technique Goal: Observe good posture as you are keystroking.

1	All letters	C. J. bought six pounds of quartz to pave my walk.
2	8	k8k k8k 8k 8k 88 kinds, 888 keys, 8 and 88 and 888
3	1	a1a a1a 1a 1a 11 ships, 111 jets, 1 and 11 and 111
4	Easy	I like my new car as it does not use too much gas.

15b Learning to Keystroke 9 and 4

5 minutes

Reach to 9
1. Strike **9** with **I** finger
2. Touch **I9I** lightly several times.
3. Lift first and second fingers slightly to give freer action.
4. Key line 1 below.

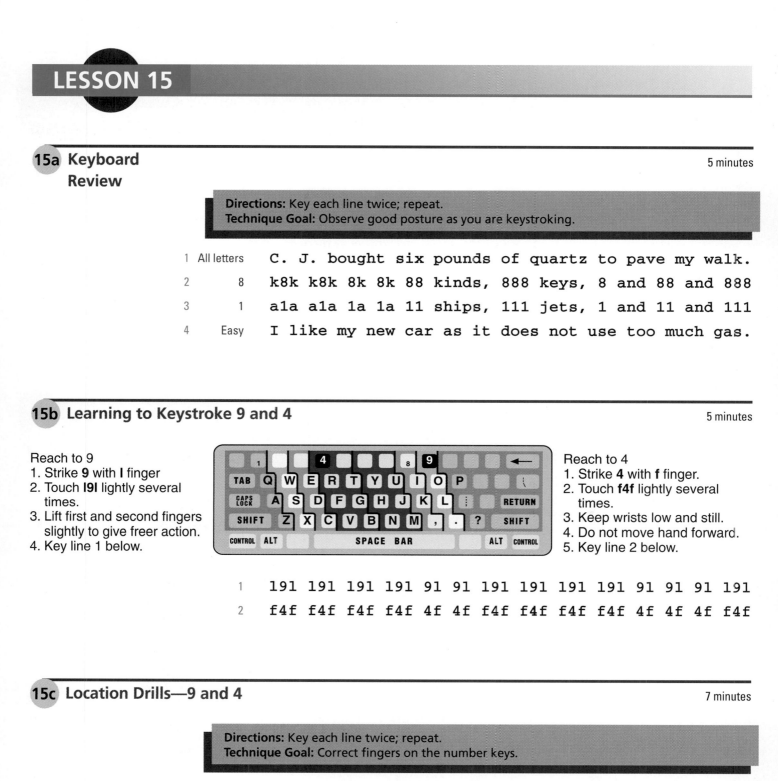

Reach to 4
1. Strike **4** with **f** finger.
2. Touch **f4f** lightly several times.
3. Keep wrists low and still.
4. Do not move hand forward.
5. Key line 2 below.

| 1 | 191 191 191 191 91 91 191 191 191 191 91 91 91 191 |
| 2 | f4f f4f f4f f4f 4f 4f f4f f4f f4f f4f 4f 4f 4f f4f |

15c Location Drills—9 and 4

7 minutes

Directions: Key each line twice; repeat.
Technique Goal: Correct fingers on the number keys.

▼ Strike **9** with the **I** finger.
▼
▼
▼
▼ Strike **4** with the **f** finger.

1	9	191 191 191 91 91 91 99 lids, 99 lights, 999 lakes
2		They have 9 lambs. Light 99 lamps. Buy 999 lids.
3	4	f4f f4f f4f 4f 4f 4f 4 floods, 44 fires, 444 forms
4		He ate 4 figs. I sent 44 furs. We need 444 feet.

65c Communication Skill Building—Spelling

5 minutes

Directions: Key each sentence twice.
Technique Goal: Study the spelling of each word shown in italics.

1 I *thought* it *advisable* to take *attendance* *before* *proceeding* on a trip.
2 The *faculty* vote was *unanimous*, and he was *appointed* to a *fourth term*.
3 *Eligible* students may *receive* *pamphlet*, *memorandum*, and *questionnaire*.
4 *College* is a *rewarding* *experience* for *students* with *established* goals.

65d Problem Formatting—Three-Column Tables

30 minutes

- **Problem 1 -** Three-Column Table With Main Heading

Directions: **1.** Format the table shown below. **2.** Position it in exact vertical and horizontal center on a half sheet of paper with the long side up. **3.** Double-space all parts. **4.** Leave 8 spaces between columns.

			words
SELECTED HEISMAN MEMORIAL TROPHY WINNERS			8
1990	Ty Detmer	Brigham Young	14
1985	Bo Jackson	Auburn	19
1980	George Rogers	South Carolina	25
1975	Archie Griffin	Ohio State	32
1970	Jim Plunkett	Stanford	37
1965	Mike Garrett	Southern California	45
1960	Joe Bellino	Navy	49
1955	Howard Cassady	Ohio State	55
1950	Vic Janowicz	Ohio State	61
1945	Doc Blanchard	Army	66

15d Key-Location Practice

8 minutes

Directions: Key each line twice; repeat. **Technique Goal:** Eyes on copy.

1 The huge farm had 49 horses, 84 pigs and 91 cows.
2 Marina Rossi sold 149 packets on December 8, 1984.
3 Please order 148 gaskets, 94 valves, and 81 rings.
4 She drove 491 miles today and 489 miles yesterday.
5 *The Rams scored 49 points, but the Raiders had 18.*
6 *Mr. Li had 49 students who scored over 818 points.*

15e Keystroking from Dictation

6 minutes

Directions: Key each line as your teacher dictates it.

1 11 14 18 19 41 44 48 49 81 84 88 89 91 94 98 99 19
2 49 89 99 41 48 49 81 84 88 89 19 18 48 49 81 91 18
3 81 191 484 819 491 849 198 481 818 948 419 181 148

15f Sustained Skill Building

14 minutes

Directions: Take 1', 2' and 3' writings on the paragraphs in 14e, page 31. Determine your *gwam*. Try to equal your 1' rate on the longer writings. For the 2' rate, use the 1' column and scale to get total words; then divide by 2. Although your main goal will be for speed on these writings, try to maintain your accuracy also.

LESSON 16

16a Keyboard Review

5 minutes

Directions: Key each line twice; repeat.
Technique Goal: Hold your hands low and keep your fingers curved.

1	All letters	Mr. Diaz gave up his new tax job and left quickly.
2	9	191 191 91 91 99 lines, 9 lots, 99 loads, 999 laws
3	4	f4f f4f 4f 4f 44 frames, 444 feet, 44 and 4 and 44
4	Easy	Jo was glad to see that she had a good test grade.

- **Problem 2 -** Two-Column Table with Main Heading

Directions: 1. Format a table with the information shown below. **2.** Position it in exact vertical and horizontal center on a half sheet of paper. **3.** Center the heading and double-space all parts. Leave 12 spaces between columns.

		words
ACADEMY AWARD BEST PICTURES		6
1929	Broadway Melody	10
1939	Gone with the Wind	15
1949	All the King's Men	19
1959	Ben Hur	22
1969	Midnight Cowboy	26
1979	Kramer vs. Kramer	31
1989	Driving Miss Daisy	35

- **Problem 3 -** Critical Thinking Skill Development—Revising a Two-Column Table

Directions: Reformat problem 2 above with the following changes. **1.** Add the following years and pictures placing the information in correct chronological sequence. **2.** Use a full sheet of paper. **3.** Place the table in exact vertical and horizontal center on the page. **4.** Double-space all parts. **5.** Leave 16 spaces between columns.

1934 It Happened One Night; 1944 Going My Way; 1954 On the Waterfront; 1964 My Fair Lady; 1974 The Godfather Part II; 1984 Amadeus

LESSON 65

65a Keyboard Review

Directions: Key each sentence three times.

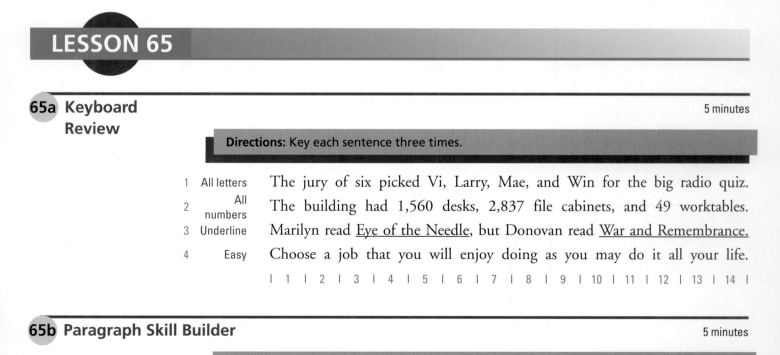

1	All letters	The jury of six picked Vi, Larry, Mae, and Win for the big radio quiz.
2	All numbers	The building had 1,560 desks, 2,837 file cabinets, and 49 worktables.
3	Underline	Marilyn read Eye of the Needle, but Donovan read War and Remembrance.
4	Easy	Choose a job that you will enjoy doing as you may do it all your life.

| 1 | 2 | 3 | 4 | 5 | 6 | 7 | 8 | 9 | 10 | 11 | 12 | 13 | 14 |

65b Paragraph Skill Builder

5 minutes

Directions: Key a 1' writing on each paragraph in 63d, page 152. Try to increase your rate on each writing by 2 to 4 words.

16b Learning to Keystroke 0 and 5

5 minutes

Reach to 0
1. Strike **0** with **;** finger.
2. Touch **;0;** lightly several times.
3. Keep elbows still.
4. Hold other fingers in position over home keys.
5. Key line 1 below.

Reach to 5
1. Strike **5** with **f** finger.
2. Touch **f5f** lightly several times.
3. Keep wrists low while reaching.
4. Avoid moving hand upward.
5. Key line 2 below.

```
1   ;0;  ;0;  ;0;  ;0;  0;  0;  ;0;  ;0;  ;0;  ;0;  0;  0;  0;  ;0;

2   f5f  f5f  f5f  f5f  5f  5f  f5f  f5f  f5f  f5f  5f  5f  5f  f5f
```

16c Location Drills—0 and 5

7 minutes

Directions: Key each line twice; repeat. **Technique Goal:** Correct keystroking.

▼ Strike **0** with the **;** finger.
▼
▼
▼
▼ Strike **5** with the **f** finger.

```
1   0   ;0;  ;0;  ;0;  0;  0;  0;  100 pets, 10 prizes, 40 parts
2       Total these numbers: 10, 80, 100, 900, and 4,000.
3   5   f5f  f5f  f5f  5f  5f  5f  55 fires, 555 feet, 55 floors
4       I have 55 files. Order 55 and 505. Sell 55 feet.
```

16d Key-Location Practice

10 minutes

Directions: Key each line once; repeat. **Technique Goal:** Hold your wrists low and steady.

```
1   The scout sold 105 of the 950 tickets last Friday.
2   He and I leave from Gate 10 at 8:50 a.m. on May 5.
3   Only 10 of the 85 dogs weighed at least 50 pounds.
4   They had 450 students at 9 a.m. and 500 at 10 a.m.
5   Please send 81 in May, 94 in June, and 50 in July.
```

6   *We sold 195 cartons of gum and 480 boxes of candy.*

7   *In 1984 only 50 teams competed in the state games.*

8   *Lucia Cruz graded 501 on Friday and 489 on Monday.*

● **Problem 1 -** Two-Column Table with Main Heading

Directions: 1. Review the steps for vertical centering from page 61. **2.** Study the steps to format a table given on page 154. **3.** Center the table as shown in the illustration below in exact vertical and horizontal position. Use a half sheet of paper with the long side up. **4.** Center the heading in all caps. **5.** Double-space all parts of the table. **6.** Leave 14 spaces between the columns.

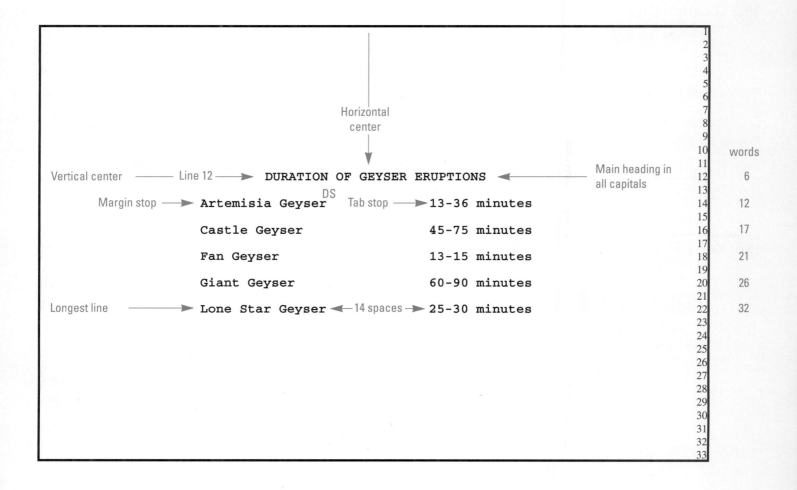

Key from Dictation

6 minutes

> **Directions:** Key each line as your teacher dictates it.

1	15 95 84 10 41 45 40 48 49 81 84 89 85 80 58 50 51
2	54 59 10 40 50 80 90 81 89 84 85 80 18 14 19 10 15
3	91 94 90 95 98 14 10 81 94 50 51 49 81 58 94 19 58
4	49 591 485 501 984 850 185 410 958 194 859 405 194

16f **Continuity Practice from Script**

12 minutes

> **Directions:** Key the entire paragraph once for practice without being timed. Then take three 1' writings. Circle your errors and determine your *gwam*. For partial lines completed, count 5 strokes as one word. Finally, key the entire paragraph again. Circle your errors.

words

All letters

75 words

1.2 si

By now you must have realized there are many — 9
varied parts to building good skill in this class. — 19
As you work, stop and see if you are doing things — 29
exactly right. All of the factors will be joined — 39
together to help you build the high rate of speed — 49
and the accuracy that you may want. You can then — 59
feel quite sure that you can reach all of the — 69
goals you have set for yourself. — 75

LESSON 17

17a **Keyboard Review**

5 minutes

> **Directions:** Key each line twice; repeat. **Technique Goal:** Correct posture.

1	All letters	The quick brown fox jumped over all the lazy dogs.
2	0	0;0 0;0 0;0 0; 0; 10 parts; 100 packs, 1,000 pages
3	5	f5f f5f f5f 5f 5f 55 fights, 555 films, 5,555 feet
4	Easy	They will go to a new beach on their spring break.

Steps in Formatting a Table

Horizontal Centering of Columns

1. Set the paper guide at 0 and insert paper into the machine.

2. Move the left and right margin stops to the ends of the scale. Clear all tab stops.

3. If the spacing between columns is not specified, decide how many spaces to leave between columns (preferably an even number such as 4, 6, or 8.)

4. Move the carrier to the center of the machine (51 elite; 42 pica).

5. Note the longest line in each column.

6. Backspace once for each 2 characters and spaces in the longest line in each column and once for each two spaces left between columns. If the longest line in one column has an extra character, combine that character with the first character in the next column for calculating purposes. A character left over after backspacing all columns is dropped.

7. Set the left margin stop at the point at which you stop backspacing. This is the point at which you will begin to key the first column.

8. From the left margin, space forward once for each character and space in the longest line in the first column and once for each space to be left between Columns 1 and 2. Set a tab stop at this point for the second column. Continue in this manner until stops have been set for all columns of the table.

9. Return the carrier. Operate the tab key to determine whether or not all the tab stops have been set.

10. Your right margin stop will remain at the end of the scale as you will not use it when formatting a table.

With computers, tables may be formatted automatically. Your teacher may give you instructions and tell you if you are to use the automatic functions on your computer to format the tables in the problems of this unit.

Vertical centering and spacing directions are given on page 61. Review the directions again.

(continued on page 155)

17b Learning to Keystroke 7 and 3

Reach to 7
1. Strike **7** with **j** finger.
2. Touch **j7j** lightly several times.
3. Make reach without arching wrist.
4. Key line 1 below.

Reach to 3
1. Strike **3** with **d** finger.
2. Touch **d3d** lightly several times.
3. Lift first finger slightly to reach easily and naturally.
4. Key line 2 below.

```
1   j7j  j7j  j7j  j7j  7j  7j  j7j  j7j  j7j  j7j  7j  7j  7j  j7j
2   d3d  d3d  d3d  d3d  3d  3d  d3d  d3d  d3d  d3d  3d  3d  3d  d3d
```

17c Location Drills—7 and 3

7 minutes

Directions: Key each line twice; repeat. **Technique Goal:** Correct keystroking.

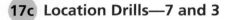

▼ Strike **7** with the **j** finger.   1
▼
▼
▼
▼ Strike **3** with the **d** finger.   3

2

4

```
7   j7j  j7j  j7j  7j  7j  7j  77 jokes, 77 jeeps, 777 jades
    I saw 77 jets.  We had 77 jobs.  She has 777 jars.
3   d3d  d3d  d3d  3d  3d  3d  33 deeds, 33 deals, 333 debts
    Only 33 may go.  I had 33 tickets.  All 33 made A.
```

17d Key-Location Practice

8 minutes

Directions: Key each line twice; repeat. **Technique Goal:** Eyes on copy.

```
1   Those 73 top runners will race on July 3 at 7 a.m.
2   Those photos are on pages 17, 43, 57, 73, and 137.
3   Our flights 397 and 587 were both 30 minutes late.
```
4   *Tony moved to 7337 Cypress Street on June 7, 1970.*

17e Keystroking from Dictation

8 minutes

Directions: Key each line as your teacher dictates it.

```
1   59 837 594 830 948 304 759 484 140 384 957 310 475
2   49 737 310 495 573 139 389 714 354 345 351 453 131
3   980 718 109 870 900 810 719 510 370 495 749 374 85
```

LESSON 64

64a Keyboard Review

5 minutes

Directions: Key each sentence three times.

1	All letters	Women quickly apply zinc oxide gel just to face to help avoid sunburn.
2	All numbers	Please turn to page 490; sing verses 2, 3, and 5 of songs 167 and 168.
3	ae, ea	What a treat to eat pear spears at both Eastern Avenue Aerobic events.
4	Easy	All teams tried to run a good race, but only one team could win today.

| 1 | 2 | 3 | 4 | 5 | 6 | 7 | 8 | 9 | 10 | 11 | 12 | 13 | 14 |

64b Paragraph Guided Writings

10 minutes

Directions: Set goals of 40 and 50 words a minute. Key two 1' writings at each rate on each paragaph. Try to reach your goal word just as time is called. Your teacher may call the quarter or half minutes to guide you. Key additional writings at the 50 word rate as time permits.

¶1
50 words
1.4 si

You are developing skills in this class that will be of value to you for the remainder of your life. Whether you apply your new skills to a typewriter or to a computer, you will find them of value in your personal life and in your professional life.

¶2
50 words
1.4 si

Keying by touch is a skill that will enhance our value in any job we have. Learning to spell is an additional value. Knowing the preferable format for a letter, a memo, or a report will put us a step in front of one who does not know these formats.

17f Sustained Skill Building

Directions: Take 1', 2', and 3' writings on the paragraph in 16f, page 35. Circle errors; determine *gwam*. Use the *words* column to figure the 1' rate. For the 2' and 3' rates, use the *words* column to get total words; then divide by 2 or 3. For partial lines, count 5 strokes for one word.

LESSON 18

18a Keyboard Review

5 minutes

Directions: Key each line twice; repeat. **Technique Goal:** Keystroke with ease.

1	All letters	Jack Benz played the sax with vim for Gilda Quinn.
2	7	j7j j7j 7j 7j 77 jars, 71 jugs, 717 jets, 17 jeeps
3	3	d3d d3d 3d 3d 33 days, 331 dogs, 31 decks, 13 dads
4	Easy	Our big dog barks at all of the birds in our yard.

18b Learning to Keystroke 6 and 2

5 minutes

Reach to 6
1. Strike **6** with **j** finger.
2. Touch **j6j** lightly several times.
3. Make reach without arching wrist.
4. Key line 1 below.

Reach to 2
1. Strike **2** with **s** finger.
2. Touch **s2s** lightly several times.
3. Lift little finger slightly to give freer action.
4. Key line 2 below.

1	j6j j6j j6j j6j 6j 6j j6j j6j j6j j6j 6j 6j 6j j6j
2	s2s s2s s2s s2s 2s 2s s2s s2s s2s s2s 2s 2s 2s s2s

18c Location Drills—6 and 2

8 minutes

Directions: Key each line twice; repeat. **Technique Goal:** Correct keystroking.

▼ Strike **6** with the **j** finger.
▼ Strike **2** with the **s** finger.

1	6	j6j j6j j6j 6j 6j 6j 66 jets, 616 jewels, 66 jumps
2	2	s2s s2s s2s 2s 2s 2s 22 suits, 122 sets, 212 ships

63c Skill Comparison

5 minutes

Directions: Key a 1′ writing on lines 1, 3, 5, and 10 in 63b, p. 151. Compare your *gwam* on the varied types of stroking.

63d Sustained Skill Building

5 minutes

Directions: **1.** Key a 5′ writing. Circle errors and determine the *gwam*. **2.** Key two 1′ writings on each paragraph. Key the first writing for speed and the second for accuracy. **3.** Finally, key another 5′ writing over all paragraphs. Circle errors and determine *gwam*. Compare the two 5′ writings and submit the better one to your teacher.

All letters

	gwam	
	1'	5'

▼ Copy difficulty level: average

1.5 si
5.8 awl
80% hfw

Text	1'	5'
A business office today is far different from an office of past	13	3	55
years. Office workers are now busy with jobs using all types of	26	5	57
software, electronic mail, fax, scanners, and modems. The outlook for	40	8	60
the future shows even more change is to come. New technology has helped	55	11	63
change the office recently.	60	12	64
In the modern office, typewriters are being replaced by computers.	13	15	67
Records once typed on paper and filed in file drawers are now keyed and	28	17	69
stored on disks. The messages once sent by the post office are now	42	20	72
sent by electronic mail. A network can store data to be accessed from	56	23	75
businesses or libraries nearby or from locations all around the world.	70	26	78
Due to new technology, office workers are now quite concerned with	13	29	81
the work environment. Ergonomics is the study of the effects of the	27	31	83
workplace on the health of those who work in it. Many factors help	41	34	86
make the office a more pleasant, productive zone for work. Restful	55	37	89
colors are used throughout.	60	38	90
In addition to the health of workers, employee safety and security	13	41	93
are also important. The degree of safety will depend on the type of	27	43	95
business, the building site, and an awareness of safety practices.	41	46	98
Accident prevention in the office will depend on office workers who	55	49	101
have good attitudes toward safety and use good safety habits while on	69	52	104
the job.	70	52	104

```
1' |  1  |  2  |  3  |  4  |  5  |  6  |  7  |  8  |  9  | 10 | 11 | 12 | 13 | 14 |
5' |        1        |        2        |        3        |
```

18d Key-Location Practice

10 minutes

Directions: Key each line twice; repeat. **Technique Goal:** Fluent keystroking.

1 Jennie sent these orders: 12, 16, 26, 62, and 66.

2 The score was 62 to 76, and Judy scored 26 points.

3 Jamie ran 26 miles in the race, but I only ran 16.

4 Their tickets are in row 26, seats 2, 4, 6, and 8.

5 She will send these sizes: 8, 10, 12, 14, and 16.

6 We sold 790 tickets, but only 356 people attended.

7 *Lyn Rue will arrive at Pier 8 on May 26 at 5 p.m.*

8 *My old code was 49310X, but the new one is 28576Z.*

18e Sentence Guided Writings

12 minutes

Directions: 1. Key each sentence for a 1' writing with the call of the guide each 20 seconds. Try to complete each sentence as the guide is called. **2.** Take the last two sentences for additional 1' writings as time permits, without the call of the guide. Work for speed and accuracy.

		words in line	gwam 20" guide
1	These lines all review proper form.	7	21
2	*Think of your form with every line.*	7	21
3	Hold your wrists low as you strike keys.	8	24
4	*Use quick strokes as you reach to a key.*	8	24
5	Hold your elbows near your body when you key.	9	27
6	*Do not twist elbows and wrists as you stroke.*	9	27
7	Sit back in the chair with your feet on the floor.	10	30
8	*You should keep your eyes on the copy in the book.*	10	30

| 1 | 2 | 3 | 4 | 5 | 6 | 7 | 8 | 9 | 10 |

18f Composing at the Keyboard

5 minutes

Directions: Compose sentences using the following words and numbers:

▼ Review directions in 13b,
▼ page 28, for composing at the
▼ keyboard.

12 dogs; 34 children; 56 bottles; 78 men; 90 boats;

148 women; 367 trees; 592 people; 1,850 books.

UNIT 13 FORMATTING TABLES

In this unit you will learn how to format two- and three-column tables with main, secondary and columnar headings. You will also continue to build your keying, communicating, composing, and proofreading skills.

General Directions: For drills and timed writ-ings use margins of 1" for elite, 1/2" for pica, and standard defaults if you are using a computer. For problems, set margins as directed. SS sentences and drill lines, and DS paragraph copy. DS between groups of repeated lines. Space problem copy as directed in each lesson.

LESSON 63

63a Keyboard Review

5 minutes

Directions: Key each sentence three times; repeat if time permits.

1	All letters	Davey Waxler hopes to make a jet flight to Brazil to acquire the land.
2	Number-symbol	The Keade Company paid a stock dividend of 7 1/2%, plus $5.30 in cash.
3	Hyphen	Her father-in-law, a well-to-do entrepreneur, is a real self-made man.
4	Easy	The best things in life do not always come to those who wait and hope.

| 1 | 2 | 3 | 4 | 5 | 6 | 7 | 8 | 9 | 10 | 11 | 12 | 13 | 14 |

63b Technique Builder—Keystroking

10 minutes

Directions: Key each line twice.

1	Right hand	You'll join my nylon mill monopoly in July. You'll ply nylon in Ohio.
2	Double letters	Jeff succeeded in getting the committee's letter to our Wilcox staff.
3	Shift keys	M. R. Nolan wrote to P. S. McNeight in Big Rapids, Michigan, in April.
4	Weak fingers	Zaza politely applauded the plays. The astronauts waited on the pads.
5	Left hand	Dave gave my car a fast grease and oil job at Steve's service station.
6	Hyphen	Faye and Lola gave a two-hour talk about their back-to-back car trips.
7	Long reach	I joined in the mountaineering fun with a hiking stick snugly in hand.
8	Dash	Your own ideas--much like your own children--are especially wonderful.
9	Numbers	I mailed order number 4958 on May 15 and order number 2736 on June 20.
10	Balanced hand	The formal goal for the city panel is to audit the problems with fuel.

| 1 | 2 | 3 | 4 | 5 | 6 | 7 | 8 | 9 | 10 | 11 | 12 | 13 | 14 |

Lesson 63 · · · · · 151

In Unit 4 you will develop efficient key-stroking of the basic symbol keys—those symbols that are used most frequently. In this unit you will also continue to build a higher level of speed and accuracy.

General Directions: Use 1" side margins or default margins for all lessons in this unit. SS sentences and drill lines and DS paragraph copy. DS between groups of repeated lines. Set a tab stop for a 5-space paragraph indention.

LESSON 19

19a Keyboard Review

5 minutes

> **Directions:** Key each line twice; repeat. **Technique Goal:** Eyes on copy.

1	All letters	Jay quizzed me at the big sneak preview in Colfax.
2	All numbers	The teacher ordered number 48576 on June 30, 1992.
3	:	We will start at 7:45 p.m. and finish by 9:30 p.m.
4	Easy	Chi did not know that he had just won a top prize.

19b Learning to Keystroke / (Diagonal) and $ (Dollar Sign)

5 minutes

Reach to /
1. Strike / with ; finger.
2. / is the lower case of **?**. To strike /, reach down with ; finger.
3. Do not space before or after diagonal.
4. Key line 1 below.

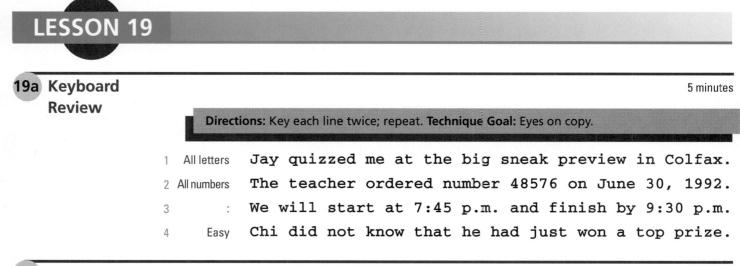

Reach to $
1. Strike $ with **f** finger.
2. Shift, then reach up to $ with **f** finger.
3. Do not space between $ sign and number following.
4. Key line 2 below.

| 1 | ;/; ;/; ;/; /; /; /;/ ;/; ;/; ;/; ;/ ;/ ;/ /;/ ;/; |
| 2 | f4f f$f f4f f$f $f $f $44 f4f f$f f4f f$ $f $f $44 |

19c Location Drills—/ and $

6 minutes

▼ Space once between a
▼ whole number and a
▼ fraction.
▼
▼ Strike / with the ; finger.
▼
▼
▼
▼ $ is the shift of **4**.

> **Directions:** Key each line twice; repeat. **Technique Goal:** Operate the shift keys with fluency.

1	/	;/; ;/; ;/; /; /; /; 2/3, 13 3/4, up 18 1/8 points
2		Be uniform in making fractions: 1/4, 2/3, or 5/8.
3	$	f4f f$f f4f f$f $f $f $44, $444, $4.38, $14 and $8
4		I owe $45. We spent $14.75. The cost was $48.40.

62d Enrichment Assignments—Memorandums

Directions: For the problems below, format the original in rough draft, edit with pen or pencil, and format a final copy.

- **Problem 1 -** Reformat the memorandum on page 145. Make appropriate changes to advertise for the following job: Executive Secretary: Position open for experienced person with outstanding skills. Ability to key 65 words a minute with accuracy; excellent spelling, punctuation, and grammar skills; strong administrative and organizational capabilities.

- **Problem 2 -** Use the formatting guides on page 144 and the sample simplified memo in the Reference Guide on page RG-14 to help you format a memo in this style. Use the information from 61d, problem 2, page 147, as the content.

Directions: Key each line twice; repeat.
Technique Goal: Eyes on copy.

▼ Strike **/** with the **;** finger.
▼
▼
▼ Strike **$** with the **f** finger.

```
1   The room is 28 1/4 feet long and 18 1/3 feet wide.
2   My new boat is 68 3/4 feet long; Kaye's is 72 1/2.
3   Dinner was $68.40, and I paid $17.10 of the total.
4   My last three bills were for $587, $392, and $641.
```

19e **Continuity Practice**
10 minutes

Directions: Key once; circle errors. Repeat if time permits.
Technique Goal: Try to develop a continuous stroking pattern.

gwam

All letters

	1'	3'

```
        The size of our world does not seem as large     9   3  31
as it once did.  We can now pick up the telephone       19   6  34
and talk with someone in another part of the world      29  10  38
just as quickly as we can talk with someone who         39  13  41
lives next door.                                        42  14  42
        The exciting event that began our new age was    9  17  45
Sputnik.  This was the first satellite to be sent       19  20  49
into space.  That was over thirty years ago, and       29  24  52
now our world has truly become what we may call a       39  27  55
global village.                                         42  29  57
```

¶1
42 words
1.2 si

¶2
42 words
1.3 si

```
1'|  1  |  2  |  3  |  4  |  5  |  6  |  7  |  8  |  9  |  10  |
3'|      1      |      2      |      3      |      4      |
```

19f **Timed Writings**
12 minutes

Directions: Take two 1' writings on each of the paragraphs in 14e, page 31. Then take two 3' writings over both paragraphs. Circle your errors. Determine *gwam* on all timings.
Technique Goal: Work for control. Try to keep your errors to a minimum on each of these timings.

• **Problem 3 -** Critical Thinking Skill Development—Revising a Memorandum

Directions: The memo below is a copy of the one you formatted in Problem 1. Make the changes marked and rekey the document.

words

TO: Regional Sales Managers   6

FROM: Van Williams, Sales Manager   13

DATE: May 1, 19--   17

SUBJECT: National Sales Meeting   23

The Annual National Sales Meeting will be held on June 4-7, 19--.   37
The location for the meeting this year is the Boston Inn and Con-   50
ference Center, 4110 Hunt Street, Boston, Massachusetts 02116-   62
1234. The phone number is (617) 555-5882. Reservations have   75
been made for ~~your arrival on June 3, 19--~~ *all sales managers.*   82

Agenda items are included below.   88

1. Opening ~~general~~ session. Well-known motivational speaker,   100
Tip Tyler, will keynote the session.   108

2. Advertising media and budget.   115

3. *of* Sales territories ~~and possible~~ reorganization.   123

4. New product ~~orientation~~ *demonstration*.   130

5. Awards luncheon. Thomas Caton, Chief Executive Officer, will   143
present the awards.   147

LESSON 20

20a Keyboard Review

5 minutes

Directions: Key each line twice; repeat.
Technique Goal: Fluent stroking.

1	All letters	Brad Jaye gave me six tickets for an LP quiz show.
2	/	I won the long jump with 23 1/2 feet 6 1/4 inches.
3	$	Her pay for March was $948, but his was only $760.
4	Easy	You need to think and to key short words as units.

20b Learning to Keystroke % (Percent), - (Hyphen), and -- (Dash)

5 minutes

Reach to %
1. Strike **%** with **f** finger.
2. Shift, then reach up to **%** with **f** finger.
3. Do not space between number and **%** sign following.
4. Key line 1 below.

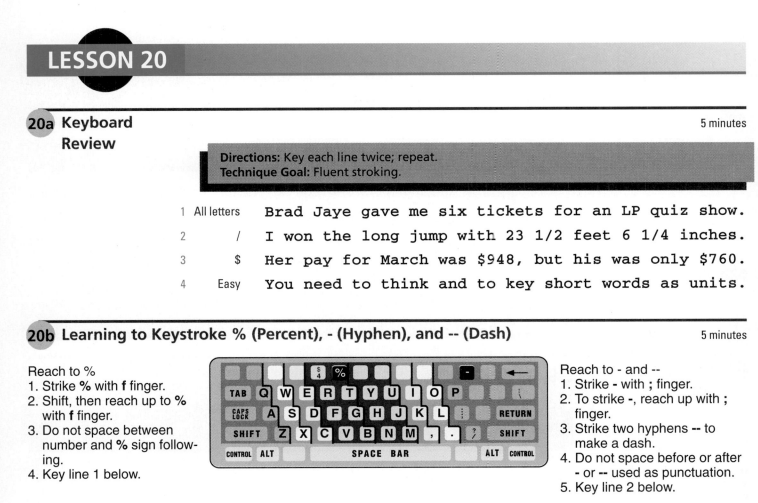

Reach to - and --
1. Strike **-** with **;** finger.
2. To strike **-**, reach up with **;** finger.
3. Strike two hyphens **--** to make a dash.
4. Do not space before or after **-** or **--** used as punctuation.
5. Key line 2 below.

| 1 | f5f f%f f5f f%f %f 55% f5f f%f f5f 5f %f %f 5f 55% |
| 2 | ;-; ;-; ;-; -; -; -;- ;-; ;-; ;-; -; -; -; -;- ;-; |

20c Location Drills—%, -, and --

8 minutes

Directions: Key each line twice; repeat if time permits.
Technique Goal: Stroke with the correct finger.

Do not space between a number and the % sign.
Do not space before or after a hyphen or a dash.

▼ % is the shift of **5**.
▼
▼
▼
▼ Strike the **-** with the **;** finger.
▼
▼
▼
▼
▼ Strike two hyphens to
▼ make a dash.

1	%	f5 f%f f5f f%f To key %, shift, then strike the 5.
2		Al got a 5% discount. Elise got 4%, and I got 7%.
3		;-; ;-; ;-; -; -; -; set-to; send-off; know-it-all
4	-	Her son-in-law had the right-of-way on the street.
5		;--; ;--; --; --; --; I will save 5%--that is $80.
6		Only two students--Ken and Jo--had perfect papers.

LESSON 62

62a Keyboard Review

Directions: Key each sentence three times.

1 All letters   A man and four boys drove quickly to the west jet to get extra prizes.

2 Number-Symbol   Ray said, "We could get 2 1/3% more for the 50# bag--a total of $846."

3 Easy   Try to do your best to win the relay race and promote our school team.

62b Skill Comparison

10 minutes

Directions: Key two 1' writings on each sentence in 62a above. Key the easy sentence first and then try to stroke all of the other sentences at the same rate.

62c Problem Formatting

30 minutes

• **Problem 1 -** Interoffice Memorandum

Directions: Format the following memorandum on a full sheet of plain paper or use an interoffice memorandum form. Follow the guidelines on page 144.

▼ Align enumerated items at margin. Space twice after numbers. If you are using a computer you may use indent function to space numbers.

	words
TO: Regional Sales Managers / FROM: Van Williams, Sales Manager /	13
DATE: May 1, 19-- / SUBJECT: National Sales Meeting	23
(¶) The Annual National Sales Meeting will be held on June 4-7, 19--. The	37
location for the meeting this year is the Boston Inn and Conference Center,	53
4110 Hunt Street, Boston, Massachusetts 02116-1234. The phone number is	67
(617) 555-5882. Reservations have been made for your arrival on June 3, 19--.	83
(¶) Agenda items are included below. 1. Opening general session. Well-known	98
motivational speaker, Tip Tyler, will keynote this session. 2. Advertising media	115
and budget. 3. Sales territories and possible reorganization. 4. New product	131
orientation. 5. Awards luncheon. Thomas Caton, Chief Executive Officer, will	147
present the awards.	151

• **Problem 2 -** Interoffice Memorandum

Directions: Format the following memorandum on a half sheet of plain paper. Follow the guidelines on page 144.

	words
TO: Mario Benitez / FROM: Van Williams, Sales Manager / DATE: May 15,	14
19-- / SUBJECT: Arrival of Mr. Tip Tyler	22
(¶) Mario, thank you for all the work you and the other regional managers in	36
the Northeast have done to make our Annual National Sales Meeting success-	51
ful. The location is great, and the speakers you suggested are planning to	66
attend.	68
(¶) Please meet Mr. Tip Tyler, our keynote speaker, at the airport. He will	83
arrive on June 4, 19--, at 10:30 a.m. on Delta Flight #1632.	95

20d Learning to Keystroke # (Number/Pounds) and & (Ampersand)

5 minutes

Reach to #
1. Strike # with **d** finger.
2. Shift, then reach up to # with **d** finger.
3. Do not space between # and number.
4. Key line 1 below.

Reach to &
1. Strike **&** with **j** finger.
2. Shift, then reach up to **&** with **j** finger.
3. Space once before and after **&** used to join names; do not space when letters are joined by **&**. **&** is used for and.
4. Key line 2 below.

```
1    d3d  d#d  d3d  d#d  #d  #d  #33  d3d  d#d  d3d  #d  #d  #d  #33
2    j7j  j&j  j7j  j&j  &j  &j  j&j  j7j  j&j  j&j  &j  &j  &j  j&j
```

20e Location Drills—# and &

6 minutes

Directions: Key each line twice; repeat.
Technique Goal: Depress and release the SHIFT keys quickly.

▼ Strike # with the **d** finger.

▼ Strike & with the **j** finger.

```
#    1    d3d  d#d  d3d  d#d  #d  #d  #33,  303#,  34# of #393,  #313
     2    Write number 343 as #343.  Write 33 pounds as 33#.
&    3    j7j  j&j  j7j  j&j  &j  &j  Lee & Roe;  PP&G;  Chi & Sons;
     4    Linda works for Rand & King.  Don works for BBD&O.
```

20f Key-Location Practice

8 minutes

Directions: Key each line twice; repeat. **Technique Goal:** Eyes on copy.

▼ Strike % with the **f** finger.

▼ Strike - and -- with the **;** finger.

▼ Strike # with the **d** finger.

▼ Strike & with the **j** finger.

```
1    We give a 10% or a 12% discount on early payments.
2    Their interest rate was 14%, but it dropped to 9%.
3    Her sister-in-law is a well-known person in Spain.
4    I toured two states--Nevada and Utah--last summer.
5    Please order 50# of cat food #8904 at a pet store.
6    The 250# of cement on order #9402 has not arrived.
7    Woo & Kim has 15 lawyers; Ross & Beck has only 12.
8    Ship the order to King & Ray on the P&O freighter.
```

20g Timed Writings

8 minutes

Directions: Key the paragraphs in 19e, page 40 once for practice; then take two 1' writings on each paragraph. Circle errors. Compute *gwam*.

61c Keying from Dictation and Spelling Checkup

5 minutes

Directions: Key the spelling words in 59c, page 141 as your teacher dictates them. Check for correct spelling. Rekey any words in which you have made an error.

61d Problem Formatting

5 minutes

• **Problem 1 -** Interoffice Memorandum

Directions: Format the following memorandum on a half sheet of plain paper. Follow the guidelines on page 144.

	words
TO: Faculty Advisors of Student Organizations / FROM: Logan Steele,	14
Department Chair / DATE: April 18, 19--/ SUBJECT: Organization Budgets	28
(¶) Please meet with your Chapter officers as soon as possible to discuss bud-	42
gets for the next school year. Items such as scholarships to be awarded, confer-	59
ences for participants, and dues for membership should be on your agenda.	74
(¶) After your meeting, please submit a budget for approval. All organization	89
financial information must be approved by the board before the new fiscal year	104
begins. We believe this will help all student organizations get off to a good	120
start next year. / xx	124

• **Problem 2 -** Interoffice Memorandum—Script

Directions: Format the following memorandum on a half sheet of plain paper. Use correct guidelines.

	words
TO: Robert Resnick / FROM: Anne Novak / DATE: April 10, 19-- / SUBJECT:	14
Decrease in Sales at South Hills Mall Store	23
(P) The total sales at our South Hills Mall store have decreased each month	37
since January (our January sales were $985,640 as compared to our March sales	53
of $723,100). Please get in contact with Ray Nugent, the manager of the store.	69
Perhaps there are problems about which we are not aware.	81
(P) Please call me before our board meeting on Monday. We need to discuss	95
any action that may need to be taken. / xx	103

• **Problem 3 -** Critical Thinking Skill Development—Composing a Memorandum

▼ Use a half sheet of plain
▼ paper.

Directions: Compose and format a memorandum to all employees from Jaye Green, Human Resources Director about the Annual Blood Drive. The Blood Drive is scheduled for Tuesday, January 10, 19--, and it will be held in the conference room. Departments will receive a schedule indicating times when employees may donate blood. Last year 73 percent of all employees participated in the donor drive.

LESSON 21

21a Keyboard Review

5 minutes

Directions: Key each line twice; repeat. **Technique Goal:** Good posture.

1 All letters Jack and Liza mixed five quarts of BHW gray paint.

2 % - - - Our hotel--rated 5-star--has a 5% discount in May.

3 # & Ann bought 100# of #485 rye seed from Lear & Wolf.

4 Easy I saw two whales as we sailed our boat to the bay.

21b Learning to Keystroke Left Parenthesis (and Right Parenthesis)

5 minutes

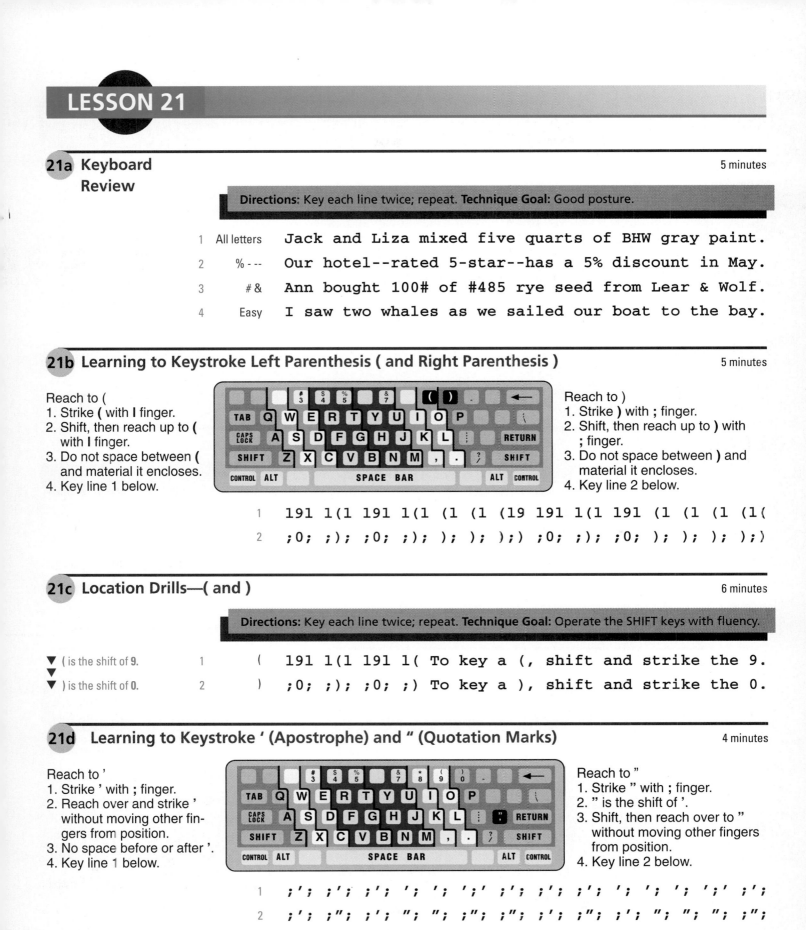

Reach to (
1. Strike **(** with **I** finger.
2. Shift, then reach up to **(** with **I** finger.
3. Do not space between **(** and material it encloses.
4. Key line 1 below.

Reach to)
1. Strike **)** with **;** finger.
2. Shift, then reach up to **)** with **;** finger.
3. Do not space between **)** and material it encloses.
4. Key line 2 below.

1 191 1(1 191 1(1 (1 (1 (19 191 1(1 191 (1 (1 (1 (1(

2 ;0; ;); ;0; ;););););) ;0; ;); ;0;););););)

21c Location Drills—(and)

6 minutes

Directions: Key each line twice; repeat. **Technique Goal:** Operate the SHIFT keys with fluency.

▼ (is the shift of **9**.

▼) is the shift of **0**.

1 (191 1(1 191 1(To key a (, shift and strike the 9.

2) ;0; ;); ;0; ;) To key a), shift and strike the 0.

21d Learning to Keystroke ' (Apostrophe) and " (Quotation Marks)

4 minutes

Reach to '
1. Strike **'** with **;** finger.
2. Reach over and strike **'** without moving other fingers from position.
3. No space before or after **'**.
4. Key line 1 below.

Reach to "
1. Strike **"** with **;** finger.
2. **"** is the shift of **'**.
3. Shift, then reach over to **"** without moving other fingers from position.
4. Key line 2 below.

1 ;'; ;'; ;'; '; '; ;'; ;'; ;'; ;'; '; '; '; ;'; ;';

2 ;'; ;"; ;'; "; "; ;"; ;"; ;'; ;"; ;'; "; "; "; ;";

- **Problem 2 -** Interoffice Memorandum

Directions: Format the memorandum shown below according to the guidelines given on page 144. Use a half sheet of plain paper.

	words
TO: Linda Haney / FROM: Richard Glenn / DATE : May 1, 19-- / SUB-	12
JECT: Cancellation of Policy Number 584-296	21
(¶) Mr. Keith Leyden called today and cancelled his policy with us. He was	35
quite unhappy about the way in which his last claim was settled.	49
(¶) As you are his agent, I thought you might want to get in contact with him	63
today and discuss the problem. The claim was handled by Saundra Michaels,	78
who is no longer with our company. Perhaps you can convince Mr. Leyden to	93
retain his policy with us.	98
xx	99

LESSON 61

61a Keyboard Review

5 minutes

Directions: Key each sentence three times.

1	All letters	Alex drove the buzzing tan jeep quickly away from the obstacle course.
2	Number-Symbol	I raised $90,670 between May 24 and 31--a 58% increase over last year.
3	Double letters	The shipping office accountant offered to send my baggage immediately.
4	Easy	Work for the gift of using words that give some life to your thoughts.

| 1 | 2 | 3 | 4 | 5 | 6 | 7 | 8 | 9 | 10 | 11 | 12 | 13 | 14 |

61b Concentration Practice—Difficult Copy

5 minutes

Directions: Key the following paragraph three times.
Technique Goal: Keystroke with ease and control.

90 words
Difficult copy:
1.8 si

	words
The National Aeronautics and Space Administration (NASA) is an	13
agency of the United States government. This agency directs civilian pro-	27
grams in aeronautics research and exploration. At the Johnson Space	41
Center in Houston, astronauts wear space suits which allow them to func-	56
tion in the airless environment of space. A space station for scientific and	71
technological work is considered the next significant step in the continued	86
exploration of space.	90

21e Location Drills—' and "

5 minutes

Directions: Key each line twice; repeat. **Technique Goal:** Avoid wrist movement.

Keystroke quotation marks without a space between them and the word(s) enclosed.
A double space follows a quotation mark when it ends a sentence.
Periods and commas should always be placed inside quotation marks.

▼ Strike ' with the ; finger.

1	'	;'; ;'; '; '; can't, didn't, isn't, wasn't, hasn't
2		Kirk didn't leave yet. Sue's brother isn't going.

▼ Shift and strike " with the ;
▼ finger.

3	"	;"; ;"; "; "; ;"; "; Use "to" and "too" correctly.
4		I saw "Alien" on VHS. It was rated "outstanding."

21f Key-Location Practice

8 minutes

Directions: Key each line twice; repeat. **Technique Goal:** Hold wrists low.

▼ Strike (with the l finger
▼ and) with the ; finger.

▼
▼
▼
▼
▼
▼ " is the shift of '.

1 We will go to Paris this summer (July) for a week.
2 Lea faxed: (1) styles; (2) sizes; and (3) prices.
3 Carl's mother and Joan's father moved from Canada.
4 Erin really doesn't like the food at Andy's Diner.
5 Anne Sexton wrote "The Bells" and "The Road Back."
6 "Congratulations," I am very proud of your awards.

21g Timed Writings

12 minutes

Directions: Take two 1' writings on each of the paragraphs in 19e, page 40. Then take two 3' writings over both paragraphs. Circle your errors. Determine *gwam* on all timings. **Technique Goal:** Work for control. Try to keep your errors to a minimum on each of these timings.

LESSON 22

22a Keyboard Review

5 minutes

Directions: Key each line twice; repeat. **Technique Goal:** Use correct fingering.

1	All letters	The gray fox jumped quickly over lazy brown ducks.
2	(and)	We will pay 10% more ($56) if our payment is late.
3	' and "	Two of Blake's poems were "To Spring" and "Night."

words

TO: Douglas Klein, Training and Recruitment   8
           DS
FROM: Barbara Knight, Administrative Services   16
           DS
DATE: April 28, 19--   19
           DS
SUBJECT: Job Openings in Word Processing   25
      DS

I need a replacement for one of our senior word processing opera-   38
tors who has been promoted to supervisor and will be leaving in   51
two weeks. I also require an additional word processor trainee.   64
Both of these are critical positions; therefore, I hope that we   77
can fill them quickly.   82
      DS
Will you please make the necessary arrangements to run advertise-   95
ments in all of the major newspapers in our area next Sunday. The   108
notices should read as follows: 115

Senior Word Processing Operator: Position open for person with a   134
minimum of three years experience in word processing. Applicant   147
must keyboard a minimum of 70 words a minute with accuracy; good   160
communication and proofreading skills required; must be experi-   173
enced in using a PC for formatting letters, memorandums, and   185
reports. Excellent salary and benefits. Equal opportunity employer. 199
Call Barbara Knight at (213) 555-9821 for an interview.   211

Word Processing Operator Trainee: Excellent opportunity to learn   230
all aspects of word processing operations. Applicant must keyboard 244
a minimum of 40 words a minute with accuracy; good communication   257
skills required; clerical experience preferred. Excellent salary   270
and benefits. Equal opportunity employer. Call Barbara Knight at   284
(213) 555-9821 for an interview.   290

Thank you for your help with these advertisements. If you have any 304
questions about the job openings, please call me at extension   316
9821.   318
      DS
xx   318

1" margin (left)   1" margin (right)

▼ A memo may be formatted on
▼ letterhead or plain paper.

Interoffice memorandum
(Shown in pica type)

BACKSPACING—The BACKSPACE key assists you in many ways. Later in this lesson you will learn how it is used when you are underlining words.

Electric Typewriter—The BACKSPACE key on most electric machines is located at the extreme right of the top row. Depress this key with your right little finger. Keep the **j** finger in its proper position and the **k** and **l** fingers in or near their home row positions.

22b Learning to Keystroke _ (Underline) and * (Asterisk)

5 minutes

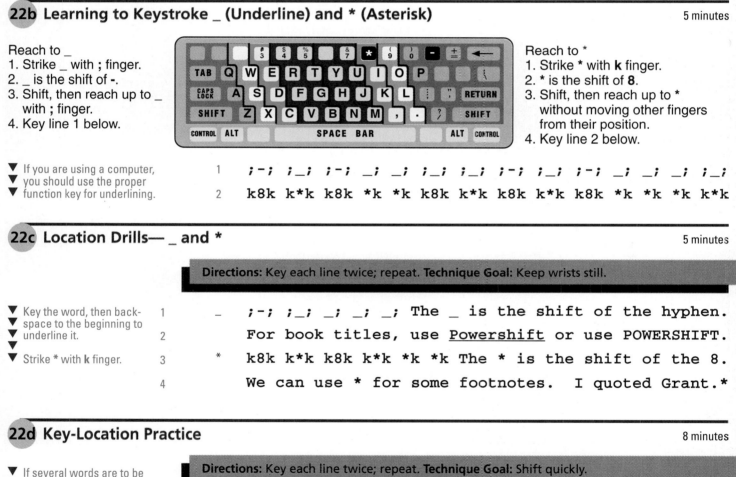

Reach to _
1. Strike _ with **;** finger.
2. _ is the shift of **-**.
3. Shift, then reach up to _ with **;** finger.
4. Key line 1 below.

Reach to *
1. Strike * with **k** finger.
2. * is the shift of **8**.
3. Shift, then reach up to * without moving other fingers from their position.
4. Key line 2 below.

▼ If you are using a computer,
▼ you should use the proper
▼ function key for underlining.

1   ;-; ;_; ;-; _; _; ;_; ;_; ;-; ;_; ;-; _; _; _; ;_;

2   k8k k*k k8k *k *k k8k k*k k8k k*k k8k *k *k *k k*k

22c Location Drills— _ and *

5 minutes

Directions: Key each line twice; repeat. **Technique Goal:** Keep wrists still.

▼ Key the word, then back-
▼ space to the beginning to
▼ underline it.
▼
▼ Strike * with **k** finger.

1   _   ;-; ;_; _; _; _; The _ is the shift of the hyphen.

2   For book titles, use <u>Powershift</u> or use POWERSHIFT.

3   *   k8k k*k k8k k*k *k *k The * is the shift of the 8.

4   We can use * for some footnotes. I quoted Grant.*

22d Key-Location Practice

8 minutes

▼ If several words are to be
▼ underlined, use the SHIFT
▼ LOCK. The underline is not
▼ broken between the words
▼ unless each word is to be
▼ considered separately.
▼
▼ With the computer, the
▼ words and the underline
▼ are keyed at the same time
▼ with the use of a function
▼ key.

Directions: Key each line twice; repeat. **Technique Goal:** Shift quickly.

1   I bought <u>Newsweek</u>, <u>People</u>, and the <u>New York Times</u>.

2   You may <u>underline</u> a word or a phrase <u>for emphasis</u>.

3   He broke all records for home runs in one season.*

4   <u>Rabbit at Rest</u>* received a Pulitzer Prize in 1991.

5   *The title may be <u>underlined</u> or keyed in ALL CAPS.

Formatting Guides for Interoffice Memorandums

The interoffice memorandum (memo) is used to send messages within a company or an organization. Its major advantages are that it is less structured and can be formatted quickly. Two styles of memorandums are commonly used: **formal** and **simplified**.

Form—Formatting guides for interoffice memorandums are listed below.

1. Use either a full or half sheet of paper.

2. Use block style.

3. Use 1" side margins.

4. Begin on line 7 (1" top margin) for half-page memorandums; begin on line 10 (1 1/2" top margin) for full-page memorandums.

5. Omit personal titles (Mr., Ms., etc.) on the memo, but do include them on the company envelope. Use the person's business title for clarity.

6. SS the body, but DS between paragraphs.

7. Key reference initials a DS below the message. Other notations (such as

Enclosure) are placed in the same position as in letters.

Formal Memorandums—Heading words, **TO, FROM, DATE,** and **SUBJECT** are keyed at the left margin followed by a colon and two spaces. Key the information following these guide words by aligning words one under the other. See the illustration on page 145. Begin on line 7 for a half sheet and line 10 for a full sheet.

Simplified Memorandums—Begin the date on line 7 for a half sheet and line 10 for a full sheet. DS between all parts of the simplified memorandum **except** after the date and after the last paragraph of the body. Quadruple space (QS) after the date and after the last paragraph of the body. Key the writer's name and business title a QS below the body. (See page RG-14 for example of this style.)

Envelopes—If a company interoffice envelope is not used, use a plain envelope and key COMPANY MAIL in the stamp position. On the envelope, include the receiver's personal title, name, and business title. Key the receiver's department a DS below the name.

- **Problem 1 -** Interoffice Memorandum

Directions: Study the memorandum illustrated on page 145 in order to format it. Use a full sheet of plain paper. Follow the directions given in the Formatting Guides above.

ADDITIONAL SYMBOLS—All keyboards have other symbols that have not been covered in this unit, and you should become familiar with those symbols. However, because they are not frequently used, you will not learn them by touch in this course.

<table>
<tr><td>Special Keys</td></tr>
<tr><td>Computer keyboards have other special keys and function keys. Their uses vary with the software. You should become familiar with these keys, but you will not learn them by touch in this course.</td></tr>
</table>

22e Critical Thinking Skill Development—Composing at the Keyboard

7 minutes

Directions: Compose sentences using the following words, numbers, and symbols:

```
50 2/3 feet; $486; 90%; brother-in-law; one person--Gail;
#178; 20#; Kaplin & Raye; ($100); haven't; "The Midnight
Ride of Paul Revere"; To Kill a Mockingbird*
```

22f Speed Ladder Paragraphs

15 minutes

Directions: Key 1' writings on the paragraphs that follow. When you can complete the first paragraph in 1', move on to the second, then the third, fourth, and fifth. Your teacher may call the 1/2' to guide you. The rate increases four words with each succeeding paragraph.

All letters are used

	gwam		
	1'	3'	

¶1
16 words
1.3 si

We communicate in many ways. Without skills — 9 | 3 | 43
to aid us, our life might be bleak. — 16 | 5 | 45

¶2
20 words
1.3 si

People may communicate as they speak, listen, — 9 | 8 | 48
write or read. Good skills are of value in all — 19 | 12 | 52
ways. — 20 | 12 | 52

¶3
24 words
1.3 si

Another way we all communicate is known as — 9 | 15 | 55
nonverbal. We do not use words. Some people say — 19 | 18 | 58
we do this the most of all. — 24 | 20 | 60

¶4
28 words
1.3 si

There are many types of nonverbal cues that — 9 | 23 | 63
we may give. For example, a smile or a frown may — 19 | 26 | 66
convey our truer feelings when a word may not. — 28 | 29 | 69

¶5
32 words
1.3 si

Many words give nonverbal signals. In the — 9 | 32 | 72
area of music, when we hear such words as jazz, — 18 | 35 | 75
rock, or rap, we all have a quick mental image of — 28 | 39 | 79
that type of music. — 32 | 40 | 80

1' | 1 | 2 | 3 | 4 | 5 | 6 | 7 | 8 | 9 | 10 |
3' | 1 | 2 | 3 | 4 |

59e Technique Builder—Balanced-Hand Words

Directions: Key each line three times. Take two 1' timings on each of the last two lines.
Technique Goal: Try to increase your speed on balanced-hand words.

1	Phrases	with them	to lend	for her	to him	and he	they may go	to the
2	Phrases	it is	in case of	as you are	for the	with us	to go	may wish
3	Sentence	A formal reply will be sent to owners by the end of the fiscal period.
4	Sentence	A new disk should be used when you key the final reports for the dean.

| 1 | 2 | 3 | 4 | 5 | 6 | 7 | 8 | 9 | 10 | 11 | 12 | 13 | 14 |

LESSON 60

60a Keyboard Review

Directions: Key each sentence three times.

1	All letters	Philip quoted lengthy excerpts from over ten books written about jazz.
2	Number-symbol	Mr. R. J. Jones (Bob) worked a total of 125 days and earned $6,397.48.
3	Shift	Ann, Kay, and Sue will go to Rome, but Dianne and Lea will go to Paris.
4	Easy	Most people can show who they are by what they do with what they have.

| 1 | 2 | 3 | 4 | 5 | 6 | 7 | 8 | 9 | 10 | 11 | 12 | 13 | 14 |

60b Skill Comparison

Directions: Key a 1' writing on each sentence in 60a, above. Key the easy sentence first and then try to key all of the other sentences at the same rate.

60c Communication Skill—Use of Colons

Directions: Key each sentence three times. The first line gives the rule; the remaining lines apply it. Capitalize and punctuate the last sentence correctly.

1	A colon is used to introduce a list and to separate hours and minutes.
2	The Scouts packed these items: compass, flashlight, hat, and canteen.
3	The French class begins at 11:30 a.m. and ends at 1:15 p.m. on Monday.
4	be here at 6 45 p m and bring these items music horn and uniform.

| 1 | 2 | 3 | 4 | 5 | 6 | 7 | 8 | 9 | 10 | 11 | 12 | 13 | 14 |

In Unit 5 you will continue to build your keying skill as well as to develop a higher rate of speed with a higher level of accuracy. You will also learn other basic keyboard operations. Common proofreader's marks are also presented in this unit.

General Directions: Use 1" side margins or default margins for all lessons in this unit. SS sentences and drill lines and DS paragraph copy. DS between groups of repeated lines. Set a tab stop for a 5-space paragraph indention.

LESSON 23

23a Keyboard Review

5 minutes

Directions: Key each line twice; repeat. **Technique Goal:** Correct keystroking.

1	All letters	Wayne or Jo quickly had five large itemized boxes expressed.
2	Number-symbol	Order #58 will cost $176.92, but #74 will only cost $103.45.
3	One hand	up we my as on be in at hip was you red ill saw oil few pull
4	Easy	You can reach the goals for this class if you try your best.

23b Symbol and Number Review

12 minutes

Directions: Key the paragraphs once; circle errors; repeat.
Technique Goal: Keystroke slowly and try to maintain good control.

words

¶1
60 words

The following information is from <u>The World Almanac</u>   11
<u>and Book of Facts</u>, 1992.*   The U.S. population increased by 9.8%   23
from 1980 to 1990.   Carl Lewis won the long jump in the 1988   36
Olympics with a distance of 28 ft. 7 1/4 in.   As of June 30,   48
1991, "Cats" was still on Broadway with 3,645 performances.   60

¶2
62 words

The building ranked #1 in the world in height is the   11
Sears Tower in Chicago--1,454 ft. (110 stories).   Procter &   23
Gamble was one of the top 20 corporations in sales in 1990.   35
"Star Wars" is one of the all-time top movies.   This film's   47
total rentals amounted to $193,500,000.   55
*Published by Pharos Books in 1991.   62

| 1 | 2 | 3 | 4 | 5 | 6 | 7 | 8 | 9 | 10 | 11 | 12 |

> **Directions: 1.** Key a 5' writing. Circle errors and determine the *gwam*. **2.** Key two 1' writings on each paragraph. Key the first writing for speed and the second for accuracy. **3.** Finally, key another 5' writing over all paragraphs. Circle errors and determine *gwam*. Compare the two 5' writings and submit the better one to your teacher.

All letters

	gwam	
	1'	5'

Correct spelling is a frequent problem for many people.   A word | 13 | 3 | 55

will be spelled wrong if a person does not see or hear it correctly. | 27 | 5 | 57

When one misspells a word mentally, it may also be misspelled on | 40 | 8 | 60

paper.   Most people can, however, develop good spelling habits that | 53 | 11 | 63

may help them remedy many errors. | 60 | 12 | 64

One habit that can be developed is to build a list of words | 12 | 14 | 66

that are frequently misspelled.   As one may become confident of | 25 | 17 | 69

Copy difficulty level: Average

proper spelling, words can be eliminated from the list.   As the list | 39 | 20 | 72

becomes shorter, one's spelling improves.   Another habit is to spell | 52 | 23 | 75

1.5 si
5.7 awl
80% hfw

a new word aloud and then write it down.   This may benefit a person's | 66 | 25 | 77

spelling them, too. | 70 | 26 | 78

A person should also develop the habit of using the dictionary. | 13 | 29 | 81

With this habit, one should never be guilty of misspelling words.   All | 26 | 31 | 83

we need is a zeal to look up words to make sure of their accurate | 40 | 34 | 86

spelling.   This not only ensures correctness, but also helps people | 53 | 37 | 89

learn to spell difficult words. | 60 | 38 | 90

Correct spelling is needed in any type of professional or | 12 | 40 | 92

personal writing.   A misspelled word jumps out at a reader and gives | 25 | 43 | 95

an impression of ignorance and carelessness.   There is no excuse that | 39 | 46 | 98

is good enough.   All must learn how to spell words correctly.   If | 53 | 49 | 101

this task seems to be impossible, then one must be willing to be chained | 67 | 51 | 103

to a dictionary. | 70 | 52 | 104

1" | 1 | 2 | 3 | 4 | 5 | 6 | 7 | 8 | 9 | 10 | 11 | 12 | 13 | 14 |
5" | 1 | 2 | 3 |

23c Technique Builder—Word Response Keystroking

5 minutes

Directions: Key each line three times. **Technique Goal:** Think words as you keystroke.

1   to do | to do it | to do the | and he | and the | and if | and she

2   if we | and if he | and if the | and if she | and if it | and the

3   to do | to do it | to do the | to form | to work | to do the work

23d Learning to Use ! (Exclamation Mark) for Punctuation

5 minutes

If your machine has an exclamation mark key (!), use your **a** finger to strike it. On any keyboard not having the ! (exclamation mark), strike the ' (apostrophe), backspace, then strike the . (period).

Directions: Key each line twice; repeat. **Technique Goal:** Strike ! with the **a** finger.

▼ Punctuation Guide:
▼ Space twice after the ! at the
▼ end of a sentence. Do not
▼ space between a word and
▼ the !.

1   Look!   Wow!   Stop!   Save!   Congratulations!   Great!   Try it!

2   Nice work!   A good job!   We won!   Our team is the very best!

23e Paragraph Guided Writings

18 minutes

Directions: 1. Key a 1' writing on ¶1. Note the *gwam*. Add four words to your *gwam* for a new goal. Take two more writings; try to reach your goal. **2.** Repeat this procedure for ¶'s 2 and 3. Your teacher may call the 1/2' guides on the 1' writings to aid you in checking your rate. **3.** Key two 3' writings. Circle errors. Determine *gwam*. Submit the better of the two writings if you are instructed to do so by your teacher.

	gwam		
	1'	3'	

	1'	3'	
We are now in a new age. In our world of today, change	11	4	38
¶1 happens so fast that we have a tough time trying to keep up	23	7	41
30 words with all that is new in our lives.	30	10	44
1.1 si This is the computer era. The low cost and the high	11	14	48
¶2 speed of this machine have now given us a whole new view of	22	17	51
34 words how we can use it. Our world will not be the same again.	34	21	55
1.2 si A future with robots and with computers that talk is	11	25	59
¶3 now much more fact than fiction. There will be changes we	22	29	63
32 words never dreamed were possible, and we may see them.	32	32	66
1.3 si			

1' | 1 | 2 | 3 | 4 | 5 | 6 | 7 | 8 | 9 | 10 | 11 | 12 |
3' | 1 | | 2 | | 3 | | 4 |

UNIT 12 INTEROFFICE MEMORANDUMS

Lessons 59-62

In this unit you will learn how to format interoffice memorandums that are used for correspondence between offices or departments within a company. You will also continue to build your keying, communicating, composing, and proofreading skills.

General Directions: For drills and timed writings, use margins of 1" for elite, 1/2" for pica, and standard defaults if you are using a computer. For problems, set margins as directed. SS sentences and drill lines, and DS between groups of repeated lines. Space problem copy as directed in each lesson.

LESSON 59

59a Keyboard Review

5 minutes

Directions: Key each sentence three times; repeat if time permits.

1	All letters	Bob's zest for speeding was quickly dimmed after his extensive injury.
2	Number-symbol	Simon & Joel's $482.36 invoice (#19750) was delivered to the cleaners.
3	Hyphen	Jae's brother-in-law, Al's father-in-law, and Tim's son-in-law played.
4	Easy	The person who has nothing to say often takes the most time saying it.

| 1 | 2 | 3 | 4 | 5 | 6 | 7 | 8 | 9 | 10 | 11 | 12 | 13 | 14 |

59b Technique Builder—Keystroking

5 minutes

Directions: Key each sentence three times.
Technique Goal: Keep your wrists and elbows quiet.

1	Home row	Hal Kaggalla and his dad had half a dish of salad and a glass of soda.
2	Third row	Peter wrote quite a true report of a wearing trip through the prairie.
3	Bottom row	Ann Vance maximized her chances on six bad exams by cramming for them.
4	Top row	Stroke 0 and 1 and 2 and 3 and 4 and 5 and 6 and 7 and 8 and 9 and 10.

59c Communication Skill—Spelling

5 minutes

Directions: Key each sentence twice.
Technique Goal: Study the spelling of each word shown in italics.

1	Seven *attorneys* asked the *sergeant* to *transfer* the *defendant promptly*.
2	The *assistant* was *conscientious* and *answered* all *correspondence daily*.
3	Six *golfers played Wednesday*, but only one had an *extraordinary score*.

LESSON 24

24a Keyboard Review

5 minutes

Directions: Key each line twice; repeat. **Technique Goal:** Eyes on copy.

1	All letters	Rex paused to see the wolf, jaguar, and zebras move quickly.
2	Number-symbol	Ty had a 58% response (12,947 questionnaires) to Survey 630.
3	Balanced hand	to he may man cut bit pep air with work busy wish girl world
4	Easy	Try to keep your eyes on your book when you stroke each key.

| 1 | 2 | 3 | 4 | 5 | 6 | 7 | 8 | 9 | 10 | 11 | 12 |

24b Sentence Skill Builder

5 minutes

Directions: Take a 1' writing on each sentence. Compute *gwam*.
Technique Goal: Keep your eyes on your copy; think and keystroke entire words.

1	We may win when we can find the key to work in the best way.
2	You can see the road to the lake if you look over that hill.
3	I know that I can do a good job if I will put my mind to it.
4	My date for the prom this year may be a new girl I just met.

| 1 | 2 | 3 | 4 | 5 | 6 | 7 | 8 | 9 | 10 | 11 | 12 |

24c Tabulator Control

6 minutes

▼ Flick the TAB key with your
▼ left little finger.

Directions: Key each sentence twice; repeat if time permits. **1.** Clear all tab stops. **2.** Key the first sentence at the left margin. **3.** Set a tab stop for the second sentence five spaces from the left margin. Set tab stops for the third, fourth, and fifth sentences as indicated.

strokes in line		On the computer these stops may be preset (default)	words
60	1	The tab key will prove to be a very useful key in your work.	12
55	2 ss	5→ Your tab stops may be set at any point along your line.	11
50	3	10——→ Use your left little finger to strike the tab key.	10
45	4	15———→ Just flick a tab key with your little finger.	9
40	5	20————→ Make the return quickly without pausing.	8

- **Problem 1 -** Continued

▼ Remember to start the head-
▼ ing on line 7 from the top of
▼ the page.

	words
Mr. Tony Scalese / Page 2 / March 28, 19--	8
(¶) Our national park tours are given throughout the year. Knowledgeable	22
guides accompany each tour to ensure that you have the best possible trip.	37
(¶) Please call any of our travel associates to schedule an appointment for	51
your video travelogue. It will make you want to see the parks for yourself.	67
Sincerely / Cheryl Marcus / Sales Associate / xx	75

- **Problem 2 -** Second Page of a Letter

Directions: Format the material below as the second page of a letter. Use the modified block style; mixed punctuation; indented paragraphs; 1" side margins; and block style heading shown on the preceding page. Address a large envelope (providing an address of your choice).

▼ Start the heading on line 7

	words
Ms. Celia Humberto / Page 2 / October 8, 19--	8
(¶) Charleston Community College is a coed institution founded in 1909. Its	23
structured and innovative curriculum ensures an education of breadth and	38
depth--a solid preparation for a constantly changing world.	50
(¶) If you have a passion for learning, an insatiable curiosity, and a spirit of	65
adventure, you will fit right in at Charleston. Call (926) 555-0613 for your	81
application packet. Take the first step to prepare for an exciting college	96
experience.	99
Sincerely, / Otis Fortson / Director of Admissions / xx	108

- **Problem 3 -** Critical Thinking Skill Development—Second Page of a Letter

Directions: Reformat Problem 1 above. Follow the same directions but this time address the envelope to Castin Tours, Inc. / 139 Old Castin Road / Russellville, AR 72932-0032 / Use the company name in the second page heading; change *you* to *your clients* in paragraph 1; in paragraph 2, delete *schedule an appointment for* and substitute *order*; change *you* to *your clients* and *yourself* to *themselves.*

58e Enrichment Assignments—Business Letters

- **Problem 1 -** Reformat the letter in Problem 1, page 137. This time, however, format it in modified block style with indented paragraphs and mixed punctuation. Use your own name in the signature lines.

- **Problem 2 -** Assume you work in the Admissions Office of a college near your home. Write a letter to Daryl Caneup and give him information on the housing arrangements for college students who wish to live on campus. Select the letter and punctuation style you prefer.

- **Problem 3 -** You are an Administrative Assistant for Dr. Jeffrey Towner, a dentist who also teaches part-time at a local dental school. Write a letter to Mr. Rodney Printz to tell him Dr. Towner will be out of town and must change his appointment from March 2 to March 16. Ask him to call you if this new date will not be convenient. Use the letter and punctuation styles you prefer. Prepare a rough draft; edit; format a final copy.

24d Spacing of Numbers and Symbols—Review

Directions: Read the explanation for each line before you key it. Key each line twice.

EXPLANATIONS

Line 1 - Do not space between the dollar sign and the number that follows it.

Line 2 - Do not space before or after the apostrophe.

Line 3 - Do not space between the quotation marks and the words they enclose.

Line 4 - Do not space between a number and the percent sign.

Line 5 - Space between a whole number and a fraction.

Line 6 - Do not space between the parentheses and the words they enclose.

Line 7 - Do not space between the number/pound sign and a number.

Line 8 - Space once before and after the ampersand used to join names; do not space when letters are joined by the ampersand.

Line 9 - Do not space before or after a hyphen or a dash.

Line 10 - Do not space between the asterisk and the word to which it refers.

SENTENCES

1 I will send you a check for $957, but I will still owe $483.

2 I'm not sure if Lou's sister can go to the teacher's office.

3 A favorite song in the play is "Don't Cry for Me Argentina."

4 That bond pays interest at the rate of 10%, but we want 12%.

5 Their shares went from 76 1/4 to 102 7/8 in only a few days.

6 Jennifer has the highest batting average (.398) on her team.

7 Our order #730 included 125# of gravel for the new driveway.

8 He decorated the new offices of Kyle & Rowe as well as CH&A.

9 My mother-in-law--Maria Crain--won a new car on a quiz show.

10 The quotation by John Naisbitt* gives very interesting data.

| 1 | 2 | 3 | 4 | 5 | 6 | 7 | 8 | 9 | 10 | 11 | 12 |

24e Timed Writings

Directions: Take three 1' writings on each of the paragraphs in 23e, page 48. For the first writing on each paragraph, push for a high rate of speed. For the second writing, work for more accuracy—slow down if necessary. On the third writing try to key at a rate that allows you to maintain both speed and accuracy.

58b Skill Comparison

5 minutes

> **Directions:** Key a 1' writing on the paragraphs in each of the following drills: 52b, page 122; 54b, page 130; 55d, page 133; 57b, page 136. Compare your *gwam* on each of these paragraphs of varied copy.

58c Communication Skill—Use of the Exclamation Point

5 minutes

> **Directions:** Key each sentence three times. The first line gives the rule, and the remaining lines apply it. Capitalize and punctuate the last sentence correctly.

1 Use the exclamation point after a word or sentence to express emotion.

2 Congratulations! Your team at Cade High won top honors in the debate!

3 Quick! Pull that marlin into the fishing boat before it can get away!

4 wonderful your performance in the final talent show was outstanding

58d Problem Formatting—Second Page of a Letter

30 minutes

Second Page of a Letter: When formatting the second page of a letter, use plain paper. Provide a heading on the top of the page, and leave at least a 1" bottom margin. When dividing a paragraph between pages, at least two lines must appear on each page. Never divide a word at the end of a page. Since 1" side margins are used for multipage letters, use 1" side margins for the second page.

Heading for the Second Page of a Letter: Begin the heading on line 7 from the top. Double-space (DS) between the heading and the body. The correct headings for a letter addressed to an individual and to a company are shown below. The Block Style heading is used for all letters.

```
        Line 7 from top of page

Mr. Michael J. Stevenson
Page 2
April 28, 19--

I hope that I have explained very clearly all of the many advantages of our pre-
ferred life insurance plan.  Let me emphasize once again the valuable feature
```

Block Style Addressed to Individual

```
Holland, McNeill, & Associates
Page 2
October 4, 19--

Our firm will conduct three estate planning seminars for residents in West-
ville.  Please send in the enclosed card if you would be interested in
```

Block Style Addressed to Company

● **Problem 1 -** Second Page of a Letter

> **Directions:** Assume that you have completed the first page of a two-page letter. Format the copy at the top of the next page as though it is the second page. Use block style; 1" side margins; and open punctuation. Key a large envelope with an address of your choice.

24f Learning to Key from Corrected Copy

5 minutes

Copy that has been keyed or printed may be corrected by the use of various proofreader's marks. Some of the most common ones are shown below. Study these marks and their uses in the following paragraph.

COMMON PROOFREADER'S MARKS

⁋ Paragraph	δ Delete	# Space	
∧ or ∨ Insert	∿ Transpose	◯ Close up	

Directions: Key the paragraph shown below. Make the corrections indicated by the marks. Repeat the paragraph if time permits.

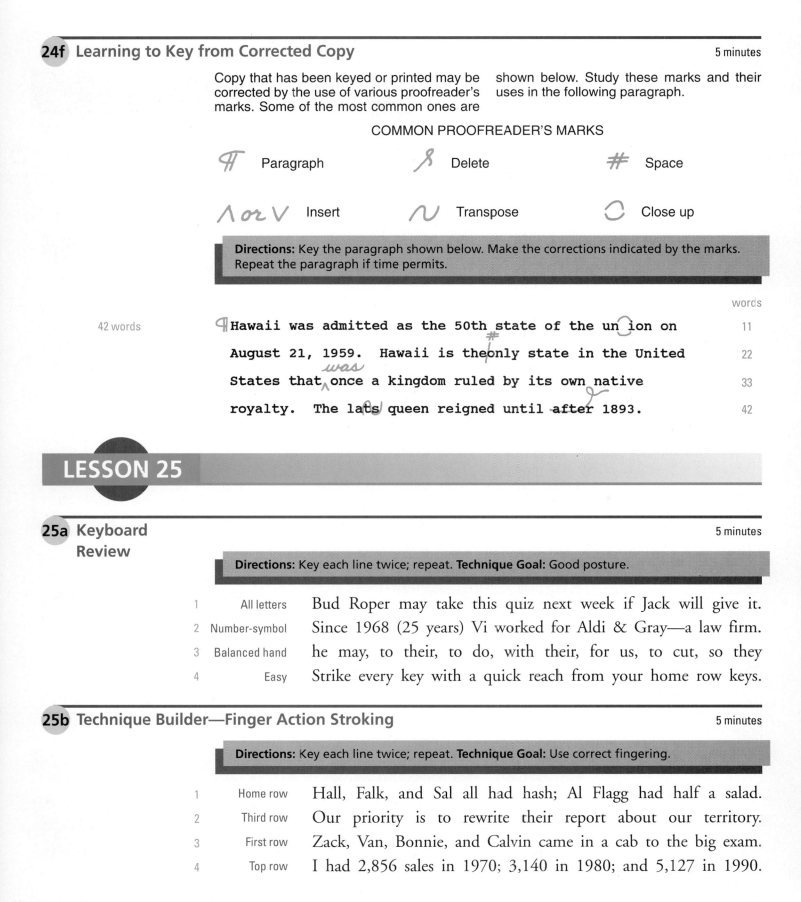

words

42 words

⁋Hawaii was admitted as the 50th state of the un◯ion on   11

August 21, 1959. Hawaii is the#only state in the United   22

States that∧ *was* once a kingdom ruled by its own native   33

royalty. The la∿ts queue reigned until after 1893.   42

LESSON 25

25a Keyboard Review

5 minutes

Directions: Key each line twice; repeat. **Technique Goal:** Good posture.

1	All letters	Bud Roper may take this quiz next week if Jack will give it.
2	Number-symbol	Since 1968 (25 years) Vi worked for Aldi & Gray—a law firm.
3	Balanced hand	he may, to their, to do, with their, for us, to cut, so they
4	Easy	Strike every key with a quick reach from your home row keys.

25b Technique Builder—Finger Action Stroking

5 minutes

Directions: Key each line twice; repeat. **Technique Goal:** Use correct fingering.

1	Home row	Hall, Falk, and Sal all had hash; Al Flagg had half a salad.
2	Third row	Our priority is to rewrite their report about our territory.
3	First row	Zack, Van, Bonnie, and Calvin came in a cab to the big exam.
4	Top row	I had 2,856 sales in 1970; 3,140 in 1980; and 5,127 in 1990.

- **Problem 2 -** Business Letter with a Postscript

Directions: Format the following letter in modified block style, mixed punctuation. Use the guide on page 123 for margins and date placement. Address a large envelope.

	words
July 8, 19-- / Mr. Derek Taylor / 1320 Old Fort Road / Billings, MT 59102-	14
2944 / Dear Mr. Taylor:	18
(¶) Thank you for your interest in a trip to Yellowstone National Park.	32
Located in Wyoming and extending into Montana and Idaho, it is the oldest	47
and largest national park in the United States.	57
(¶) Our travel agency will be happy to arrange group trips for a visit to	71
Yellowstone. We use the most up-to-date coaches equipped with many luxu-	85
ries. We can arrange day trips as well as extended visits with overnight accom-	101
modations.	104
(¶) Enclosed are brochures explaining the various tours. Please call me when	119
you are ready to make arrangements.	126
Sincerely yours, / John Hentzler, Travel Associate / xx / Enclosures	139
(¶) Coupons will be awarded for a special dinner for two when you book a	152
tour of four days or longer.	158/170

- **Problem 3 -** Business Letter with a Postscript

Directions: Reformat the letter in Problem 1, page 137. Follow the same directions given for that problem. This time, however, you are giving a reference for Ms. Tamara Barrineau. Also change eight years to seven years; $750 to $850; and change male pronouns to female.

🖳

Computer Note: When reprinting or merging the same letter with different information (known as variables), be careful to see that the new information is correct in each letter.

LESSON 58

58a Keyboard Review

5 minutes

Directions: Key each sentence three times.

1	All letters	Julian may have paid for the exquisite zigzag sewing machine by check.
2	All numbers	A $12,857.90 bill for the awards banquet included an error of $346.50.
3	Shift	Dr. Sue Anne Carston will speak at the Wichita Booster Club on Monday.
4	Easy	We are not able to take it with us if we spend all of it before we go.

25c Spacing After Punctuation Marks—Review

8 minutes

Directions: Read the explanation for each line before you key it. Key each line twice.

EXPLANATIONS

Line 1 - Space twice after end-of-sentence punctuation.

Line 2 - Do not space after a period within an abbreviation. Space once after a period that ends an abbreviation, twice if that period ends a sentence.

Line 3 - Space once after a comma.

Line 4 - Space twice after a colon. Exception: Do not space before or after a colon in stating time.

Line 5 - Strike the dash by keying two hyphens, without spacing before or after.

Line 6 - Space once after a semicolon.

SENTENCES

1 Will he leave now?   Please hurry!   He went alone.   I can go.

2 I saw him at 10 a.m.   Jerry will leave on the 9 p.m. flight.

3 Thomas may go to Rome, Paris, Tokyo, and Moscow on his tour.

4 We checked these sizes: 6, 8, and 10.   We left at 5:17 p.m.

5 Only two students--Carlos and Maria--had perfect attendance.

6 The students achieved high goals; they will get good grades.

| 1 | 2 | 3 | 4 | 5 | 6 | 7 | 8 | 9 | 10 | 11 | 12 |

25d Learning to Key from Corrected Copy

5 minutes

In 24f, page 51, some of the most common proofreader's marks were presented. Some additional ones are shown below. Study the marks below as well as the ones shown on page 51 and see how they are used in the following paragraph.

COMMON PROOFREADER'S MARKS

⊙ Insert period

⌐ Move right

Cap or ≡ Capitalize

ᵛⁿ Insert quotation marks

⌐ Move left

lc or / Lowercase

Directions: Key the paragraph shown below. Make the corrections indicated by the marks. Repeat if time permits.

words

¶
Alaska was admitted to the union as the 49th state on   11

January 3, 1959. The wild grandeur of alaska has intrigued   23

people for hundreds of years In fact, there are many   34

people who who still think of Alaska as the Last Frontier.   45

45 words

• **Problem 1 -** Rough Draft Letter with a Postscript

Directions: Format the following letter, making all necessary corrections. Use 1 1/2" side margins and date on line 16. Address a large envelope.

xx
Mr. Ryan's account with us also in
teenage daughter.

A postscript in a business letter is placed a double space below the reference initials. Omit the letters P.S. at the beginning of the postscript. Indent to block the postscript according to the style of the other paragraphs in the letter.

words

_____ April 12, 19-- 3

Ms. Maria Anderson *Credit Department* 7 / 10
The Fashion Store *Center* 14
6101 Clifton Road 18
Atlanta, GA 30333-6901 23
Dear Ms. Anderson: 26

Double space

I am pleased to give you a reference for Mr. Martin M. Ryan who has 40
filed an application with you for an account. He had an excellent 53
credit rating with our company. During the last eight years he pur- 67
chased merchandise from us on a regular basis and had account balances 81
as high as $750. His payments was always made regularly, and he 94
reduced his balance to 0 before moving to your city. 106

We enjoyed doing business with Mr. Ryan. I am sure that he will 119
prove to be an excellent credit customer for your company. 131

Double space

Yours truly, 133

Marcos Sanchez, Credit Department 140

xx 157/176

Mr. Ryan's account with us also included credit privileges for his teenage daughter.

25e Critical Thinking Skill Development—Composing at the Keyboard

Directions: Compose a complete sentence from each of the following:

1. There were 860 tickets. . .
2. Over 492 passengers were. . .
3. The 7% discount ($15) was. . .
4. We shipped 14 3/4 pounds of. . .
5. The book <u>Gone with the Wind</u> is. . .
6. Two people--Carol and Kay-- were. . .
7. Help!. . .
8. My father's car was. . .
9. "How to Hang Glide" was the article that. . .

25f Paragraph Guided Writings

17 minutes

Directions: 1. Key a 1' writing on ¶ 1. Note the *gwam*. Add four words to your *gwam* for a new goal. Take two more writings. Try to reach your new goal. **2.** Repeat step 1 for ¶'s 2 and 3. **3.** Your teacher may call the 1/2' guides to aid you in checking your rate. **4.** Key two 3' writings. Circle errors. Determine *gwam*. Submit the better of the two writings if you are instructed to do so by your teacher.

		gwam	
		1'	3'
	As you build a new skill in this course, you must also	11	4	44
	improve your basic skill in the use of the English language.	24	8	48
¶1	You cannot apply your new skill unless you punctuate and	35	12	52
38 words 1.3 si	spell correctly.	38	13	53
	In all that we write, punctuation marks help us to make	11	16	56
	what we are saying much clearer. There are some important	23	20	60
¶2	rules we must follow if we are to punctuate correctly, and	35	24	64
40 words 1.3 si	we must learn those rules.	40	26	66
	Spelling can be a problem for some of us. English is	11	30	70
	not always an easy language to use. For instance, words	22	33	73
¶3	are not always spelled the way they sound. Also, a word	34	37	77
42 words 1.3 si	with double letters can be most confusing.	42	40	80

1' | 1 | 2 | 3 | 4 | 5 | 6 | 7 | 8 | 9 | 10 | 11 | 12 |
3' | 1 | 2 | 3 | 4 |

LESSON 57

Directions: Key each sentence three times.

1	All letters	Zena Jan Co. posted profits quickly on its big new x-ray view machine.
2	All numbers	Flower arrangements included 14 gold, 236 red, 89 white, and 570 pink.
3	ex	Executives may exempt the extra exams by making exactly enough points.
4	Easy	Key with eyes on the copy, fingers curved, and both feet on the floor.

| 1 | 2 | 3 | 4 | 5 | 6 | 7 | 8 | 9 | 10 | 11 | 12 | 13 | 14 |

57b Paragraph Skill Builder—Rough Draft   5 minutes

Directions: Key four 1' writings on the paragraph below.
Technique Goal: Work for control on these writings.

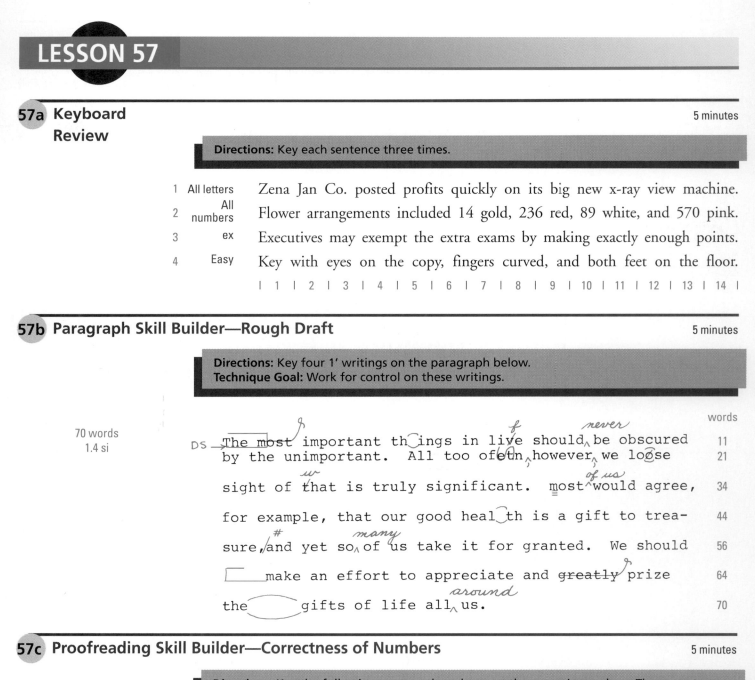

70 words
1.4 si

words

DS → The most important things in live should be obscured by the unimportant. All too often, however, we loose	11 / 21
sight of that is truly significant. most would agree,	34
for example, that our good health is a gift to trea-	44
sure, and yet so of us take it for granted. We should	56
make an effort to appreciate and ~~greatly~~ prize	64
the gifts of life all us.	70

57c Proofreading Skill Builder—Correctness of Numbers   5 minutes

Directions: Key the following paragraph and correct the errors in numbers. The correct numbers are as follows: 1970 should be 1870; 200 should be 100; 31 to 33 should be 21 to 23.

66 words

words

Old Faithful is the world's most publicized geyser. Since it was dis-   14
covered in 1970, it has been remarkably consistent. Its thermal heights,   29
intervals, and length of spray have changed little in 200 years. Old Faithful   45
erupts 31 to 33 times each day. The column of water averages 130 feet but   60
has sometimes reached 184 feet.   66

• PART 2 •
DEVELOPING PERSONAL COMMUNICATION SKILLS

Lessons 26-50

Your basic keying skills should now be evolving into complete keyboard proficiency. In Part Two, you will learn how to apply this proficiency to the formatting of a variety of personal papers.

● **ANNOUNCEMENTS AND INVITATIONS**

You will learn how to format these types of papers and center them horizontally as well as vertically.

● **OUTLINES, SHORT REPORTS, AND BOOK REPORTS**

In formatting these papers, you will use commonly accepted guides.

● **LONG REPORTS**

You will learn the format for long reports as well as the internal citation reference method. You will also learn how to format bibliographical and note cards.

● **PERSONAL BUSINESS LETTERS, RESUME, AND APPLICATION LETTER**

Acceptable form and content will be emphasized in these various papers.

● **CORRECTING ERRORS**

Instructions for correcting errors will be given in Lesson 33. Your teacher will tell you if you are to correct errors on problems in lessons following Lesson 33.

● **BASIC SKILL DEVELOPMENT**

There will be continued emphasis on basic skills. The ideal is to be able to keystroke so well that you forget the machine and concentrate on the papers you are preparing.

● **COMMUNICATION SKILL DEVELOPMENT**

Many of the drills, spelling aids, and capitalization guides will help you to achieve a major goal of improving your written communication skills. You will also continue to develop your composing skills at your machine.

● **ENRICHMENT ASSIGNMENTS**

Problems will be given at the end of each unit for you to complete if you finish your work ahead of schedule. These problems are designed to help you enhance your critical thinking skills.

56d Problem Formatting—Business Letters with Special Parts

- ### Problem 1 - Business Letter with Attention Line

Directions: Format the following letter in block style with mixed punctuation. Use the letter placement chart on page 123 to determine margins and date placement. Address a large envelope.

▼ An attention line is used to
▼ direct a letter to a particular
▼ person. It is keyed as the first
▼ line of the letter and envelope
▼ address. Ladies and
▼ Gentlemen is the proper salu-
▼ tation because the letter is
▼ addressed to a company.

> Attention Ms. Carmelo Perez
> Perez and Miranda, Inc.
> 1028 Windward Way
> Wrightsville Beach, NC
> 28480-1028

	words
June 23, 19-- / Attention Ms. Carmelo Perez / Perez and Miranda, Inc. / 1028	14
Windward Way / Wrightsville Beach, NC 28480-1028 / Ladies and Gentlemen:	28
(¶) Thank you for joining the Wrightsville Beach Chamber of Commerce.	42
Our town has had great participation this year. The support of area businesses	58
enables us to provide services to the community.	68
(¶) On August 15, 19--, the Chamber of Commerce will sponsor	79
Wrightsville Beach Scene--a festival highlighting cultural events, business	94
services, industrial products, and local resources. We invite you to participate	111
in this festival by sponsoring a booth in the Wrightsville Civic Center. The	126
cost for rental of each booth is $500.	134
(¶) We hope you will participate in Wrightsville Beach Scene. For more infor-	149
mation and registration materials, please call Julia Morales or Janet Guthrie at	165
453-2900. Sincerely, / Louis C. Smith, Director / xx	175/193

- ### Problem 2 - Business Letter with Subject Line

Directions: Format the following letter in block style with mixed punctuation. Use letter placement chart on page 123 to determine margins and date placement.

▼ Place the subject line a dou-
▼ ble space below the saluta-
▼ tion. If the body paragraphs
▼ are blocked, block the subject
▼ line. If the body paragraphs
▼ are indented, indent the sub-
▼ ject line the same number of
▼ spaces or center the subject
▼ line.

> Dear Mr. Walker
>
> SUBJECT: Before Christmas
> This letter is our special invi

	words
November 12, 19-- / Mr. Melvin Walker / 6701 Lake Road / Morgan, GA	12
31755-0845 / Dear Mr. Walker: / SUBJECT: Before Christmas Sale	25
(¶) This letter is our special invitation to you, our preferred charge customer,	41
to our special one day before Christmas sale on December 1. We will give you	56
a special fifteen percent discount on any merchandise you purchase that day	71
on your account. You will not be billed for these items until February 1.	86
(¶) Mr. Walker, this is our way of saying "thank you" for your business during	101
the past year. Please bring this letter with you on December 1 to show to our	117
sales personnel when you make your purchases. We look forward to seeing you	132
at this special sale.	137
Sincerely yours, / Hector Ramos, Manager / xx	145/155

- ### Problem 3 - Composing a Business Letter

Directions: Assume you are Carmelo Perez and you have received the letter in Problem 1. Write a letter in response. Address it to Mr. Louis C. Smith, Director, Chamber of Commerce / Wrightsville Beach, NC 28480-1638. In your letter tell Mr. Smith that your company, Perez and Miranda, Inc., will participate in the festival on August 15. Your company will provide a display of its safety products and will need electrical outlets to set up a video display. Include other information or questions you consider relevant. Format a rough draft; edit; format a final copy. Choose the letter and punctuation styles you prefer. Use your judgement to determine margins or use standard computer defaults. Use line 16 for the date.

UNIT 6 FORMATTING ANNOUNCEMENTS AND INVITATIONS

Lessons 26-30

In this unit, you will learn how to format various types of announcements and invitations. You will center them horizontally and vertically. Some will be prepared on a half page and others on a full page. You will also continue to build your basic keying skill.

General Directions: For drills and timed writings, use the following side margins:

Computer: Default margins with use of word wrap to complete line unless your teacher directs you to change your default margins. For this process, refer to your user's guide or follow your teacher's instructions.

Typewriter: Elite—1"
Pica—½"

Directions for setting margins on the typewriter are given on page RG-3. For problems, set margins as directed in each lesson. SS sentences and drill lines, and DS paragraph copy. DS between groups of repeated lines. Space problem copy as directed.

Placement Guide

Side Margins	Margin Settings
1" Elite	12–90*
½" Pica	5–80*

*Plus 5 spaces for end-of-line signal

LESSON 26

26a Keyboard Review

5 minutes

Directions: Key each line twice; repeat if time permits.

1	All letters	David and Jake Craig were quite happy for a month in Texas and Brazil.
2	Number-symbol	Tickets for the concert cost $35, $25, or $15; Luz spent $100 on them.
3	Fourth Finger	Paula quickly quizzed the pupils; prizes were awarded for the puzzles.
4	Easy	Words are the keys that we must use to open our minds to other people.

| 1 | 2 | 3 | 4 | 5 | 6 | 7 | 8 | 9 | 10 | 11 | 12 | 13 | 14 |

26b Sentence Skill Builder

5 minutes

Directions: Key four 1' writings on sentence 4 in 26a. Determine *gwam;* try to increase your rate on each writing of this easy sentence.

55e Sustained Skill Building

Directions: 1. Key a 5' writing on the copy on page 121. Circle your errors and determine your *gwam*. **2.** Key two 1' writings on each paragraph. Key the first for speed and the second for control. **3.** Finally, key another 5' writing over all paragraphs. Circle your errors and determine *gwam*. Compare the number of errors and the *gwam* on the two 5' writings. Submit the better of the two to your teacher.

LESSON 56

56a Keyboard Review

5 minutes

Directions: Key each sentence three times.

1	All letters	In July begin quick exams of each product so we may have zero defects.
2	Number-symbol	Flowers for $4 each will be $268--10% of all the cash and carry items.
3	Hyphen	Their new Bock-Crane fax machine is one of the most up-to-date models.
4	Easy	An old adage says that you get what you pay for, and this may be true.

| 1 | 2 | 3 | 4 | 5 | 6 | 7 | 8 | 9 | 10 | 11 | 12 | 13 | 14 |

56b Skill Comparison

5 minutes

Directions: Key a 1' writing on each sentence in 56a. Compare *gwam* on each sentence.

56c Communication Skill—Placement of Semicolons Between Independent Clauses

5 minutes

Directions: Key each sentence three times. The first line gives the rule; the remaining lines apply it.

1. Use semicolons between independent clauses not joined by conjunctions.

2. Bella completed a major in accounting; then she finished the CPA exam.

3. Send a resume with the application; this will provide additional data.

26c Technique Builder—Flowing Rhythm Practice

5 minutes

Directions: Key each sentence twice on the response level indicated in the left margin.

Stroke Response—Think and strike each letter as a separate unit.

Word Response—Think and keystroke each word as a unit.

Combination Response—Think and keystroke the short, balanced-hand words as units. Keystroke the one-hand and difficult words letter by letter. Combine the two response levels into a natural, flowing, rhythmic pattern.

1	Stroke	Communication is a complex process of many varied critical components.
2	Word	We need to write, read, speak, hear, and see to deal with our new era.
3	Combination	We can communicate if we will recognize the needs of the other person.
4	Combination	In the information society, communication is more important than ever.

26d Communication Skill—Keying Book Titles

5 minutes

Directions: Key each line twice. The first line gives the rule; the remaining lines apply it. Capitalize and punctuate the last sentence correctly.

1 The title of a book may be underlined or keyed in all capital letters.

2 <u>Doctor Zhivago</u> and <u>War and Peace</u> are on my reading list this semester.

3 Two good books for your term paper are POWERSHIFT and MEGATRENDS 2000.

4 mrs sumida is requiring her students to read jane eyre this semester.

26e Keying from Corrected Copy

5 minutes

Directions: Key the paragraph twice. Make all corrections that are indicated by the proofreaders's marks. Review the marks presented in 24f, page 51 and 25d, page 52.

words

Southern california is a great place for a summre vacation.   12

There are so very many places to go: the beach, the mountains,   24

TV Shows, or theme parks. Some of the most popular parks are   36

disneyland, Knott's Berry Farm, SixFlags Magic Mountain, and   49

Univeral studios. A person can spend a day, or even two or   61

75 words   three days, at any of these parks with thier exciting rides and shows.   75

55b Speed Ladder Sentences

Directions: Key each sentence for 1' as the guides are called. Your teacher will call the return of the carrier every 10, 12, or 15 seconds. **Technique Goal:** Return the carrier quickly without looking away from the copy. Start keying immediately after returning the carrier.

		gwam		
		15"	12"	10"
1	Plan soon for the career of your choice.	32	40	48
2	Career options open to trained men and women.	36	45	54
3	It is said people will change careers three times.	40	50	60
4	One must work to be successful at small and large jobs.	44	55	66
5	Many positions now require workers to move to new locations.	48	60	72
6	Learning keyboarding skills will be valuable to the new employee.	52	65	78
7	Most people can agree that hard work and a little luck bring benefits.	56	70	84

| 1 | 2 | 3 | 4 | 5 | 6 | 7 | 8 | 9 | 10 | 11 | 12 | 13 | 14 |

55c Keystroking from Dictation and Spelling Checkup

5 minutes

Directions: Key the spelling words in 53b, page 127 as your teacher dictates them. Check for correct spelling. Rekey any words in which you have made an error.

55d Continuity Practice from Script

5 minutes

Directions: Key the paragraph below as many times as you can in the time allowed. Try not to make errors. After each writing of the paragraph, circle any errors you may have made. Key correctly three times the word in which you made an error along with the word preceding and the word following it.

words

64 words
1.5 si

Many people believe that the computer is the most important	12
invention of this century. Whether or not that is true, it has most	26
definitely changed all of our lives, and it has had a profound effect	40
on almost everything we ever do. Many people also believe that the	52
future of the computer may be just as exciting as its past.	64

Directions: **1.** Key a 1' writing on ¶1. Note the *gwam* and add 4 words for a new goal. Key a second 1' writing on ¶1 and try to reach your new goal—stroke for speed. Key a third writing on ¶1 at your original rate. Keystroke for control—fewer errors. **2.** Repeat this procedure for ¶'s 2 and 3. Alternate your practice for speed and for control. **3.** Key two 3' writings over all paragraphs. Figure your *gwam*. Submit the writing with the higher rate.

All letters

| | *gwam* |
| | 1' | 3' |

	1'	3'
¶1 36 words 1.2 si	If we want to be able to convey our thoughts to other people, we	13	4	42
	should be able to speak and write well. These are critical skills in	27	9	47
	our lives, and we must master them with zeal.	36	12	50
¶2 38 words 1.3 si	Giving a speech in public is easy for some people, but many of	13	16	54
	us feel it is quite a major issue. Fear is a normal part of such an	26	21	59
	event, but fear can be controlled if we want to be expert.	38	25	63
¶3 40 words 1.4 si	Other people fear writing. They may have great trouble in just	13	29	67
	taking a thought and putting it onto a sheet of paper. This is also	27	34	72
	a very normal fear. With much work, however, they can overcome it.	40	38	76

```
1' |  1  |  2  |  3  |  4  |  5  |  6  |  7  |  8  |  9  |  10  |  11  |  12  |  13  |  14  |
3' |        1        |        2        |        3        |        4        |        5        |
```

LESSON 27

Directions: Key each sentence twice; repeat.

1	All letters	If we get the vast zoo job done quickly, the next project may be ours.
2	Number-symbol	Some banks are only paying 7% interest, but mine is now paying 8 1/2%.
3	One hand	Tax rates on oil trade were set. Best rates were based on exact data.
4	Easy	We all had great fun in the city park with our senior class last week.

```
| 1 | 2 | 3 | 4 | 5 | 6 | 7 | 8 | 9 | 10 | 11 | 12 | 13 | 14 |
```

27b Skill Comparison

5 minutes

Directions: Key a 1' writing on each sentence in 27a. Key the easy sentence first. Try to keep the same rate on the others.

- **Problem 2 -** Business Letter in Modified Block Style

> **Directions:** Format the letter below in modified block style, with indented paragraphs and mixed punctuation. Use the table on page 123 to determine margin settings and dateline placement. Address a large envelope.

▼ A modified block letter may
▼ be formatted with blocked or
▼ indented paragraphs.

	words
April 22, 19-- / Mr. Donald Framing / 129 Inlet View Drive / Charleston,	13
SC 29408-0129 / Dear Mr. Framing:	20
(¶) Thank you for accepting our invitation to be the keynote speaker at the	34
Young Business Entrepreneur Conference. We know your motivational talk	49
will be a highlight of this meeting.	56
(¶) The banquet will be held in the Grand Ballroom of the Omni Hotel on	70
April 19, 19--, at 7:00 p.m.	76
(¶) As soon as our programs are printed, we will send one to you.	89
Sincerely yours, / Dianne Kell, President / xx (words in body: 69)	97/110

- **Problem 3 -** Business Letter in Modified Block Style

> **Directions:** Reformat the Letter in Problem 2, above. Use the same directions. This time, however, address it to: Mrs. Teresa Lazaro / 2006 Longview Court / Riverside, CA 92504-2006. Also, in this letter change the conference to Women in Construction Conference at the Homestead Hotel.

LESSON 55

55a Keyboard Review

5 minutes

> **Directions:** Key each sentence three times.

1	All letters	Grady and Jill must take the quiz, but very few of us expect to do so.
2	All numbers	Enclosed is personal check 3927 for the premium on Policy No. 814-650.
3	Shift	The Rockies, Smokies, and Grand Tetons are mountain ranges in the USA.
4	Easy	I know the man and woman who are in the last row of the movie theater.

| 1 | 2 | 3 | 4 | 5 | 6 | 7 | 8 | 9 | 10 | 11 | 12 | 13 | 14 |

27c Speed Ladder Sentences

Directions: Key 1' writings on each sentence. Your teacher will call the return every 15 seconds. Try to finish each sentence as the return is called. **Technique Goal:** Follow the suggestions in the sentences, and make sure you are using the correct techniques.

		words in line	gwam 15" guide
1	You must now be using proper techniques.	8	32
2	Place your book at the right of your machine.	9	36
3	Sit back in your chair; hold your shoulders erect.	10	40
4	Be sure that you hold the elbows in and near your body.	11	44
5	Hold your wrists low; don't rest your hands on your machine.	12	48
6	Keep your fingers well-curved, and hold them over your home keys.	13	52
7	Is your head turned toward your book; are your eyes held on your copy?	14	56
8	Make sure your feet are flat on the floor with one ahead of the other.	14	56

| 1 | 2 | 3 | 4 | 5 | 6 | 7 | 8 | 9 | 10 | 11 | 12 | 13 | 14 |

27d Learning to Center Horizontally

Centering material so that there will be equal left and right margins is called horizontal centering.

Horizontal Centering Steps

Step 1—Check the placement of the paper guide to see that it is set on 0. Turn to page 5 and read the directions for adjusting the paper guide.

Step 2—Move to the center point. When using 8 1/2" x 11" standard size paper, use 51 as the center point for elite and 42 as the center point for pica type.

Step 3—Backspace once for every two letters or spaces in the line to be centered. If there is one letter left over, do not backspace for it. Begin to key.

If you are using a computer or an electronic typewriter, your teacher may give you different instructions for horizontal centering. With word processing software, centering may be accomplished automatically.

• **Problem 1 -** Practicing Centering Lines Horizontally

Directions: Using practice paper, horizontally center each line shown below.

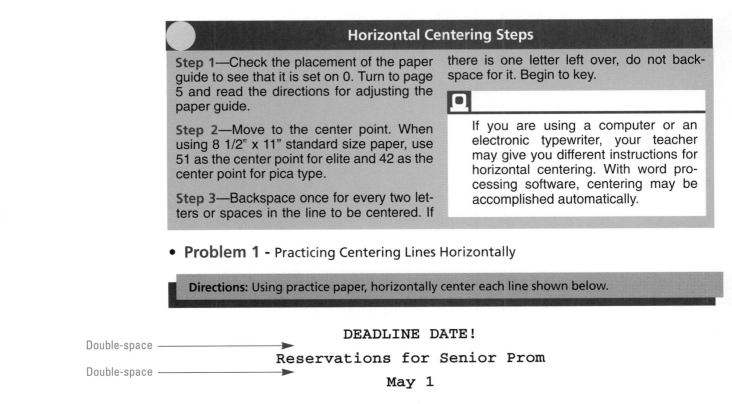

```
                     DEADLINE DATE!
Double-space ──────────▶
                 Reservations for Senior Prom
Double-space ──────────▶
                         May 1
```

- **Problem 1** - Business Letter in Block Style

Directions: Format the letter below in block style with open punctuation. Use the table on page 123 to determine margin settings and dateline placement. Address a large envelope.

words

May 12, 19-- 3

Miss Sallie Gunter 6
306 Regatta Road 10
Charleston, SC 29412-0306 15

Dear Miss Gunter 18

Are you interested in obtaining money for college tuition, books, and other 34
expenses? If you are, you may want to consider our Earn While You Learn 48
Program. 50

The Earn While You Learn Program is an employment opportunity for col- 64
lege students who have keyboarding skills. Our office employs students to 79
format and keyboard letters, mailing lists, and other documents for alumni 94
organizations. 97

Simply complete the enclosed application form and mail it to us. We will 112
then contact you to arrange a time for our skills assessment. If you meet the 128
performance requirements, you'll be on your way to a rewarding position-- 143
and money for college expenses. 149

Sincerely 151

Joel S. Patrick 154
Program Coordinator (words in body: 131) 158

xx 159

Enclosure 161/173

▼ Double-space between each
▼ line in Problems 2, 3, 4, and 5.

- **Problem 2** - Centered Invitation

Directions: Use a half sheet of paper, long side up. Follow the example in Problem 1 to center the lines below. Begin keying on line 15.

Community Advisory Council Breakfast
DS
Friday, April 28, 7 a.m.
DS
Faculty Lounge

- **Problem 3** - Centered Announcement

Directions: Center the lines below. Follow the same directions that were given for Problem 2.

CHAMPIONSHIP BASEBALL GAME
DS
Kennedy High vs Granada Hills High
DS
City Park Field, May 26, 3 p.m.

- **Problem 4** - Centered Announcement

Directions: Center each line below. Follow the same directions that were given for Problem 2 except place the first line on line 14 from the top.

BAKE SALE
Western Hills Garden Society
Crestview Shopping Center
Saturday, May 1, 9 a.m. to 3 p.m.

- **Problem 5** - Centered Invitation

Directions: Center each line below. Follow the same directions that were given for Problem 4.

Honor Society Spring Dance
Hamilton High Gymnasium
Friday, May 1, 7 to 11 p.m.
Tickets: $3 each

LESSON 28

28a Keyboard Review

5 minutes

Directions: Key each sentence twice.

1	All letters	Jack Mavis will specialize in shipping quantities of goods by express.
2	Number-symbol	Orders #85930 and #71642 will be shipped to us next week (January 15).
3	Easy	Do not use a long word if a short one will give the very same meaning.

| 1 | 2 | 3 | 4 | 5 | 6 | 7 | 8 | 9 | 10 | 11 | 12 | 13 | 14 |

28b Paragraph Guided Writing

5 minutes

Directions: Key the paragraph below for four 1' writings. Try stroking exactly 40 words a minute. Your teacher will call the quarter-minute marks to help you guide your keying on this easy copy (1.1 si).

40 words
1.1 si

words

How will you use your new skills from this class? ^{1/4} You may use   13

them in another class, and you may use them when you go to college.   26

Maybe you could even use them in a new job you may find this summer.   40

| 1 | 2 | 3 | 4 | 5 | 6 | 7 | 8 | 9 | 10 | 11 | 12 | 13 | 14 |

LESSON 54

54a Keyboard Review

5 minutes

Directions: Key each sentence three times.

1 All letters   The two key firm executives quibbled over major property zone changes.

2 All numbers   I saw 369 flutes, 20 trombones, 1 drum, 48 clarinets, and 57 trumpets.

3 Underline   <u>The Washington Post</u> and <u>The New York Times</u> are large daily newspapers.

4 Easy   Be aware of change which is a constant factor in our lives day by day.

| 1 | 2 | 3 | 4 | 5 | 6 | 7 | 8 | 9 | 10 | 11 | 12 | 13 | 14 |

54b Paragraph Skill Builder—Straight Copy

5 minutes

Directions: Key four 1' writings on this paragraph. Work for both speed and accuracy.

60 words
1.5 si

      There are many exciting jobs for which we may prepare. Some of these jobs demand a college degree, but for others a high school education is enough. It is certainly true, however, that more training is required today for success than was needed many years ago. This trend seems likely to continue.

54c Proofreading Skill Builder—Letter Transposition Errors

5 minutes

Directions: In the sentences below, find the words with transposition errors. Key each sentence correctly. Repeat. Each sentence has two words with errors.

1 Many expereinced as well as new employees recieve on-the-job training.

2 Varoius methods of transportatoin are used to ship goods to consumers.

3 Individaul financial statements should be sent for each fiscal peroid.

4 Produtcion figures were given for domestic as well as foriegn markets.

5 Will you plaese add an appropraite salutation for each of the letters?

28c Technique Builder—Flowing Rhythm

5 minutes

Directions: Key each line three times. Try to feel the difference in stroking the balanced-hand and the one-hand words. **Technique Goals:** Develop a smooth, rhythmic keystroking pattern.

1   they are | for her | their address | with the case | and the date | for you

2   she saved it | and the fact | if it were | they fear | for the only | as it

3   and she | if they look | and the union | to the state | the facts | for him

4   they grade | and imply | if they saw | and may trade | they were | the case

28d Problem Formatting

30 minutes

▼ If you are using a typewriter,
▼ be sure that your paper guide
▼ is set at 0 when you are cen-
▼ tering horizontally.
▼
▼ If you are using a computer,
▼ your teacher will give you
▼ instructions on how you may
▼ center automatically with a
▼ function key.

• Problem 1 - Centered Invitation

Directions: 1. Review the steps for horizontal centering on page 58. **2.** Use a half sheet of paper long side up and key the invitation which appears below. **3.** Double-space between every line. **4.** Start to key on line 9 from the top edge of your paper. **5.** Center each line horizontally.

Mr. and Mrs. Ray Genson

cordially invite you to a party

honoring

Kay Genson and Roberto Asato

on their engagement to be married

Saturday, March 16, 19--, 8 p.m.

13957 West Mountainview Road

Scottsdale, Arizona

RSVP

• Problem 2 - Centered Announcement

Directions: 1. Use a half sheet of paper long side up and key the announcement which appears below. **2.** Double-space between every line. **3.** Start to key on line 9 from the top edge of your paper. **4.** Center each line horizontally.

El Camino High School

Open House

Monday, October 15, 19--,

7 to 9 p.m.

Refreshments served by the

Parent-Teacher-Student Association

in the

Cafeteria at

8:30 p.m.

• Problem 3 - Centered Announcement

Directions: 1. Use a half sheet of paper long side up and key the announcement at the right. **2.** Double-space between every line. **3.** Start to key on line 11 from the top edge of your paper. **4.** Center each line horizontally.

Recycling Drive
sponsored by
the Westside Sports Club
405 Bayside Drive
Saturday, June 24
9 a.m. to 4 p.m.
Cans and bottles only

- **Problem 2 -** Business Letter in Modified Block Style

Directions: Format the letter below in modified block style, blocked paragraphs and open punctuation. Use the table on page 123 to determine margin settings and dateline placement. Address a large envelope. Students using computers should follow teacher's directions for margins.

	words
November 4, 19--	3

Dr. Ramona Morales | 7
628 Stuart Lane | 10
Ada, OK 71201-8212 | 14

Dear Dr. Morales | 18

Thank you for your interest in our new computer software program for den- | 32
tal records. We are enclosing a demonstration disk which gives you a sample | 48
of features. | 50

Dent-U-Pack has been tested for two years in 42 dental practices. Dentists | 66
report a savings of six to nine hours weekly on the time it takes to maintain | 81
dental charts and other records. Our representative, Mr. John Stephens, will | 97
be happy to demonstrate the software and tell you about its special features. | 113

Please call Mr. Stephens to arrange a time for the demonstration. He will also | 129
provide information on discounts available to large dental offices such as | 144
yours. We look forward to helping you with your records management needs. | 159

Sincerely | 161

Miss Joanne Taylor | 165
New Products Manager | 169

(words in body: 141)

xx | 169

Enclosure | 171/181

- **Problem 3 -** Business Letter in Modified Block Style

Directions: Reformat the letter in Problem 2, above. Use the same directions given for that letter. This time, however, address it to: Dr. Vernon C. Tapper / Box 83269 / Tulsa, OK 74104-3269.

29a Keyboard Review

5 minutes

Directions: Key each line twice.

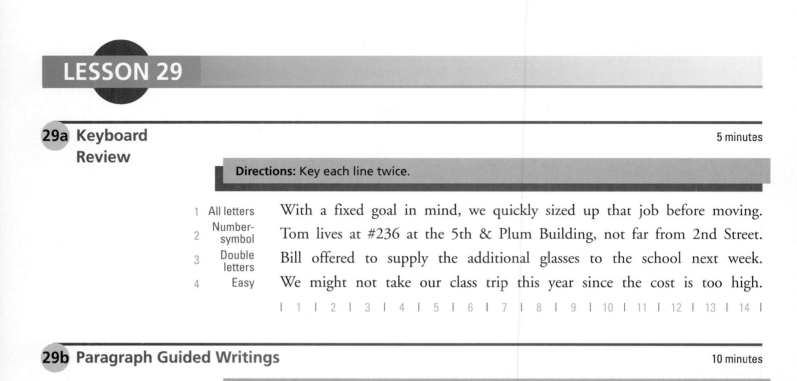

1	All letters	With a fixed goal in mind, we quickly sized up that job before moving.
2	Number-symbol	Tom lives at #236 at the 5th & Plum Building, not far from 2nd Street.
3	Double letters	Bill offered to supply the additional glasses to the school next week.
4	Easy	We might not take our class trip this year since the cost is too high.

| 1 | 2 | 3 | 4 | 5 | 6 | 7 | 8 | 9 | 10 | 11 | 12 | 13 | 14 |

29b Paragraph Guided Writings

10 minutes

Directions: 1. Key a 1' writing on ¶1, in drill 26f, page 57. Note the *gwam* and add 4 words for a new goal. Key a second 1' writing on P1 and try to reach your new goal—keystroke for speed. Key a third writing on ¶1 at your original rate. Keystroke for control—fewer errors. Repeat this procedure for ¶'s 2 and 3. Alternate your practice for speed and control.

29c Learning to Center Vertically

30 minutes

Centering copy on a page so that there are equal top and bottom margins is called vertical centering.

▼▼▼▼▼▼▼▼▼ If you are directed to center the problem in reading position, subtract 2 lines from the normal top margin attained in Step 3; then move on to Step 4. Reading position is used only when formatting on a full sheet of paper.

Vertical Centering Steps

Step 1—Count the lines in the copy to be centered. Be sure to count all blank lines in double-spacing.

Step 2—Subtract the total lines to be used from the lines available on the paper you are using. There are 6 lines to a vertical inch; therefore, when using standard size paper, 8½" by 11", a half sheet with the long side up has 33 lines and a full sheet 66 lines.

Step 3—After subtracting, you will know exactly how many blank lines you will have on the paper. Divide these remaining lines by 2. Disregard any fraction. The answer is the number of blank lines in the top and bottom margins.

Step 4—Insert your paper so that the top edge is exactly even with the alignment scale. Roll the paper up the proper number of lines (the answer from Step 3). Begin to key on the next line so that you retain the correct number of blank lines in the top margin.

If you are using a computer, your teacher may give you different instructions for vertical centering. With word processing software, vertical centering may be done automatically.

Business letter in modified block style
(Shown in pica type)

TAYLOR AND ASSOCIATES, INC.
1836 River Drive
Savannah, GA 31402-4312
(912) 324-4312

Center point

words

November 20, 19-- ← Line 16   4

QS

Ms. Peggy S. Strickland   First line of letter   8
Word Processing Department   address on fourth line   14
Lowcountry Realtors, Inc.   space (QS) below the   19
Letter address → 1521 Coligny Circle   dateline   23
Hilton Head Island, SC 29928   29
DS
Salutation → Dear Ms. Strickland: 33
DS
I am pleased to give you the information that you re-   44
quested about the modified block letter style. This   54
rather traditional format is very popular with many   65
companies. I have used it in this letter to you.   75
DS
Body of letter → In the modified block style the date is formatted to   1½" margin   85
begin at the center of the page. The closing lines   96
are also formatted to begin at the center point in   106
line with the date. You will notice that the para-   116
graphs are blocked and mixed punctuation is used.   126
It would be equally correct, however, to indent the   137
paragraphs or to use open punctuation.   145

1½" margin
You may wish to experiment with a variety of letter   155
styles until you find the one that you like best. Let   166
me know if I may give you additional information that   177
might be of value in your word processing operations.   188

DS
Complimentary close ──────────────→ Sincerely,   190
QS
Handwritten name ──────────────→ *Jennifer Cole*
(Signature)

Typewritten name and title ──────→ Jennifer Cole, Consultant

Reference → pe   195/221
initials

Center point

(words in body: 156)

- **Problem 1 -** Centered Announcement

Directions: Using a half sheet of plain paper long side up, center vertically and horizontally the problem illustrated below. Follow the steps given on page 61 for vertical centering. Double-space the problem. If necessary, refer to page 58 for a review of the steps to be followed for horizontal centering.

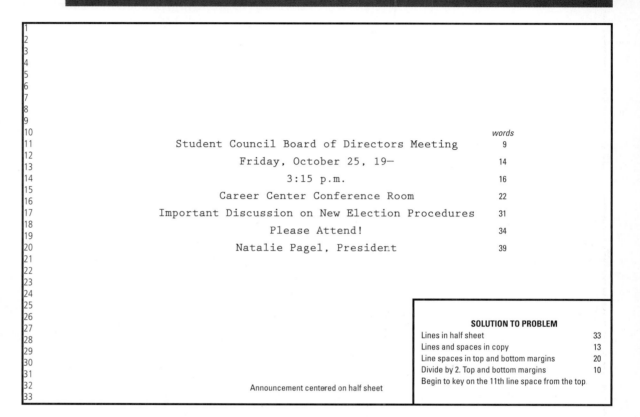

	words
Student Council Board of Directors Meeting	9
Friday, October 25, 19—	14
3:15 p.m.	16
Career Center Conference Room	22
Important Discussion on New Election Procedures	31
Please Attend!	34
Natalie Pagel, President	39

Announcement centered on half sheet

SOLUTION TO PROBLEM

Lines in half sheet	33
Lines and spaces in copy	13
Line spaces in top and bottom margins	20
Divide by 2. Top and bottom margins	10
Begin to key on the 11th line space from the top	

- **Problem 2 -** Centered Invitation

Directions: Using a half sheet of paper long side up, key the problem below. Center it vertically and horizontally. Double-space.

	words
Kevin W. Marino	3
requests the pleasure of your company	11
at a dinner celebrating his acceptance to medical school	22
Saturday, the thirtieth of December	29
at seven o'clock	33
Country Inn Restaurant	37
171 Old River Road	41
Arlington, Virginia	45
RSVP	46

53b Communication Skill—Spelling

Directions: Key each sentence twice.
Technique Goal: Study the spelling of each word shown in italics.

These are words that are frequently misspelled in business letters. Learn to spell them correctly.

1   *Apparently* room *accommodations* for both board meetings were *excellent.*

2   You may *schedule* an *interview* after you complete the *application* form.

3   *Information processing personnel* use keyboards for much of their work.

4   The *superintendent* issued *congratulations* to the *athlete* who competed.

5   *Whether* they travel by bus or plane will depend on *weather conditions.*

53c Paragraph Guided Writings

5 minutes

Directions: Key a 1' writing to establish your base rate. Key three additional 1' writings. Try to reach the exact letter of your base rate on each writing. ½' guides will be called. Keystroke at a controlled rate.

60 words
1.4 si

You probably believe that luck is simply that good fortune which happens purely by chance. Perhaps you are right, but it is wishful thinking to believe that the success others enjoy just happens. This world's greatest optimist is the person who waits for a ship to come in when it was not sent out.

53d Problem Formatting

30 minutes

- **Problem 1 -** Business Letter in Modified Block Style

Directions: Study the modified block style letter shown on page 128 and then format it. Use mixed punctuation. Follow all directions given on the illustration. Address a large envelope.

A modified block letter may be formatted with mixed or open punctuation.

- **Problem 3 -** Centered Announcement—Reading Position

> **Directions:** Key the announcement shown below on a full sheet of paper. Center it vertically in reading position. Center each line horizontally. Double-space.

	words
The Crescent Heights Community Orchestra	8
presents	10
AN EVENING WITH TCHAIKOVSKY	16
Symphony No. 4	19
Overture 1812	21
Piano Concerto No. 1	26
Antonio Cisneros, Guest Pianist	32
February 26, 19--	35
8 p. m.	37
University Performing Arts Center	44

LESSON 30

30a Keyboard Review

5 minutes

> **Directions:** Key each sentence twice.

1	All letters	Rita packed two dozen boxes of very good tarts filled with quince jam.
2	Number-symbol	Order #1492 (File 385-C) for $670 must be shipped in June to Sue Hill.
3	Easy	We build our skills by hard work and by setting goals we try to reach.

| 1 | 2 | 3 | 4 | 5 | 6 | 7 | 8 | 9 | 10 | 11 | 12 | 13 | 14 |

30b Technique Builder—Keystroking

5 minutes

> **Directions:** Key each line twice; repeat.

1	Double letters	The bookkeeper listed the assets in a letter she had for my committee.
2	Weak fingers	We were puzzled by the manager's lack of aptitude for the appointment.
3	One hand	Face facts. You'll get rewarded only after you exceed my best grades.
4	Flowing rhythm	The main reason that we fail to learn is that we stop before we start.

Folding Letters for Large Envelopes

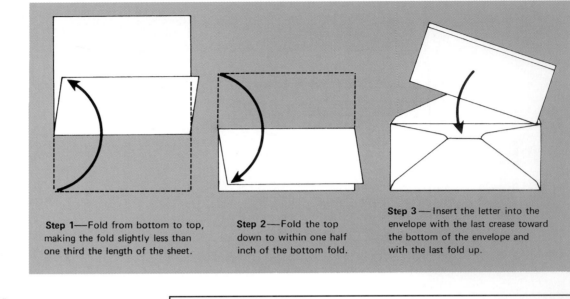

Step 1—Fold from bottom to top, making the fold slightly less than one third the length of the sheet.

Step 2—Fold the top down to within one half inch of the bottom fold.

Step 3 — Insert the letter into the envelope with the last crease toward the bottom of the envelope and with the last fold up.

▼ Refer to page 105 for spacing
▼ directions on formatting a
▼ large envelope

- **Problem 3 -** Business Letter in Block Style

Directions: Reformat the letter in Problem 2, page 124. Use the same directions given for that letter. This time, however, address it to: Mr. Daniel Cates | 4391 Old River Road | Claxton, GA 31106-4225

Be sure to change the salutation.

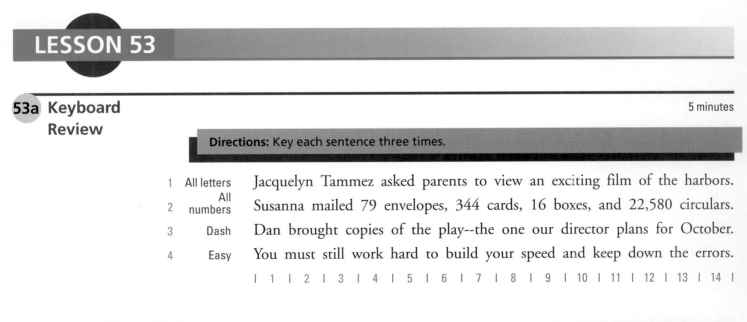

```
TAYLOR AND ASSOCIATES, INC.
1836 River Drive
Savannah, GA 31402-1836




                           MR. FRANK M. MITCHELL MANAGER
                           INFORMATION SERVICES DEPARTMENT
                           HARRISON INSURANCE SERVICES
                           8970 HARRISON ROAD
                           SAVANNAH, GA 31402-8970
```

Large envelope formatted as recommended by U.S. Postal Service

LESSON 53

53a Keyboard Review

5 minutes

Directions: Key each sentence three times.

1	All letters	Jacquelyn Tammez asked parents to view an exciting film of the harbors.
2	All numbers	Susanna mailed 79 envelopes, 344 cards, 16 boxes, and 22,580 circulars.
3	Dash	Dan brought copies of the play--the one our director plans for October.
4	Easy	You must still work hard to build your speed and keep down the errors.

| 1 | 2 | 3 | 4 | 5 | 6 | 7 | 8 | 9 | 10 | 11 | 12 | 13 | 14 |

30c Paragraph Guided Writing

5 minutes

Directions: 1. Key a 1′ writing on the following paragraph. Note your *gwam*. Add four words for a new goal. **2.** Take second and third writings. Try to reach new speed levels. **3.** Take a fourth writing with ease and control. Your goal on this writing will be improved accuracy. Your teacher may call the 1/2′ guides to aid you in checking your rate.

	words
A top keyboarding skill is a real asset when one tries to find a	13
job. Knowing how to use computer software is an added value. There	27
is a great need for these skills in all types of companies. Some stu-	41
dents have found that the summer jobs can sometimes turn into full-	54
time jobs after they graduate.	60

60 words
1.3 si

| 1 | 2 | 3 | 4 | 5 | 6 | 7 | 8 | 9 | 10 | 11 | 12 | 13 | 14 |

30d Problem Formatting

30 minutes

- **Problem 1 -** Centered Invitation

Directions: Key the invitation shown below on a full sheet of paper. Center it vertically in reading position. Center each line horizontally. Double-space. Make the corrections that are needed as you key the invitation.

	words
The Students and faculty o f	6
Punahou school	9
Honolulu, Hawaii	12
Request The Pleasure Of Your Compnay At	20
Honors Night	23
May 29, 19--, 7 pm	27
in the school Auditor ium	30

- **Problem 2 -** Critical Thinking Skill—Composing and Formatting an Invitation

Directions: Compose an invitation for a birthday party for you or for a friend. Refer to some of the problems in this unit for examples of information that you could use on the invitation. Take the rough draft from your typewriter or print a copy if you are using a computer. Edit your copy by making corrections with a pen or pencil, and then rekey your edited copy. Center each line horizontally and center the entire invitation vertically in reading position on a full sheet of paper.

TAYLOR AND ASSOCIATES, INC.
1836 River Drive
Savannah, GA 31402-1836
(912) 324-4312

words

March 17, 19--   ← Line 16   3

QS

Mr. Frank M. Mitchell, Manager   ← First line of letter address   9
Information Services Department   on fourth line space (QS)   16
Harrison Insurance Services   below the date line   21
Letter address → 8970 Harrison Road   25
Savannah, GA 31402-8970   30
DS
Salutation → Dear Mr. Mitchell   33
DS
Thank you for your interest in our services. I believe   45
that I may be able to help you with the communication   55
functions in your company, specifically regarding the   66
implementation of the block letter style.   75
DS
I think you will be pleased with this style for your   85
Body of letter → company correspondence. As you can see, I use it for my   97
own correspondence. The form has become very popular   108
because of its efficiency. The date line, letter   118
address, salutation, and closing lines are all format-   128
ted to begin at the left margin. Paragraphs are not   139
indented.   141

The block letter style is often combined with the open   152
1½" margin   punctuation style as illustrated in this letter.   1½" margin   162
Consequently, no mark of punctuation follows the salu-   173
tation or the complimentary close. However, the mixed   184
punctuation style is also acceptable to use with the   195
block letter format.   199

Please let me know if there are additional ways that I   210
might help you with your communication needs.   219
DS
Complimentary   221
close → Sincerely

(words in body: 186)

Susan Monson   ← Handwritten name (Signature)

Typewritten name
and title → Susan Monson, Consultant   ← Name of writer is shown in keyed   226
DS   form 4 spaces (QS) below the compli-
Reference → xx   mentary close.   227/253
initials

The writer's title may either follow the typewritten
name or be placed on the line below, depending on
the length of the name and the title.

- **Problem 3 -** Centered Poem

Directions: Key the following poem in exact vertical center on a full sheet of paper. Single-space the lines in the poem. Double-space after the title and between the last line and the poet's name. Determine the left margin stop by centering the poem horizontally according to the longest line. Center the title. Begin to key the name of the poet at the horizontal center point of the page.

This poem is inscribed at the main entrance to the pedestal of the Statue of Liberty.

▼ If you prefer, and if your
▼ teacher permits, you may
▼ wish to position the poem in
▼ reading position rather than
▼ in exact vertical center.

THE NEW COLOSSUS

Not like the brazen giant of Greek fame,
With conquering limbs astride from land to land.
Here at our sea-washed, sunset gates shall stand
A mighty woman with a torch, whose flame
Is the imprisoned lightning, and her name
Mother of Exiles. From her beacon-hand
Glows world-wide welcome; her mild eyes command
The air-bridged harbor that twin cities frame.
"Keep, ancient lands, your storied pomp!" cries she
With silent lips. "Give me your tired, your poor,
Your huddled masses yearning to breathe free,
The wretched refuse of your teeming shore.
Send these, the homeless, tempest-tost to me,
I lift my lamp beside the golden door!"

Emma Lazarus

30e Enrichment Assignments—Horizontal and Vertical Centering

- **Problem 1 -** Key the announcement (as shown below) on a half sheet of paper in exact vertical center. Center each line horizontally. Double-space. Repeat the problem; however, center it vertically in reading position on a full sheet of paper.

	words
GARAGE SALE	2
Saturday, October 20, 19--	8
9 a.m. to 4 p.m.	11
4938 West Ridgely Road	16
BARGAINS! BARGAINS! BARGAINS!	22
Toys, Books, Clothing, Furniture	29

- **Problem 2 -** Compose an original invitation to an event at your school to which you could invite your parents or friends. Center your invitation vertically and center each line horizontally. Double-space your invitation. Use your own judgement regarding whether or not you wish to use a half or full sheet of paper.

• **Problem 1** - Business Letter in Block Style

> **Directions:** Study the block style letter shown on page 125 and then format it. Use open punctuation. Follow all directions as given on the illustration. For this problem and all problems that follow, if you are using plain paper instead of paper with a letterhead, assume that there is a letterhead. Address a large envelope or paper cut to envelope size ($9\frac{1}{2}$" x $4\frac{1}{8}$"). For this problem and all problems that follow, assume that the return address is printed in the upper left-hand corner of the envelope. The final figure in the word count at the bottom of the letter on page 125 shows the total words in the letter plus the word count for the envelope. Fold the letter for inserting into a large envelope. Follow the directions on page 126 for folding letters for large envelopes.

Follow the style recommended by the U.S. Postal Service for addressing envelopes for the business letters in this unit. All words in the address are fully capitalized and no punctuation is used. Use two-letter state abbreviations shown on page RG-6. This style is illustrated on page 126.

• **Problem 2** - Business Letter in Block Style

> **Directions:** Format, in block style, the letter shown below. Use open punctuation. Use the table on page 123 to determine margin settings and dateline placement. Address a large envelope.

For the remaining letters in the book, use your initials as the reference initials.

Your teacher will give you additional instructions for the formatting and printing of business letters and envelopes if you are using a computer. When using a computer, envelope addresses are frequently printed on sheets of labels. Your teacher will give you instructions if you are to use this technique.

▼ A block letter may be formatted with open or mixed punctuation.

▼ An enclosure notation is used when something is sent with the letter. Key this notation a double space below the reference initials. Use the plural (Enclosures) if more than one item is enclosed.

	words
March 20, 19--	3
QS	
Ms. Christine Pruitt	7
Johnson and Pruitt Personnel Services	15
34 Skagway Island Boulevard	20
Savannah, GA 31402-0034	25
DS	
Dear Ms. Pruitt	28
DS	
Welcome to Savannah. We are happy to have Johnson and Pruitt Personnel	43
Services join the business community.	51
DS	
Enclosed are several complimentary items you may find helpful--a Savannah	65
Business Directory, a county map, and a catalog listing our office products	81
and services. Should you need any of those products or services as you begin	96
business operations, we can open an account for you and deliver orders to	111
your office each day.	116
DS	
Please consider us for all of your communication needs. Let us know if we	130
may help your business prepare successful documents.	141
DS	
Sincerely	143
QS	
Susan Monson, Consultant	148
DS	
xx (words in body: 113)	149
DS	
Enclosures	151/172

UNIT 7 · FORMATTING OUTLINES AND SHORT REPORTS

In this unit you will learn how to format outlines, one-page reports, and book reports. You will also continue to build your keying and your communication skills. Methods for correcting errors are also presented in this unit.

General Directions: For drills and timed writings, use 1" side margins with elite type and 1/2" with pica. With a computer, use default margins. For problems, set margins as directed. SS sentences and drill lines. DS paragraph copy and between groups of repeated lines. Space problem copy as directed.

LESSON 31

31a Keyboard Review

5 minutes

> **Directions:** Key each sentence twice.

▼ Always remember to
▼ repeat all drills more
▼ than twice if time
▼ permits.

1	All letters	Zinna W. Jacobson faxed a letter hoping to get her money very quickly.
2	All numbers	Before October 19, Flights 483 and 76 will arrive in Reno by 2:50 p.m.
3	Shift keys	Ms. T. Chi and Mr. L. Eto flew to Cincinnati, Ohio, to see Dr. P. Lee.
4	Easy	Use the words that say just what you want to say in the very best way.

| 1 | 2 | 3 | 4 | 5 | 6 | 7 | 8 | 9 | 10 | 11 | 12 | 13 | 14 |

Formatting Guides for Business Letters

Letter Styles—The two most widely used letter styles are the block and the modified block. They are illustrated on pages 125 and 129.

Punctuation Styles—The two most commonly used punctuation styles are open and mixed. In open, no punctuation marks are used after the salutation or the complimentary close. In mixed, a colon is placed after the salutation and a comma after the complimentary close.

Stationery—Most business letters are prepared on standard-size ($8\frac{1}{2}$" by 11") letterhead paper with the company name, address, and telephone number printed at the top.

Envelopes—Most firms use large envelopes (No. 10) for one-page letters, although small envelopes (No. 6 3/4) may be used. A large envelope should be used, however, for two-page letters and when items are enclosed. Company envelopes usually have the return address printed in the upper left corner.

Copies—One or more copies are usually made of business letters. They are usually made by a photocopier, but may be done with carbon paper.

Margins—Many business firms use standard margin defaults set on computers for all letters. To make the letter appear more balanced on the page, however, margins which vary according to the length of the letter should be used. Use the following chart for letters in this unit.

> Computer: Use standard default unless your teacher directs you to change margins.

Length	5-Stroke Words in Letter Body	Side Margins	Margin Setting Elite	Pica	Dateline
Short	Up to 100	2"	24–78*	20–65*	18
Avg.	101–200	$1\frac{1}{2}$"	18–84*	15–70*	16
Long	201–300	1"	12–90*	10–75*	14
2-page	More than 300	1"	12–90*	10–75*	14

* Add 5 spaces for end-of-line signal.

Basic Letter Parts—The various parts of a business letter are described in order of their occurrence.

Heading—This part is printed as a letterhead at the top of the paper and includes the name, address, and telephone number of the company.

Date—Vertical placement of the dateline varies according to the letter length. If a deep letterhead prevents placing the date on the line indicated in the table in column 1, place it a DS below letterhead.

> If you use default margins on your computer, you will need to place the dateline further down on the page when formatting short and average length letters.

Letter Address—This address should begin on the fourth line space (QS) below the date. A title (Mr., Mrs., Miss, Dr., etc.) should be used as a courtesy to the person to whom a letter is addressed. When a woman's preferred title is not known, use Ms. as her personal title. Use the standard two-letter state abbreviations as shown on page RG-6.

Salutation—The salutation (greeting) should be placed a double space (DS) below the letter address. If the letter is addressed to a company rather than an individual, the salutation Ladies and Gentlemen should be used.

Body—The body (message) of the letter begins a double space (DS) below the salutation. Paragraphs are single-spaced (SS) with a double space between them. They are most frequently blocked, but they may be indented in the modified block style letter.

Complimentary Close—The complimentary close (farewell) should be placed a double-space below the body.

Name of the Writer—The name of the writer should be keyed on the fourth line space (QS) below the complimentary close. The title of the writer may be keyed on the same line as the name preceded by a comma, or the title may be keyed on the line below the writer's name. The name of the writer is signed between the complimentary close and the typewritten name.

Reference Initials—The initials of the keyboard operator are keyed a double space (DS) below the writer's name.

Enclosure Notation—The word Enclosure, which indicates that something is included with the letter, is placed a double space below the reference initials. Use the plural Enclosures if more than one item is enclosed.

Special Letter Parts—A letter may also contain one or more of certain special parts such as an attention line, a subject line, or a postscript. The correct placement of these parts will be illustrated in other lessons of this unit.

31b Skill Comparison

5 minutes

Directions: Key a 1' writing on each sentence. Compare *gwam* on the four writings. Try to maintain the rate you set on the first sentence.

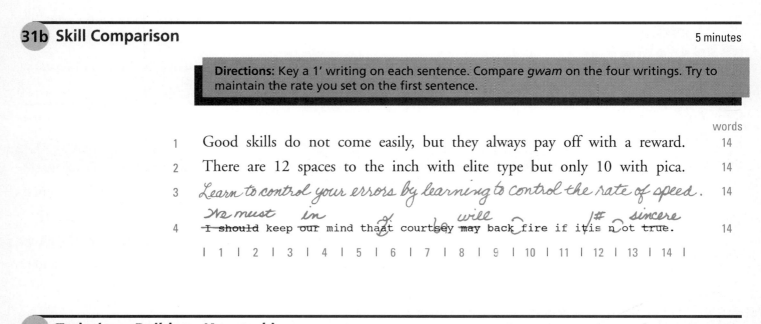

words

1　Good skills do not come easily, but they always pay off with a reward.　14

2　There are 12 spaces to the inch with elite type but only 10 with pica.　14

3　*Learn to control your errors by learning to control the rate of speed.*　14

4　I should keep our mind that courtesy may back fire if it is not true.　14

| 1 | 2 | 3 | 4 | 5 | 6 | 7 | 8 | 9 | 10 | 11 | 12 | 13 | 14 |

31c Technique Builder—Keystroking

5 minutes

Directions: Key each line three times.

1　One hand　refer you | saw him | we saw | look upon | as you were | my grade | dress up

2　Balanced hand　they did | with them | and the | and then | and they did | if she | for them

3　Combination　and look | the case | for only | for him | did look | she saw him | see them

4　Combination　and the joy | she did jump | and did regard | to hop | to see him | for you

31d Communication Skill—Spelling

5 minutes

Directions: Key each sentence twice.

Correct spelling is basic to accurate keying. Study the spelling of each word shown in italics below as you key it. These words and those in other spelling drills are words that are frequently misspelled.

1　My *instructor* gave me the *secret* to help me *excel* and *achieve success.*

2　The *registrar* shall *determine* if that *license* is *valid* and *acceptable.*

3　I cannot *exaggerate relevant* skills I *possess* to *succeed* in my *career.*

4　We *prefer* an *estimate* of the *consistency* needed to *guarantee strength.*

| 1 | 2 | 3 | 4 | 5 | 6 | 7 | 8 | 9 | 10 | 11 | 12 | 13 | 14 |

LESSON 52

52a Keyboard Review

5 minutes

Directions: Key each sentence three times.

1	All letters	Wilbur Jackson explained the quick-freezing process to every customer.
2	All numbers	On August 28, she wrote a check for $705.96 in payment of invoice 134.
3	Long reach	About once every night, Ben checks the barometer on that bottom level.
4	Easy	Build speed by keying shorter words by the word and not by the letter.

| 1 | 2 | 3 | 4 | 5 | 6 | 7 | 8 | 9 | 10 | 11 | 12 | 13 | 14 |

52b Paragraph Skill Builder—Statistical Copy

5 minutes

Directions: Key four 1' writings. Try to increase your rate on each writing by 1 to 2 words, but also maintain your accuracy on each writing.

60 words
1.4 si

Your order for 12 dozen turkeys was filled today.   The shipment should reach you by December 14, in time for your Christmas shoppers. I shall be happy to give you a standard 5% discount if you pay the balance within 8 days.   The total amount of the invoice, after deducting the discount, is $760.39.

52c Communication Skill—Capitalization in Business Letter Parts

5 minutes

Directions: Read the explanations for capitalizing words in various parts of business letters. Key each line three times. Repeat if time permits.

Line 1—Capitalize the first word, titles, and proper names used in the salutation.
Line 2—Capitalize only the first word of the complimentary close.
Line 3—Capitalize all titles appearing in the address.
Line 4—Capitalize a title that follows the name of the writer in the closing line.

1   Dear Marshall: Dear Mr. Lugo: Ladies and Gentlemen: Dear Ms. Utako:

2   Sincerely yours, Very truly yours, Cordially yours, Very respectfully,

3   Dr. Yan Huang, Professor; Mr. Terry Tucker, Manager; Cpt. Jerrod Kent;

4   Barbara Gordon, President; Jo Hamer, Chairperson; David Rankin, Judge;

Directions: 1. Key a 1' writing on ¶1. Note the *gwam*. Add four words to your *gwam* for a new goal. Take two more writings. Try to reach your new goal. **2.** Repeat step 1 for ¶'s 2 and 3. Your teacher may call the 1/2' guides on the 1' writings to aid you in checking your rate. **3.** Key two 3' writings over all paragraphs. Figure your *gwam*. Submit the better of the two writings.

All letters

words

	1'	3'

¶1
60 words
1.3 si

Baseball has often been called the most popular sport in this   12 | 4
country.   Thousands of fans go to pro games each day of the season,   26 | 9
and millions more hear games on radio or watch them on television.   40 | 13
Amateurs of all ages play, and some dream of being stars.   This   52 | 17
game is now played all over the world.   60 | 20

¶2
60 words
1.3 si

Soccer is thought to be the most widely played team game in the   13 | 24
world.   It is also the most popular of spectator sports.   Millions of   27 | 29
fans seem to love their favored teams and stars, and they are known   40 | 33
to be zealous and excited to win.   Amateur soccer has become quite a   54 | 38
popular sport in our country.   60 | 40

¶3
60 words
1.3 si

Basketball is another sport judged to be one of the most popular   13 | 44
in the world.   This is true for the players as well as for the spec-   27 | 49
tators.   It is a favorite because of the fast action and the high scor-   41 | 54
ing.   This sport has long been popular in high schools and in   53 | 58
colleges both for men and for women.   60 | 60

1'	1	2	3	4	5	6	7	8	9	10	11	12	13	14
3'		1		2		3		4		5				

> **Directions: 1.** Key a 5' writing. Circle your errors and determine your *gwam*. **2.** Key a 1' writing on each paragraph. Key the first and third paragraphs for speed and the second and fourth for control. **3.** Finally, key another 5' writing over all paragraphs. Circle your errors and determine *gwam*. Compare the number of errors and the *gwam* on the two 5' writings. Submit the better of the two to your instructor.

All letters

	gwam	
1'	5'	

Copy difficulty level: Average

In the job market today, good communication skills will help you compete with success.   To get the job you want, you may need to prepare several messages: a resume or data sheet, a cover letter, and a follow-up message.   A good data sheet and cover letter can be one of the first steps to acquire that desired job.

1'	5'	
14	3	53
29	6	56
45	9	59
61	12	63
63	13	63

▼ For the remaining 5´ skill
▼ building writings in this book,
▼ the copy will be controlled
▼ not only for the average sylla-
▼ bles per word (or syllable
▼ intensity—si), but also for
▼ the average word length
▼ (awl) and for the percent
▼ of common words (or high-
▼ frequency words—hfw) used.
▼ These controls should give
▼ you an accurate evaluation of
▼ your 5´ speed and accuracy
▼ skills.

The data sheet tells about your knowledge and skills and should be written to fit your job goal.   The data sheet should contain several major parts.   One part should be made up of personal data such as name, address, and phone number.   Other sections list skills, education, work experience, and school activities.

13	15	66
28	18	69
43	21	72
58	24	75
63	25	76

Good communication skills will enable you to compose an effective letter to send with your data sheet.   The purpose of the cover letter is to help you get an interview.   Begin the letter with a topic sentence which will draw favorable attention to you.   Pique the reader's interest with zeal to know more about you.

13	28	78
28	31	81
44	34	84
59	37	87
63	38	88

After the interview, a prompt follow-up letter should be sent.   A thank-you letter can be used to keep the person aware of your interest and skill.   The thank-you letter can reinforce the application, data sheet, and interview.   Employers are always looking for qualified persons, and that person could just be you.

13	40	91
28	43	94
43	46	97
59	50	100
63	52	101

1.5 si
5.7 awl
80%hfw

1' | 1 | 2 | 3 | 4 | 5 | 6 | 7 | 8 | 9 | 10 | 11 | 12 | 13 | 14 |
5' | 1 | 2 | 3 |

31f Horizontal and Vertical Centering—Review

5 minutes

Directions: Key the announcement shown below on a half sheet of paper. Center it in exact vertical position. Center each line horizontally. Double-space. Make all corrections shown.

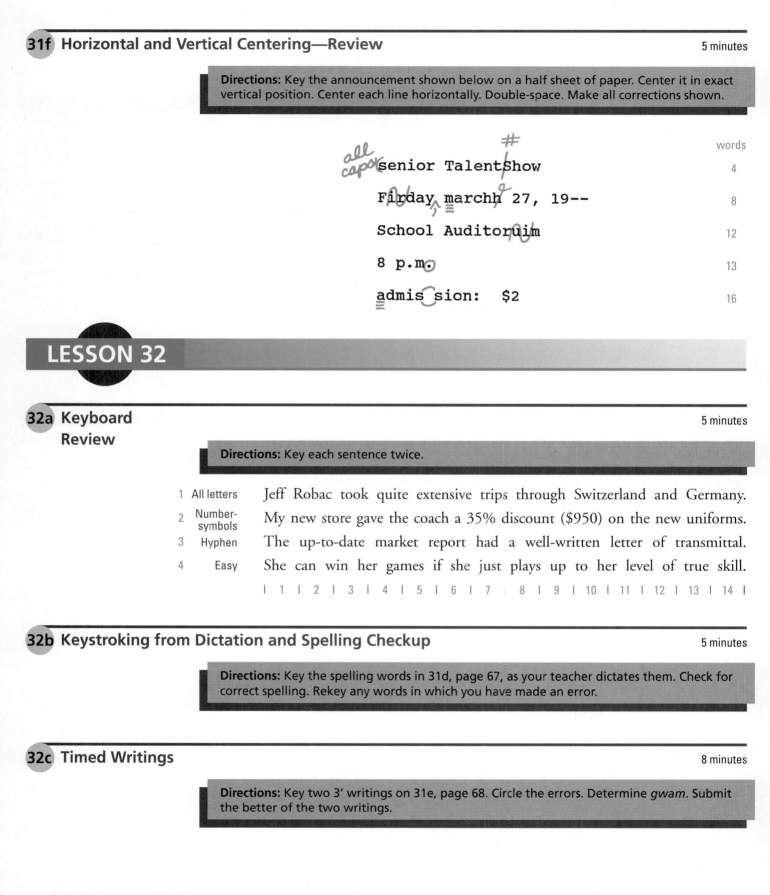

	words
all caps senior Talent Show #	4
Firday marchh 27, 19--	8
School Auditoruim	12
8 p.m.	13
admission: $2	16

LESSON 32

32a Keyboard Review

5 minutes

Directions: Key each sentence twice.

1	All letters	Jeff Robac took quite extensive trips through Switzerland and Germany.
2	Number-symbols	My new store gave the coach a 35% discount ($950) on the new uniforms.
3	Hyphen	The up-to-date market report had a well-written letter of transmittal.
4	Easy	She can win her games if she just plays up to her level of true skill.

| 1 | 2 | 3 | 4 | 5 | 6 | 7 | 8 | 9 | 10 | 11 | 12 | 13 | 14 |

32b Keystroking from Dictation and Spelling Checkup

5 minutes

Directions: Key the spelling words in 31d, page 67, as your teacher dictates them. Check for correct spelling. Rekey any words in which you have made an error.

32c Timed Writings

8 minutes

Directions: Key two 3' writings on 31e, page 68. Circle the errors. Determine *gwam*. Submit the better of the two writings.

Proofreading Techniques

Proofreading is a very important element in the correct formatting of business and professional documents. Each document should be proofread carefully before it is taken out of the machine or stored on the computer disk.

A person must look closely for a variety of possible errors. These include: typographical, spelling, punctuation, and grammatical errors; transposition of letters and lines; errors in page numbers, in meaning, in uniformity of names and numbers, in exact- ness of names and addresses, and inconsistency of styles.

Proofread your printed copy again after removing it from the machine or printing a hard copy from the computer. You may wish to read it to a co-worker who will check it against the original as you read. For some types of copy, particularly that containing statistics, two people should always proofread; one person reads the copy aloud from the original and the other checks the accuracy of the information just keyed.

Directions: Find the incorrectly spelled word in each sentence. Key the sentence, spelling the word correctly. Key the sentences again.

▼ All of the incorrect words in
▼ this drill are frequently mis-
▼ spelled. Learn to spell all of
▼ them correctly.

1   Students can acheive higher scores for exams if they study diligently.

2   The personnell manager will interview applicants for an accounting job.

3   Some of the coldest months each year are January, Febuary, and March.

4   Drivers entered the tracks through seperate gates and started engines.

5   Writers should use correct grammer when they write letters or reports.

6   Business executives may purchase new calenders at the end of the year.

7   Please do not dissappoint Catherine with poor performance at the track.

8   Job discriptions were sent to former employees of the accounting firm.

- **Problem 1 -** Topic Outline

Directions: Key the topic outline shown below. Use a full sheet of paper. Leave a 2" top margin (place the title on line 13). Use 1" side margins. Center the heading. Indent, space, capitalize, and punctuate exactly as shown in the problem.

This outline gives the basic elements and format for the book report that you will key in Problem 1, Lesson 35.

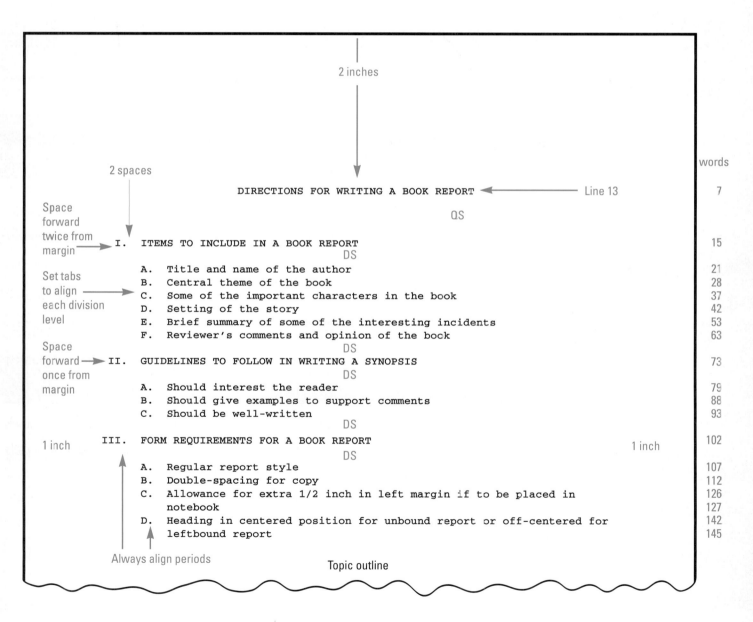

2 inches

words

2 spaces

DIRECTIONS FOR WRITING A BOOK REPORT ← Line 13	7
QS	

Space forward twice from margin

I.	ITEMS TO INCLUDE IN A BOOK REPORT	15
	DS	

Set tabs to align each division level

A.	Title and name of the author	21
B.	Central theme of the book	28
C.	Some of the important characters in the book	37
D.	Setting of the story	42
E.	Brief summary of some of the interesting incidents	53
F.	Reviewer's comments and opinion of the book	63
	DS	

Space forward once from margin

II.	GUIDELINES TO FOLLOW IN WRITING A SYNOPSIS	73
	DS	
A.	Should interest the reader	79
B.	Should give examples to support comments	88
C.	Should be well-written	93
	DS	

1 inch

III.	FORM REQUIREMENTS FOR A BOOK REPORT	102
	DS	

1 inch

A.	Regular report style	107
B.	Double-spacing for copy	112
C.	Allowance for extra 1/2 inch in left margin if to be placed in	126
	notebook	127
D.	Heading in centered position for unbound report or off-centered for	142
	leftbound report	145

Always align periods

Topic outline

UNIT 11 BUSINESS LETTERS

In this unit you will learn how to format business letters in various styles and with special features. You will also continue to build your keying, communicating, and composing skills.

General Directions: For drills and timed writings, use margins of 1" for elite, 1/2" for pica, and standard default margins if you are using a computer; your teacher may instruct you to change your default margins. For problems, set margins as directed. SS sentences and drill lines, and DS paragraph copy. DS between groups of repeated lines. Space problem copy as directed in each lesson. For computers, use the standard default margins for the letters.

LESSON 51

51a Keyboard Review

5 minutes

Directions: Key each sentence three times; repeat if time permits.

1 All letters   Mary Johnson packed five more bags with one dozen boxes of quail each.

2 All numbers   By May 13, 968,547 fans will have attended over 20 of my team's games.

3 Shift keys   Milwaukee, Madison, and Green Bay are three large cities in Wisconsin.

4 Easy   You should keep your reader in mind when you write a letter or a memo.

| 1 | 2 | 3 | 4 | 5 | 6 | 7 | 8 | 9 | 10 | 11 | 12 | 13 | 14 |

51b Technique Builder—One-Hand Words

10 minutes

Directions: Key each line three times. Take two 1' timings on each of the last two lines.
Technique Goal: Try to increase your speed on one-hand words.

1 Phrases   as my | as we see | as you join | at a | see her | we see | as we see | saw a

2 Phrases   as he sees | we were only | we were aware | as you look | we see them only

3 Sentence   Molly and Garrat saw several endangered animals at the Riverbanks Zoo.

4 Sentence   I was aware of a few exaggerated opinions given on the phony monopoly.

| 1 | 2 | 3 | 4 | 5 | 6 | 7 | 8 | 9 | 10 | 11 | 12 | 13 | 14 |

• **Problem 2 -** Topic Outline

Directions: On a full sheet of paper, key the outline shown below. Use a 2" top margin and 1" side margins. Refer to the outline illustrated on page 70 and follow the guidelines shown there for indenting, spacing, capitalizing, and punctuating.

▼ This outline describes the
▼ content of the resume (also
▼ known as a personal data
▼ sheet) that you will learn to
▼ format in Lesson 48.

CONTENT OF A RESUME

I. PERSONAL INFORMATION

A. Name

B. Address

C. Phone number

II. EDUCATION

A. Schools attended

B. Date of graduation

C. Major field of study

D. Grade point average (if good)

E. Honors and activities

III. EXPERIENCE

A. Title of job held

B. Name of company

C. Address of company

D. Dates worked

E. Description of job duties

IV. REFERENCES

A. Name and title

B. Address

C. Phone number

V. ACTIVITIES AND INTERESTS

A. Clubs, volunteer work, etc.

B. Sports, music, etc.

LESSON 33

33a Keyboard Review

5 minutes

Directions: Key each sentence twice.

1	All letters	The ski jumper walked quickly over the breezeway while fixing his ski.
2	All numbers	The invoice number of the shipment was 403718, and my cost was $95.26.
3	Right shift	The Rams, Giants, Cowboys, Raiders, Bills, and Colts play today on TV.
4	Easy	In your work you now do in this class, try for both speed and control.

| 1 | 2 | 3 | 4 | 5 | 6 | 7 | 8 | 9 | 10 | 11 | 12 | 13 | 14 |

• PART 3 •
DEVELOPING PROFESSIONAL COMMUNICATION SKILLS

Lessons 51-75

In Part Three you will learn how to apply your keying proficiency to the formatting of a variety of business and professional documents. You will be keying the types of materials most frequently encountered in the business office as well as in other professional situa-tions. The problems in this part of the book will give you an opportunity to sample career applications and will provide a transition to a more advanced keyboarding course leading to an occupational goal.

● Letters

You will learn to format business letters in both block and modified block styles. You will also learn how to format special features of letters such as the attention line, subject line, postscript, and correct second-page heading.

● Memorandums

You will learn the correct format for keying memorandums that are used for correspon-dence between offices or departments within a company.

● Tables

You will learn to format tables with two and three columns. These tables will also use main and secondary headings.

● Reports

You will learn to format reports with foot-notes, endnotes, and internal citations. You will also learn how to format reports which include tables.

● Correcting Errors

Your teacher will tell you the methods to use to correct errors.

● Basic Skill Development

The drills and timed writings are designed to help you put the finishing touches on your keystroking skills. The 5´ timings are triple-controlled.

● Communication Skill Development

A continued emphasis will be placed on spelling, capitalization, and punctuation.

● Proofreading

A variety of proofreading exercises will be presented. Proofreading is an important skill you should develop.

● Composing

Additional emphasis will be given to helping you develop your composition skills. Exer-cises will provide practice in composing a va-riety of documents.

● Enrichment Assignments

Problems will be given at the end of each unit for you to complete if you finish your work ahead of schedule. These problems are designed to be challenging and to help you enhance your critical thinking skills.

33b Skill Comparison

5 minutes

Directions: Key a 1' writing on each sentence in 33a. Key the easy sentence first. Try to keep the same rate on the others.

33c Paragraph Guided Writings

5 minutes

Directions: Set a goal for a 1' writing. Key a 1' writing on each paragraph. Try to reach your word goal just as time is called. Keystroke no faster or slower than is required by the goal you select.

All letters

¶1
60 words
1.3 si

Good skills are not quite all that we need in order to be able to get and keep a job. An excellent attitude and a zeal for hard work are both needed if one ever hopes to be successful. People lose their jobs more often because of a personal problem or a poor social skill than for any other reason.

¶2
60 words
1.3 si

One of the best habits we could develop is an ability to analyze our work with a clear eye. We could be proud of our work, but we must not be satisfied with it. If we are, we will never excel at anything we do. Sometimes a person does not see what lies in the future with a job, and may even quit.

¶3
60 words
1.3 si

People who quit one job after another because they see no future may be closer to an answer than they know. There is no real future in a job. The future begins within a job holder. A person must have a strong desire to improve, and the desire must be kept alive for one to be a success in any job.

| 1 | 2 | 3 | 4 | 5 | 6 | 7 | 8 | 9 | 10 | 11 | 12 | 13 | 14 |

50d Problem Formatting—Critical Thinking Skills

30 minutes

- **Problem 1 -** Composing and Formatting Your Personal Resume

Directions: Complete your own personal resume that you began in Lesson 48.

- **Problem 2 -** Composing and Formatting Your Personal Letter of Application

Directions: Compose and format your own personal letter of application in response to the advertisement shown at right. Use the letter on page 115 as a guide. Use correct personal business letter format. Select the letter and punctuation styles you prefer. Assume that you will attach your resume to this letter. Address a large envelope.

▼ Key a draft copy; edit carefully; rekey a final copy.

▼ Assume this advertisement appeared in the classified section of a recent edition of your local newspaper. For this problem, use your own street address but assume that you live in Baton Rouge, LA.

WORD PROCESSING SPECIALIST

A mid-size CPA firm has an immediate opening for a word processing specialist. We are looking for a person with the following qualifications:

Excellent keyboarding skills;
Outstanding proofreading ability;
Knowledge of WordPerfect or a
similar software;
Exceptional communication skills,
spelling, grammar, and
punctuation;
Good organizational ability.

Experience helpful but not required.

Excellent salary and benefits.

Send your resume with a letter of application to:

Ms. Catherine Gwinn, Administrative Manager
Rosebrock and Associates
1702 Spring Street, Suite 601
Baton Rouge, LA 70801-4042

AN EQUAL OPPORTUNITY EMPLOYER

50e Enrichment Assignments—Employment Documents

- **Problem 1 -** Assume that you have had an interview with Ms. Catherine Gwinn from Problem 2 above. Compose and format an interview follow-up letter that you could send to Ms. Gwinn. Address a small envelope.

- **Problem 2 -** Find an advertisement in your local newspaper for a job that you might find of interest. Compose and format a letter of application for this job. Attach your resume. Address a large envelope.

- **Problem 1 -** Outline

Directions: On a full sheet of paper, key the outline shown below. Use a 2" top margin and 1" side margins. Refer to the outline illustrated on page 70 and follow the guidelines shown there for indenting, spacing, capitalizing, and punctuating.

In future lessons you will be formatting some lines of copy that are either longer or shorter than those for which your margin is set. If you are using a typewriter, you will need to listen for a line-end signal and to divide long words correctly to keep fairly even right margins. NOTE: On some electronic typewriters and on computers, the writing line will wrap automatically to the next line when you reach your margin. Your teacher or your equipment and software manual will give you information on word division procedures.

WORD-DIVISION GUIDES

I. DIVIDE ONLY BETWEEN SYLLABLES

▼ As you key these guidelines,
▼ read them carefully. They will
▼ help you make decisions
▼ about dividing words.

    A. Con-flict
    B. Dif-fer-ent

II. DIVIDE HYPHENATED COMPOUNDS AT POINT OF HYPHENATION

    A. Cross-file
    B. Son-in-law

▼ Consult a dictionary when
▼ you are in doubt about the
▼ proper division of a word.

III. DO NOT DIVIDE WORDS OF ONE SYLLABLE

    A. Thought
    B. Straight

IV. DO NOT DIVIDE WORDS OF FIVE OR FEWER LETTERS

    A. Only
    B. Every

V. DO NOT DIVIDE A ONE-LETTER SYLLABLE FROM THE REST OF A WORD

    A. Enough
    B. Ready

VI. DO NOT DIVIDE ABBREVIATIONS OR NUMBERS

    A. Corp.
    B. $3,850,000

VII. DO NOT DIVIDE A WORD BETWEEN TWO PAGES

LESSON 50

50a Keyboard Review

5 minutes

Directions: Key each sentence three times.

1 All letters   The quick-mix angel food cake Yvonne just baked won first prize today.

2 Number-Symbol   My E-mail access number is 031/&82/#45, and the password is DINOSAURS.

3 Underline   I think you will like Michael Crichton's exciting book, <u>Jurassic Park</u>.

4 Easy   Your new skill will be of much value to you for the rest of your life.

| 1 | 2 | 3 | 4 | 5 | 6 | 7 | 8 | 9 | 10 | 11 | 12 | 13 | 14 |

50b Communication Skill—Placement of Commas Between Independent Clauses

5 minutes

Directions: Key each sentence three times. The first line gives the rule, and the remaining lines apply it. Capitalize and punctuate the last sentence correctly.

1   Place a comma before a conjunction that separates independent clauses.

2   Kenneth reached his new speed goal, and he also had excellent control.

3   Elaine and Chi will leave today, but Olivia will not go until Tuesday.

4   keri read the book for her english class but she did not do her math

50c Keying on Ruled Lines

5 minutes

Many companies require that an application form be completed when a person applies for a job. In some cases the applicant may be asked to complete the form in longhand, and in other cases the applicant may wish to key the information onto the form. This drill on keying on ruled lines should be of value when keying on an application form as well as when keying on other types of preprinted forms.

Directions: 1. Set the line-space selector for double spacing. **2.** Using the underline, on a sheet of paper key three lines about 3" long. Pica: 30 strokes; Elite: 36 strokes. **3.** Notice the position of the line in relation to the top of the aligning scale. **4.** Remove the paper, then reinsert it. **5.** Align the paper, using the variable line spacer to key on the first line. **6.** Key the lines shown below.

If you are using a computer, format this problem by using the automatic underlining feature of your software as you key the three lines below.

Mr. Carlo Roberto

18992 Cliffview Drive

San Diego, CA 92110-1310

Correcting Errors

Errors made in reports, letters, and other papers should be corrected. Therefore, you should learn how to correct errors properly.

With electronic typewriters, methods may vary, but a key is usually used to remove errors from the electronic window. With a computer, the incorrect characters are removed from the screen with the backspace or delete key.

With other typewriters, errors may be cor-rected with automatic correction tape, correction paper, correction liquid, or an eraser.

Techniques for making corrections are described in the outline in Problem 2, below, and in the report in Problem 2, page 77. Read this information carefully.

Your teacher will tell you if you are to correct errors made in keying problems that follow and which method or methods you should use.

• **Problem 2 -** Topic Outline

Directions: Format the outline shown below. Use all the guidelines for formatting outlines that you have used in the previous problems.

▼ An outline is frequently devel-
▼ oped before one writes a
▼ report. The outline is then
▼ very useful in helping collect
▼ and organize the information
▼ before writing the final report.
▼ For example, this outline was
▼ used for writing the report in
▼ Problem 2, page 77.

THE CORRECTION OF ERRORS

I. ELECTRONIC TYPEWRITERS AND COMPUTERS
   A. Special key to remove errors
   B. Backspace key
   C. Delete key

II. TYPEWRITERS
   A. Automatic correction tape
   B. Correction paper
   C. Correction liquid
   D. Eraser

• **Problem 3 -** Critical Thinking Skill—Composing and Formatting an Outline

Directions: Using the information on horizontal and vertical centering found on pages 58 and 61 in your book, compose and format an outline. Use the same guidelines for outlines that you have used in previous problems. Develop an appropriate title for your outline.

```
19528 Rimrock Drive                                                          4
Lincoln, NE 68504-3976                                                       9
June 5, 19--                                                                11

QS

Ms. Kara Walter, Manager                                                    16
Mountain States Insurance Agency                                            23
693 University Avenue                                                       27
Lincoln, NE 68504-3976                                                      32

Dear Ms. Walter                                                             35

My counselor, Mr. R. W. Loudamy, at Lincoln High School has informed me     51
about an opening you have for an entry-level clerk.  He told me that the     65
job requires both keyboarding and filing skills.  I believe that my high    80
school business courses and my summer work experience have given me a good  95
background for this position.                                              100

In my Personal Keyboarding course, I developed my skill to a level of 50   115
words a minute with high accuracy.  I also learned how to format letters,  129
memorandums, and reports.  I improved my composition skills in my Business  144
English class, and I am especially careful with spelling, grammar, and     160
punctuation.  In my Computer Applications in Business course, I learned a  175
variety of software including Lotus, dBase, and WordPerfect.               186

Last summer in my job with Great Plains Manufacturing, I became quite pro- 201
ficient at preparing sales orders through automated forms software.  I     216
also learned an alpha-numeric filing system controlled by a computerized   231
index.  My enclosed resume will give you more details on my background,    246
and it also lists the names of three people who have given me permission   262
to use them as references.                                                 264

May I have an appointment for an interview?  You can reach me at the        280
address given above or by phone at (402) 295-9981.  I look forward to       295
hearing from you.                                                          296

Sincerely                                                                  298
QS
Adam J. Dolan
Adam J. Dolan                                                              301

Enclosure                                                             302/322
```

Letter of Application (Shown in elite type)

LESSON 34

34a Keyboard Review

5 minutes

Directions: Key each sentence twice.

1 All letters   If Judge Ruiz acquires the papers, he may solve the robbery next week.

2 Number-symbol   Our questionnaire was completed by 1080 women (54%) and 920 men (46%).

3 Left shift   Ken, Paul, Harold, Mike, Ira, Nick, and Luis all play for the Packers.

| 1 | 2 | 3 | 4 | 5 | 6 | 7 | 8 | 9 | 10 | 11 | 12 | 13 | 14 |

34b Technique Builder—Keystroking

5 minutes

Directions: Key each sentence twice.
Technique Goal: Stroke on the response level indicated.

1 Letter   I realize there are significant errors I should correct in my outline.

2 Letter   This season's television programs have some fascinating personalities.

3 Word   Old words which we now use in a new way are bit, bug, mouse, and menu.

4 Combination   Please order the customized software for a new electronic mail system.

34c Paragraph Guided Writing

5 minutes

Directions: Set a goal for a 1' writing. Key a 1' writing on each paragraph in 33c, page 72. Try to reach your word goal just as time is called. Keystroke no faster or slower than is required by the goal you select.

34d Learning to Format Short Unbound Reports

30 minutes

- **Problem 1 -** One-Page Unbound Report

Directions: 1. Read the report shown on page 76. **2.** Key it on a full sheet of paper following the suggested guidelines. **3.** Use a top margin of 2" (begin to key on line 13) and side margins of 1". **4.** Double-space the report and indent paragraphs 5 spaces. Quadruple-space after the title. Proofread and correct errors if your teacher instructs you to do so.

The illustration on page 76 is shown in pica type. If you are using a typewriter with elite type, be sure that you key by your line-end signal and not line-for-line from the illustration.

- **Problem 1 -** Letter of Application

> **Directions:** Using block style and open punctuation, format the letter of application that follows on page 115. Begin the return address with the standard placement (line 14). Use 1" side margins because the letter is long. Address a large envelope. *Refer to page 99, if necessary, for information on formatting a personal business letter.*

Remember, the word Enclosure is used when an item is being sent with a letter. In this case, the resume is being sent.

- **Problem 2 -** Interview Follow-up Letter

> **Directions:** Using block style and open punctuation, format the letter shown below. Begin the return address with the standard placement. Use 1½" side margins because the letter is average in length. Address a small envelope.

words

19528 Rimrock Drive	4
Lincoln, NE 68504-3976	9
June 16, 19--	11
QS	
Ms. Kara Walter, Manager	16
Mountain States Insurance Agency	23
693 University Avenue	27
Lincoln, NE 68504-3976	32

Dear Ms. Walter — 35

Thank you for giving me an opportunity to meet with you yesterday to discuss the opening you have in your agency for an entry-level clerk. I appreciated the hospitality that you extended to me. I also enjoyed meeting the other people with whom I would be working if you were to decide to offer the job to me. — 50 65 80 95 98

I am still very interested in the clerical position. After our discussion, I think I have a clear understanding of the job, and I believe that I have the background to be successful in it. I was especially pleased to hear about the opportunities for growth and promotion that are available after six months. — 114 130 145 160

Please let me know if there is any additional information you may need from me. I am looking forward to hearing from you regarding your decision. — 175 190

Sincerely — 192
QS
Adam J. Dolan — 194/214

2″

FORMAT FOR A SHORT REPORT ◄———— Line 13   5

Quadruple-space (QS) ————————►

Students who prepare research papers, essays, book reports,   17
and other types of personal work should know the correct format   30
for these documents. The content of a report will be enhanced   43
with a good format.   47

A short report that will not be put in a cover or a binder   59
is called an unbound report. This type of short report is for-   71
matted with standard 1″ side margins (12 spaces for elite; 10   84
for pica). The top margin on the first page should be 2 inches.   97
1″ margin   Therefore, a good position for the title of the report is line 13   1″ margin   110
from the top edge of the page.   116

All pages after the first should have a top margin of 1 inch.   129
Thus, the first line of text should be keyed on line 7 from the   142
top edge. A bottom margin of at least 1 inch should be used on   155
all pages.   157

The title of a report should be keyed in all capital let-   168
ters. The body should be a quadruple space (QS) below the title,   182
leaving 3 blank lines between the title and the body. Double-   194
spacing is usually preferred in the body of a report, and para-   207
graphs should be indented 5 spaces.   214

If these format guidelines are followed when writing a   225
report, the appearance will always impress the reader. Also, the   238
report will be easier and faster for people to read.   249

At least 1″

One-page unbound report
(shown in pica type)

• **Problem 2 -** Composing and Formatting a Resume—Critical Thinking Skill

Directions: Compose and format your own personal resume. Use the illustration on page 112 to guide you. Key the first copy in draft form and edit it carefully. Rekey a copy in final form. You will be given time in Lesson 50 to complete your resume.

LESSON 49

49a Keyboard Review

5 minutes

Directions: Key each sentence three times.

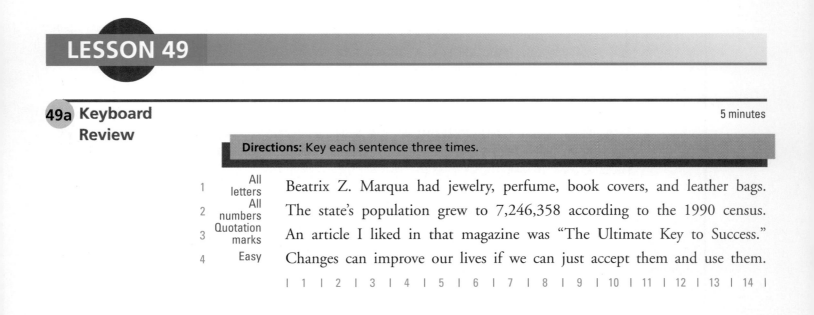

1	All letters	Beatrix Z. Marqua had jewelry, perfume, book covers, and leather bags.
2	All numbers	The state's population grew to 7,246,358 according to the 1990 census.
3	Quotation marks	An article I liked in that magazine was "The Ultimate Key to Success."
4	Easy	Changes can improve our lives if we can just accept them and use them.

| 1 | 2 | 3 | 4 | 5 | 6 | 7 | 8 | 9 | 10 | 11 | 12 | 13 | 14 |

49b Keying from Dictation and Spelling Checkup

5 minutes

Directions: Key the spelling words in 47c, page 109 as your teacher dictates them. Check for correct spelling. Rekey any words in which you have made any error.

49c Correcting Errors by Spreading Words

5 minutes

▼ If you are using a computer,
▼ move the cursor to the space
▼ where the t was keyed in ext-
▼ tra, and use the delete func-
▼ tion key to delete the t.

Directions: 1. Key the first sentence below just as it appears. **2.** Remove the word that contains an extra letter. **3.** Backspace to the position of the first letter of the word you removed. **4.** Use the half-space mechanism or the electronic incremental backspacer to move the carrier a half space to the right and then rekey the word correctly. **5.** If you do not have either of these mechanisms on your machine, operate the paper release lever and move the paper a half space to the left. Rekey the word correctly so that the first letter is 1½ spaces to the right of the last letter of the preceding word. **6.** Repeat this process for practice if time permits.

▼ In correcting errors, it is often
▼ possible to spread a word to
▼ fill extra space.

With error   An exttra letter appears in one of the words.

Corrected   An extra letter appears in one of the words.

Directions: Refer to page 76 for format guides. Key the report on a full sheet of paper. Use a top margin of 2" and side margins of 1". Double-space. Indent paragraphs 5 spaces. Quadruple-space after the title. Correct errors if your teacher instructs you to do so.

THE CORRECTION OF ERRORS

Errors that are made in documents should be corrected. Several different methods may be used.

With an electronic typewriter, a special key is often used to remove errors from an electronic window. With a computer, incorrect characters are removed from the screen with the backspace or delete key.

With typewriters, four methods may be used: automatic correction tape, correction paper, correction liquid, eraser. In the first method, when a special correction key is depressed, the tape will lift the error off the page. With correction paper, backspace to the beginning of the error, insert the paper between the ribbon and the error, rekey the error exactly as it was made, and then remove the paper. Backspace to the point where the correction begins and key the new copy.

When using a liquid, turn the platen up a few spaces and apply a small amount of the liquid over the entire error. Allow the liquid to dry completely, then key the correction. With an eraser, move the carrier to the right or left, roll the paper up, and hold it firmly against the platen while erasing. Brush the eraser crumbs away from the machine.

All of these methods have advantages and disadvantages. Choose the one that is the most appropriate for each situation.

ADAM J. DOLAN ◄──── Line 7 (1" top margin) ────
19528 Rimrock Drive
Lincoln, Nebraska 68504-3976
(402) 295-9981

QS

EDUCATION

DS

Lincoln High School, Lincoln, Nebraska; Graduated, June, 19--

Indent 5 ──► Grade Point Average: 3.8
Extracurricular Activities: Vice president, Senior Class;
Treasurer, National Honor Society; Member, Key Club; Member,
Football Team; Captain, Tennis Team
Honors: Graduated with High Honors--Gold Seal Bearer
Business Courses Completed: Personal Keyboarding;
Computer Applications in Business; Business English

DS

EXPERIENCE

General Clerk, Great Plains Manufacturing Company, Lincoln,
Nebraska; Summer of 19--; Duties: Preparing sales orders
and filing invoices

Salesperson, Akins Pharmacy, Lincoln, Nebraska; Summer of 19--;
Duties: Serving customers throughout the store; delivering
orders

1" margin

Recreation Assistant, Lincoln City Park Administration, Lincoln,
Nebraska; Summer of 19--; Duties: Supervising park activities for children; teaching tennis to children

REFERENCES

Ms. Anne Taylor, Chairperson, Business Department, Lincoln High
School, Lincoln, NE 68504-3976
Phone: (402) 339-9045

Mr. Dan O'Neill, Director of Marketing, Great Plains
Manufacturing Company, Lincoln, NE 68504-3976
Phone: (402) 336-2904

Mr. Sam Akins, Owner, Akins Pharmacy, Lincoln, NE 68504-3976
Phone: (402) 299-4106

ACTIVITIES AND INTERESTS

Volunteer, Lincoln Hospital Junior League; amateur guitarist

20

32
37
49
61
68
79
89
100

104

116
128
132

145
157
158

171
183
192

197

210
216
220

231
240
245

257
262

272

284

1" margin

Resume (shown in elite type)

LESSON 35

35a Keyboard Review

5 minutes

Directions: Key each sentence twice.

1	All letters	Jim had very quickly put labels on six coils of wire going to the zoo.
2	All numbers	Ana Cruz flew 105,783 miles last year but only 92,460 miles this year.
3	Hyphen	He read a ten-page booklet on the use of large-scale computer systems.
4	Easy	She did help their team win over all the other teams they had to play.

| 1 | 2 | 3 | 4 | 5 | 6 | 7 | 8 | 9 | 10 | 11 | 12 | 13 | 14 |

35b Sentence Guided Writings

10 minutes

Directions: Key each sentence as a 1' writing with the return called every 15 or 20 seconds.
Technique Goal: Do not hesitate; return with the call and begin keystroking at once. Keep your eyes on the copy.

		words in line	gwam 20" guide	gwam 15" guide
1	Reports are documents we all write.	7	21	28
2	Write reports that interest the readers.	8	24	32
3	Try to make a report complete in its content.	9	27	36
4	An outline might help us to write a better report.	10	30	40
5	A report must always be correct in the facts presented.	11	33	44
6	Clear writing is a very important aspect of any good report.	12	36	48
7	A good format should make a report easier for any person to read.	13	39	52
8	Try to keep these aspects in mind and do a good job with your reports.	14	42	56

| 1 | 2 | 3 | 4 | 5 | 6 | 7 | 8 | 9 | 10 | 11 | 12 | 13 | 14 |

35c Problem Formatting

30 minutes

• Problem 1 - A Book Report

▼ The content of this book
▼ report is based on the outline
▼ you formatted in Lesson 32.

Directions: Key the book report shown on the next page using the report format that has been used in the previous lessons. Leave a 2" top margin and 1" side margins. The illustration of the book report is shown in pica type. If you are using elite, be sure that you key by your line-end signal or use your automatic wrap if you are using a computer.

48c Correcting Errors by Squeezing Words

5 minutes

▼ With a computer you may use
▼ the insert function to add the
▼ additional letter to the word
▼ needing the correction.

Directions: 1. Key the first sentence below just as it appears. **2.** Remove the word in which a letter has been omitted. **3.** Backspace to the position of the first letter of the word you removed. **4.** Use the half-space mechanism or the electronic incremental backspacer to move the carrier a half space to the left and then rekey the word correctly. **5.** If you do not have either of these mechanisms on your machine, operate the paper release lever and move the paper a half space to the right. Rekey the word correctly so that the first letter is in half of the space following the preceding word, and the final letter is in half of the space following the corrected word. **6.** Repeat this process for practice if time permits.

▼ In correcting errors, it is often
▼ possible to squeeze a word
▼ into less space.

With error   `A   leter   is   omitted   from   one   of   the   words.`

Corrected   `A   letter   is   omitted   from   one   of   the   words.`

48d Learning to Format Employment Documents

30 minutes

A Resume, A Letter of Application, and an Interview Follow-up Letter

A resume, which is also known as a personal data sheet, and a letter of application are very important papers for anyone who may be looking for a job. These documents should be designed to help a person get an interview. The follow-up letter is important to write after an interview has been completed.

Resume: The resume should be prepared first and should include any information that may be of value in getting an interview. The resume should include the complete name, address, and telephone number of the applicant as well as the educational background and work experience. It may also include references and other personal data that may be of interest to the potential employer. A one-page resume is usually preferable, although it may be longer if necessary.

Letter of Application: A one-page letter should accompany the resume. The letter should be addressed to the person who may be responsible for arranging an interview. The letter should emphasize the major points from the resume.

Interview Follow-up Letter: A letter should be written immediately following the interview. This letter should express appreciation for the interview and show continued interest in the job and in the company. This letter should be concise.

Format: An appropriate format should be followed for both of these letters and for the resume. Also, they should be proofread very carefully for correct spelling, grammar, and punctuation.

A resume will be prepared in this lesson and a letter of application and an interview follow-up letter will be prepared in Lesson 49.

● **Problem 1 -** Resume

Directions: Format the resume that is illustrated on the following page. Use 1" top and side margins and use spacing as directed on the illustration.

2 "

BOOK REPORT--LONESOME DOVE

5

QS

Larry McMurtry, the author of LONESOME DOVE, has written

DS

many popular novels about Texas and the Southwest. He was

awarded the Pulitzer Prize for fiction in 1986 for this book.

LONESOME DOVE is filled with many interesting and colorful

characters, but the two main ones are Augustus (Gus) McCrae and

W. P. Call. These two men have very different personalities.

However, they are good friends who have shared many dangerous

1" margin — experiences, and they know they can always count on each — 1" margin

other. They are former Texas Rangers; and as the story begins,

they are partners in a Texas cattle ranch.

Gus is a romantic, easygoing man while Call is a driven,

demanding person with no patience for weakness. Call is

obsessed with a dream of creating a cattle empire. Gus and many

other people are drawn into Call's plan to make a cattle drive

from Texas to Montana to establish a ranch there. Some of the

characters who play important roles in this cattle drive are

Lorena, whom Gus loves; Elmira, the wife of an Arkansas sheriff;

Blue Duck, an Indian; Newt, a young cowboy; Jake, a dashing ex-

ranger; and July Johnson, husband of Elmira.

The reader can recognize the research that went into the

writing of LONESOME DOVE. As a mixture of fiction and history,

the novel is educational as well as entertaining.

Book report
(shown in pica type)

47e Speed Ladder Sentences

Directions: Key each sentence for 1'. Try to return the carrier as the guides are called at 15-, 12-, or 10-second intervals. **Technique Goal:** Return the carrier quickly without looking away from the copy. Start keystroking immediately after the return.

		words a minute
		15"	12"	10"

		15"	12"	10"
1	You build your skills in many ways.	28	35	42
2	We need three levels of stroke response.	32	40	48
3	A beginner always strokes on the first level.	36	45	54
4	On level one we think each letter as we stroke it.	40	50	60
5	This is necessary when key locations are being learned.	44	55	66
6	We should move up to the next level which is the word level.	48	60	72
7	When one strokes on the word level, each word is read as a whole.	52	65	78
8	At the third level you combine letters and words for a smooth pattern.	56	70	84

| 1 | 2 | 3 | 4 | 5 | 6 | 7 | 8 | 9 | 10 | 11 | 12 | 13 | 14 |

LESSON 48

48a Keyboard Review

Directions: Key each sentence three times.

1	All letters	Dexter Jacques may give the prize for the best novel to Wilma Jackson.
2	Number-Symbol	The big graduation party cost us $483.25, and Joe's share was $176.90.
3	pol	A political poll was the policy of any polite and polished politician.
4	Easy	Try to learn that luck is on the side of one who does not count on it.

| 1 | 2 | 3 | 4 | 5 | 6 | 7 | 8 | 9 | 10 | 11 | 12 | 13 | 14 |

48b Technique Builder—Flowing Rhythm Practice

Directions: Key each line three times.

1	Letter	Expert systems in new computer technologies may be absolutely amazing.
2	Word	We should learn to use words that will give some life to our thoughts.
3	Word	A goal of our lives should be to do the best we can with what we have.
4	Combination	A major objective of new computer programs is to be friendly to users.

| 1 | 2 | 3 | 4 | 5 | 6 | 7 | 8 | 9 | 10 | 11 | 12 | 13 | 14 |

- **Problem 2 -** One-Page Unbound Report from Rough Draft

> **Directions:** Key the report shown below. Use the correct report format that you have used in previous report problems. Make the corrections that are indicated by the proofreader's marks. Key by your line-end signal or use your automatic word wrap. If necessary, refer to the report format shown on page 76 and the proofreader's marks shown on pages 51 and 52.

Halley's comet) *Caps*

A highly publicized event of 1985 and 1986 was return of Halley's comet. Although there are many known comets Halley's is the most popular and the talked about because it hsa been in existence for hundreds of years.

A british scientist Sir Edmund Halley, did much comet research and he calculated that the comets of 1531, 1607, and 1682 all seemed move to in the the same orbit. he concluded that they were all the comet that had orbited the Sun over a period of about 86 years. Because of research the Comet was named after halley.

Chinese records confirm that halleys Comet did ap pear as early as 240 B. C. Its return in 1066 was also heavily documented because of the a sociation of the Comet with the battle of Hastings. In 1910 the return expecially exciting because the Earth passed through the comets tail, causing a meteor shower.

Much new research was done durnig the return 1985–86. For example the first photograph were taken of the nucleus of active comet. The comet was not easy to see however. Many amateur comet watchers had to far far out into the country away from the big city lights, and even then the view of the comet was faint. Halleys is now back its way out to the edges of the solar systme and will stay there until 2061 when will vis it the Earth.

- **Problem 3 -** Critical Thinking Skill—Composing and Formatting a Book Report

> **Directions:** In the next lesson, you will be asked to compose and format a book report about a book you have read recently. Bring this book with you, if possible, for use in your next lesson.

47c Communication Skill—Spelling

5 minutes

Directions: Key each sentence twice.
Technique Goal: Study the spelling of each word shown in italics.

1 I *deferred* the *surprise announcement* until the *recipient* was *definite*.
2 *Treacherous circumstances* may have been a *basis* for the *fiery tragedy*.
3 My team *received* his *congratulations* for our *truly excellent research*.
4 We *occasionally* have the *privilege* to *fulfill* an *irresistible pursuit*.

47d Skill Building

20 minutes

Directions: 1. Key a 5' writing. Circle your errors; note your *gwam*. **2.** Key a 1' writing on each paragraph. Try to add 10 words to your gwam on each paragraph. **3.** Key another 5' writing. Circle errors and determine *gwam*. **4.** Compare your *gwam* and your number of errors on the two 5' writings.

All letters

	gwam	
	1'	5'

¶1
60 words
1.4 si

The goal of a good resume and letter of application is to help a person get a job interview, but the interview is what leads to a job offer. A probe is made into all of the varied aspects of the ability and personality of an applicant. What you may say and what you may do are both quite important.

13	3	51
27	5	53
41	8	56
54	11	59
60	12	60

¶2
60 words
1.4 si

An attitude of the applicant plays a most important part in the success of an interview. Show a high level of confidence in yourself. Be zealous about the job and about your ability to do it. Do not give any hint of arrogance. Have a sense of humor. Show that you can get along well with people.

13	15	63
27	17	65
41	20	68
55	23	71
60	24	72

¶3
60 words
1.4 si

The first few minutes of an interview may be the most critical. Negative behavior could result in a quick rejection of the applicant. Always be on time. Dress in the correct way. Use a firm handshake. Maintain direct eye contact. These are some factors that can lead to a good first impression.

13	27	75
27	29	77
41	32	80
55	35	83
60	36	84

¶4
60 words
1.4 si

An applicant must always know what to expect in the interview. If a person is prepared well, there should be no real surprises. Have a good knowledge of the company, and know what the job requires. Be prepared to answer difficult questions because the answers may be the major keys to a job offer.

13	39	87
27	41	89
41	44	92
55	47	95
60	48	96

1' | 1 | 2 | 3 | 4 | 5 | 6 | 7 | 8 | 9 | 10 | 11 | 12 | 13 | 14 |
5' | 1 | 2 | 3 |

LESSON 36

36a Keyboard Review

5 minutes

Directions: Key each sentence twice.

1   All letters   Our amazed executive, Fay Quante, kept our goodwill by the adjustment.

2   Number-Symbol   Chi Liang's note (due May 28) for $35,764 was discounted at 10% today.

3   Apostrophe   Christy's sister made three A's and three B's on her last report card.

4   Easy   The way you play the game may tell them just how hard you want to win.

| 1 | 2 | 3 | 4 | 5 | 6 | 7 | 8 | 9 | 10 | 11 | 12 | 13 | 14 |

36b Timed Writings

12 minutes

Directions: Key a 1' writing on each paragraph of 31e, page 68. Then key two 3' writings over all paragraphs. Circle your errors. Determine *gwam*. Submit the better of the 3' writings.

36c Problem Formatting

28 minutes

- **Problem 1 -** Critical Thinking Skill—Composing and Formatting a One-Page Unbound Report

Directions: Key the paragraph in 24f, page 51 and the paragraph in 25d, page 52 into a one-page report. Compose a short introductory paragraph and a short closing summary paragraph. Use the following title for your report or you may choose a title you prefer: THE TWO NEWEST STATES OF THE UNION. Use the correct report format that you have used in the other report problems.

- **Problem 2 -** Critical Thinking Skill—Composing and Formatting a Book Report

Directions: You were instructed in your preceding lesson to bring a book that you have read recently with you to class today. Prepare a book report on this book. You may be able to submit this assignment in your English class. Discuss this possibility with your English and keyboarding teachers to determine if this would be acceptable. Use the content for a book report suggested in the outline in 32d, Problem 1, page 70, or you may use a different content that is preferred by your English teacher. Use the illustration on page 76 for the correct format. You may not be able to complete this problem today. If not, you may have to complete it on your own time, or your teacher may give you additional time in a future class period.

UNIT 10 FORMATTING EMPLOYMENT DOCUMENTS

Lessons 47-50

In this unit you will learn how to format employment documents: a resume, a letter of application, and an interview follow-up letter. Emphasis will be continued on developing your skills in keying, communicating, and critical thinking.

General Directions: For drills and timed writings, use side margins of 1" (elite) or 1/2" (pica). Use default and word wrap with a computer, or change default margins. For problems, set margins as directed. SS sentences and drill lines. DS paragraph copy and between groups of repeated lines. Space problem copy as directed in each lesson. Correct errors in problems if your teacher tells you to do so.

LESSON 47

47a Keyboard Review

5 minutes

Directions: Key each sentence three times.

1 | All letters | J. W. Brill got his faxed copy of the zoning document from K. V. Quan.
2 | All numbers | Attendance at the picnic on July 4 was 10,578; last year it was 9,236.
3 | Shift keys | NFL teams included the Packers, Saints, Oilers, Rams, Jets, and Bears.
4 | Easy | Do not use a long word if a short one will give the very same meaning.

| 1 | 2 | 3 | 4 | 5 | 6 | 7 | 8 | 9 | 10 | 11 | 12 | 13 | 14 |

47b Paragraph Skill Builder—Numbers

5 minutes

Directions: Key four 1' writings. Try to increase your rate on each writing by 1 to 2 words, but also maintain your accuracy on each writing.

60 words
All numbers used

Columbus sighted land on October 12, 1492. Cabot explored the northeast coast to Delaware in 1497. Ponce de Leon explored the coast of Florida in 1513, and then de Soto landed in Florida on May 28, 1539. The California coast was explored in 1540. Menendez founded St. Augustine, Florida, in 1565.

UNIT 8 FORMATTING MULTIPLE PAGE REPORTS

Lessons 37-41

In this unit you will learn how to format longer reports that are bound at the left margin. You will also learn to key copy using the internal citation method including keying a list of references at the end of the report and a title page at the beginning. You will format bibliographical and note cards. Your development of keying and communication skills will also be continued.

General Directions: For drills and timed writings, use 1" side margins with elite type and 1/2' with pica. With a computer, use default margins and word wrap or change default margins. For problems, set margins as directed in each lesson. SS sentences and drill lines. DS paragraph copy and between groups of repeated lines. Space problem copy as directed in each lesson. Your teacher will tell you whether or not you are to correct errors made in problems in this unit.

LESSON 37

37a Keyboard Review

5 minutes

Directions: Key each sentence three times; repeat.

1	All letters	Joey knew that extra quiz should prove to be a true challenge for him.
2	All numbers	We had 485 students to graduate in 1993, 367 in 1992, and 290 in 1991.
3	Quotation marks	When Karen was in New York, she saw "Phantom of the Opera" and "Cats."
4	Easy	Do the work right the first time and you will not have to do it again.

| 1 | 2 | 3 | 4 | 5 | 6 | 7 | 8 | 9 | 10 | 11 | 12 | 13 | 14 |

37b Technique Builder—Carrier/Cursor Return and Tabulator Control

15 minutes

Directions: 1. Clear the tab stops as directed on page 21 or change default tabs as explained in your user's guide. **2.** See that your margins are set for 1" or default. **3.** Set the first tab stop for the second column 25 spaces from the left margin. Set the second tab stop 25 spaces from the first one. **4.** Begin to key at the left margin and continue across the page. Use double-spacing. Key the list of computer terms once; repeat.

Margin stop	Tab stop	Tab stop
——— 25 spaces →	——— 25 spaces →	
mainframe	minicomputer	microcomputer
system	hardware	software
network	bit	byte
database	spreadsheet	word processing
disk	modem	printer
mouse	cursor	window
delete	word wrap	default

- **Problem 3 -** Critical Thinking Skill—Composing a Personal Business Letter

Directions: Assume that you have received the same letter sent to Ms. Carter in Problem 2, page 106. Also, assume that you have decided to join the Booster Club. Compose and format a letter that you could send to Mario Silva. In your letter tell him that you are joining, you have completed the application form and are enclosing it, and you are also enclosing a check for $20. Include any other information you think is appropriate. Use the letter and punctuation styles you prefer. Decide on appropriate margins.

46d Enrichment Assignments—Personal Business Letters

- **Problem 1 -** Format the following letter from rough draft. Make all needed corrections. Use modified block style, indented paragraphs, and mixed punctuation. Use 2" side margins and begin the return address on line 14.

	words
4598 Westport Road	4
Crafton, M D 21114-2330	8
January 25, 19--	12
Director, National Park Services	18
U.S. department of The Interior	25
Washington DC 20240-6143	30
dear Director:	33
Will you please send me lists of the films and posters taht	43
you have available on Yellowstone national park. I am preparing a	57
speech for one of my classes and I like to illustrate my speech.	71
I will really appreciate hearing from you as I must give my speech	84
on March 15.	87
Sincerly	89
Bradley Lewiston	92

- **Problem 2 -** Compose and format a letter to the President, Chamber of Commerce, Santa Fe, NM 87501-5309. Request information for a paper you are writing on the topic "Interesting Cities in the United States." Use the letter and punctuation styles you prefer. Decide on appropriate margins.

- **Problem 3 -** Compose and format a letter to the Director, National Park Service (see Problem 1 above for the address). Request information on summer jobs that are available in various national parks. Use the letter and punctuation styles you prefer. Decide on appropriate margins.

37c Building Skill on Numbers and Symbols

5 minutes

Directions: Key each sentence three times. **Technique Goal:** Work for control.

1 Our total income was $4,830.29 for January and $5,176.49 for February.

2 My discount on the order is 10% if I pay in 15 days but 6% in 30 days.

3 We leave at 10 a.m. (Flight #384) and return at 11 p.m. (Flight #692).

| 1 | 2 | 3 | 4 | 5 | 6 | 7 | 8 | 9 | 10 | 11 | 12 | 13 | 14 |

37d Speed Ladder Paragraphs

15 minutes

Directions: Key 1' writings on the paragraphs. When you can complete the first paragraph in 1', key the second one; then the third, and so forth. Climb the speed ladder. See if you can reach the top. Finally, key two 3' writings over all paragraphs combined. Submit the better writing to your teacher.

All letters

	words		
	1'	3'	

¶1
32 words
1.3 si

	1'	3'	
When we write a report, we must be quite exact with our spelling,	13	4	55
grammar, and punctuation. We should also choose the best words that	27	9	60
can send a clear message.	32	11	62

¶2
36 words
1.3 si

Spelling is a skill we should all master for good writing. Peo-	13	15	66
ple can be quite critical of our work when we spell poorly. We	26	19	70
should not be too lazy to make use of our dictionary.	36	23	74

¶3
40 words
1.3 si

The use of correct grammar is one of the other vital keys for	12	27	78
good writing skills. Poor grammar shows a lack of interest in trying	27	32	83
to help our readers get a quick and clear meaning of our message.	40	36	87

¶4
44 words
1.3 si

Speakers use pauses and inflections in their voices to help send	13	40	91
a clear message just as writers use punctuation marks. We might not	27	45	96
be clearly understood if we do not use the correct marks in all of the	41	50	101
work that we do.	44	51	102

| 1' | 1 | 2 | 3 | 4 | 5 | 6 | 7 | 8 | 9 | 10 | 11 | 12 | 13 | 14 |
| 3' | | 1 | | 2 | | 3 | | 4 | | 5 | | | |

37e Communication Skill—Spelling

5 minutes

Directions: Key each sentence twice. **Technique Goal:** Study the spelling of each word in italics.

1 One's good *appearance* is a *definite requirement* for *achieving success.*

2 The *athlete* was an *aggressive competitor* and *received* the *endorsement.*

3 His *argument* was *wholly irrelevant* and did not *persuade* the *attorneys.*

4 We *apologize* for the *embarrassing quantity* of *facilities* in *exist*

5 I am *truly surprised* at a *noticeable* lack of *safety* in the *i*

46c Problem Formatting—Envelopes and Personal Business Letters

- **Problem 1 -** Small and Large Envelopes

Directions: Format a small and a large envelope for each of the addresses shown below. Use envelopes or paper cut to correct size. Use your name and address as the sender. Follow the directions given on the envelopes illustrated on pages 104 and 105.

```
MS CATHERINE CAMERON
CAMERON REALTY COMPANY
8749 UNIVERSITY AVENUE
SYRACUSE NY 13210-1246

MISS KATHLEEN GUILLORY
15802 CRESCENT PLACE
PALATINE IL 60067-6325
```

```
DR WILLIAM WIPFF
340 MAIN STREET APT 12
LINCOLN NE 68504-3976

MR TONY FIELDS MANAGER
ELECTRONICS SERVICES CORP
759 RIVER ROAD
LITTLE ROCK AR 72204-1099
```

- **Problem 2 -** Personal Business Letter in Block Style, Open Punctuation

Directions: Format the following letter in block style with open punctuation. Use 2" side margins and begin the return address on line 14. Refer to the guidelines on page 99 if necessary. Address a large envelope.

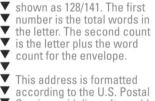

▼ The total word count is shown as 128/141. The first number is the total words in the letter. The second count is the letter plus the word count for the envelope.

▼ This address is formatted according to the U.S. Postal Service guidelines. It would also be correct, however, in the format shown in the letters illustrated on pages 100 and 103.

▼ An enclosure notation is used when an item (or items) is sent with the letter. Place the word Enclosure a double space below the typewritten name at the left margin. Use the plural enclosures if more than one item is enclosed.

	words
3950 Stone Bridge Road	5
Billings, MT 59102-2944	9
September 9, 19--	13
QS	
MS JUANITA CARTER	17
829 SPRING CREEK LANE	21
BILLINGS MT 59102-2944	26
Dear Ms. Carter	29

I am the president of the Booster Club of Billings High School. — 42
We help provide special support for all of the athletic programs. — 55
The cost of membership is only $20 a year, and all the money we — 68
raise goes to buy special items for various teams. — 78

Please join us! I am enclosing an application form. Just return — 92
it to me with your check for $20, or bring it to our next meeting — 105
on Wednesday, September 20, at 7 p.m. in the gym. I look forward — 118
to seeing you then. — 122

Sincerely	124
QS	
Mario Silva	127
Enclosure	128/141

lesson 46 106

LESSON 38

38a Keyboard Review

5 minutes

Directions: Key each sentence three times.

1 All letters   Fred M. Quigg spoke subjectively and expressed hot opinions with zeal.

2 Number-symbol   Her fare for Flight #2016 is only $398, but your fare is more at $475.

3 Double letters   Nell Brooks will sell her zoology books to Tommy Mann of Fayetteville.

4 Easy   You can now fly to almost any place in the world in only a short time.

| 1 | 2 | 3 | 4 | 5 | 6 | 7 | 8 | 9 | 10 | 11 | 12 | 13 | 14 |

38b Technique Builder—Keystroking

5 minutes

Directions: Key each sentence three times.
Technique Goal: Keystroke on the response level indicated.

1 Letter   Each individual should see our environmental problems as very serious.

2 Letter   Decreasing levels of stratospheric ozone are of concern to scientists.

3 Word   We must all work hard to do our own small part to help save our world.

4 Combination   I cannot think only of myself; I must think of our future generations.

5 Combination   Our action is needed now for a clean environment for the next century.

| 1 | 2 | 3 | 4 | 5 | 6 | 7 | 8 | 9 | 10 | 11 | 12 | 13 | 14 |

38c Communication Skill—Placement of Quotation Marks

5 minutes

Directions: Key each sentence three times. The first line gives the rule, and the remaining lines apply it. Capitalize and punctuate the last sentence correctly.

1   Periods or commas are placed inside, not outside, the quotation marks.

2   Huxley stated, "Facts do not cease to exist because they are ignored."

3   "The hardest thing about a job," he stated, "is the work it requires."

4   alvin toffler believes a new civilization is emerging in our lives

- **Problem 2 -** Addressing a Large Envelope

Directions: 1. Address a large envelope for the letter on page 103. **2.** Follow the placement directions given on the illustration shown below. **3.** Use a large envelope or paper cut to the proper size (9 1/2" x 4 1/8"). **4.** Follow the procedures for folding letters to insert into large envelopes as shown in the Reference Guide, page RG-7.

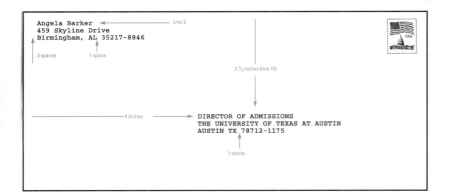

Addressing a Large Envelope:
1. A large envelope is usually prepared for business letters, for letters of more than one page, or if items are enclosed. Place the writer's name and return address as you did on a small envelope and as shown on the illustration at the left.
2. Begin the receiver's name and address 2 1/2" (line 15) from the top and 4" from the left edge of the envelope.
3. Use block style and single spacing as you did for a small envelope.

This address is also shown in the format recommended by the U.S. Postal Service. This all caps unpunctuated format may also be used for the address on the letter when window envelopes are used or when the computer is used for preparing envelope addresses.

- **Problem 3 -** Composing and Formatting a Personal Business Letter

Directions: Edit the rough draft of your own personal letter that you composed and formatted in 44d, Problem 3, page 102. Format a final copy. Address a small envelope for your letter. Use the guidelines shown on page 104.

LESSON 46

46a Keyboard Review
5 minutes

Directions: Key each sentence three times.

1	All letters	The lazy fox was very quick to get away before the dogs jumped on him.
2	All numbers	Total points possible were 1,540; Kara scored 973, and Jim scored 862.
3	Dash	Only two of our students--Louise Lee and Robin Martino--were selected.
4	Easy	Words are the keys that we must use to open our minds to other people.

| 1 | 2 | 3 | 4 | 5 | 6 | 7 | 8 | 9 | 10 | 11 | 12 | 13 | 14 |

46b Speed Ladder Paragraphs
10 minutes

Directions: Key 1' writings on the paragraphs in 42c, page 97. When you can finish one at the rate shown, move to the next. *Push for speed.* **Alternate procedure:** Follow the directions above, but move from one paragraph to the next only when you can finish one at the rate shown without errors. *Work for control.*

● **Problem 1** - Bibliographical Card

> **Directions: 1.** Study the bibliographical card below and format a copy of it on a 5" x 3" card or paper cut to this size. **2.** Place the first item on the card about three spaces from the top edge and three spaces in from the left edge.

▼ If you are using a computer,
▼ rule the outline of the card
▼ size on your printer paper.
▼
▼ Much of the information that
▼ is used in reports comes from
▼ such sources as books,
▼ magazines, and newspapers.
▼ Bibliographical cards contain
▼ information about references
▼ to be used in a report.

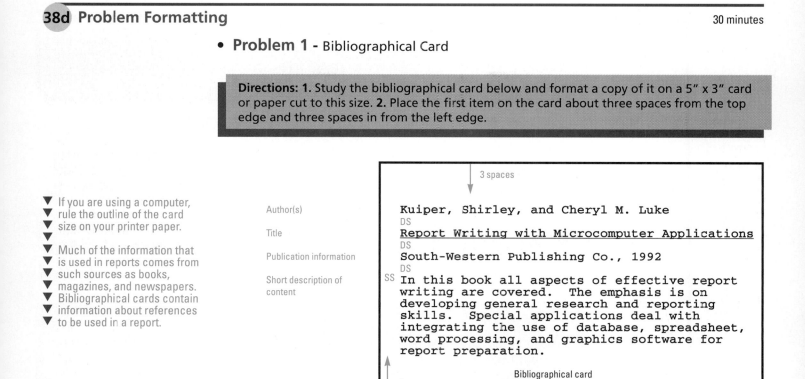

● **Problem 2** - Note Card

> **Directions: 1.** Study the note card shown below. Format a copy of it on a 5" x 3" card or paper cut to this size. **2.** Place the heading about three spaces from the top edge of the card and three spaces in from the left edge.

▼ If you are using a computer,
▼ rule the outline of the card
▼ size on your printer paper.

▼ Note cards contain ideas,
▼ facts, and quotations to be
▼ used in preparing the body of
▼ a report. They are also very
▼ useful in preparing a speech.

45b Paragraph Guided Writing

5 minutes

> **Directions:** Set a goal for a 1' writing. Key four 1' writings on the paragraph in 43c, page 98. Try to reach your word goal just as time is called. Key no faster or slower than is required by the goal you select.

45c Alignment of Paper—Horizontal and Vertical

5 minutes

▼ You may sometimes find it
▼ necessary to reinsert paper
▼ to correct an error. This drill
▼ will help you learn how to
▼ align your paper correctly.

If you are using a computer, repeat drill 44b, page 101, instead of this drill.

> **Directions: 1.** Key the following sentence:

A good alignment takes practice!

> **2.** Before removing the paper from your machine, find the aligning scale (No. 2). Its location will depend on the type of machine you are using. Note the relationship of the scale to the bottom of the letters. Also note how the scale lines up with the letters **i** and **l**. **3.** Remove the paper from the machine and reinsert it, aligning horizontally first by using the paper release lever and moving the paper to the left or right until the lines on the scale are brought into alignment with the letters **i** and **l**. **4.** Align vertically using the variable line spacer. **5.** Rekey the sentence over the first one. **6.** Repeat the problem for practice.

45d Learning to Format Envelopes

30 minutes

▼ If you are using a computer,
▼ your teacher will give you
▼ additional instructions for for-
▼ matting envelopes.

- **Problem 1 -** Addressing a Small Envelope

> **Directions: 1.** Address a small envelope for the letter on page 100. **2.** Follow the directions for the placement of the return address and the letter address as shown in the illustration following. **3.** Use a small envelope or paper cut to the proper size (6 1/2" x 3 5/8"). **4.** Follow the procedures for folding letters to insert into a small envelope as shown in the Reference Guide, page RG-7.

Guidelines from the U.S. Postal Service show that every word in the address is written in all capital letters with no punctuation. This is preferred for the envelope address because optical character recognition (OCR) equipment is used to sort and process mail.

```
Michael Harrison ◄───── Line 2
16984 Ridgeview Road
Los Angeles, CA 90042-5022

3 spaces        1 space

                        2 inches (line 12)


─2 ½ inches ──────►  DR ANNA MARCUS PROFESSOR
                     DEPARTMENT OF BIOLOGY
                     UNIVERSITY OF SOUTHERN CALIFORNIA
                     LOS ANGELES CA 90089-0001

                              1 space
```

Addressing a Small Envelope:
1. Place the writer's name and return address in the upper left corner. Begin on the second line space from the top edge and 3 spaces from the left edge.
2. Place the receiver's name 2" (line 12) from the top of the envelope and 2 1/2" from the left edge.
3. Use block style and single spacing for all addresses.
4. Key the city, 2-letter state abbreviation, and ZIP code on one line in that order. Leave one space between the state and ZIP code. A complete list of the state abbreviations is shown on page RG-6 in the Reference Guide.

- **Problem 3 -** Composing and Formatting Bibliographical and Note Cards

> **Directions:** Prepare a bibliographical card and a note card from information you can find in a textbook you are now using in one of your courses. Format a rough draft copy of each card. Edit and format a final copy. Use the illustrations on page 85 to guide you.

LESSON 39

39a Keyboard Review

5 minutes

> **Directions:** Key each sentence three times.

1	All letters	Becky Mallard expects to quiz Vance Wolfe about the jade gem he found.
2	All numbers	Carol Ann had 267,380 frequent flyer miles, but Adam had only 145,940.
3	Fourth finger	Alex Pasqual and Pam Squires are away at a political meeting in Azusa.
4	Easy	Our air can be clean and pure if we all work hard to keep it that way.

| 1 | 2 | 3 | 4 | 5 | 6 | 7 | 8 | 9 | 10 | 11 | 12 | 13 | 14 |

39b Communication Skill—Titles of Articles

5 minutes

> **Directions:** Key each sentence three times. The first line gives the rule, and the remaining lines apply it. Capitalize and punctuate the last sentence correctly.

1   As a rule, the titles of articles should be placed in quotation marks.

2   "New Ways to Finance a College Education" is an article you might use.

3   He thought "Lost Beneath the Sea" was a very exciting article to read.

4   A good article for my term report would be robots in a computer age.

39c Keying from Dictation and Spelling Checkup

5 minutes

> **Directions:** Key the spelling words in 37e, page 83 as your teacher dictates them. Check for correct spelling. Rekey any words in which you have made an error.

▼ Mixed punctuation is used in
▼ this letter. A colon follows the
▼ salutation, and a comma fol-
▼ lows the complimentary
▼ close.

		words
Return address ——— (Center point) ——→	**459 West Skyline Drive**	5
	Birmingham, AL 35217-8846	10
Dateline ————————————→	**September 16, 19--**	14

Operate return
4 times (QS)

Letter address ——————→	**Director of Admissions**	18
	The University of Texas at Austin	25
	Austin, TX 78712-1175	29
	DS	
Salutation ——————→	**Dear Director:**	33
	DS	

SS	**I am interested in applying for admission to**	42
	your university for next fall. Please send	51
	me all of the forms that I will need to com-	60
	plete and return to you when I apply.	67
	DS	

Body of
letter ——————→ **Also, please send me current information** 75
about fees and living expenses. I am espe- 84
cially interested in knowing the cost of 93
out-of-state tuition since I am not a resi- 101
dent of Texas. I would also appreciate 111
information on scholarships, grants, and 119
loans that are available. 122
DS

2"
margin   2"
                          margin

Your cooperation will be most appreciated. 131
DS

Complimentary close ——————————→	**Sincerely,**	133

Operate return
4 times (QS)

Signature ——————————→ *Angela Barker*

Typewritten name ——————————→	**Miss Angela Barker**	137

2" Tab

▼ In the modified block style let-
▼ ter, the paragraphs may be
▼ blocked, or they may be
▼ indented five spaces.

Personal business letter in modified block style (Shown in pica type)

FORMATTING LEFTBOUND REPORTS

Many reports are placed in ring binders or heavy paper covers with clasps. These are referred to as "leftbound" reports and an extra half inch of space is needed in the left margin for the "binding." Follow the directions shown below in preparing leftbound reports.

Margins—Set the margin stops for a 1 1/2" left margin (pica, 15 spaces; elite, 18 spaces) and a 1" right margin (pica, 10 spaces; elite, 12 spaces).

Leave a top margin of 2" on the first page. A good standard placement for the title on both pica and elite machines is on line 13 from the top edge. Pages after the first should have a top margin of 1". Leave a bottom margin of at least 1" on all pages.

Spacing—The body of the report should be double-spaced, and paragraphs should be indented 5 spaces throughout the report.

Title—The title of the report should be centered in all capitals over the line of writing. To find the horizontal center for a leftbound report, add the numbers at the left and right margins and divide by 2. (This procedure places center 3 spaces to the right of the point normally used.) Quadruple-space (QS) after the title.

Quotations—Short quotations (fewer than four lines) should be placed within the text material and enclosed by quotation marks.

Long quotations (four or more lines) should be single-spaced and indented five spaces from the left margin. Double-space above and below the quotation.

Paging—The first page of the report is not numbered. On the second and following pages, the number is placed 1" from the top (line 7) at the right margin. Double-space below the number before keying the first line of the body of the report on that page.

When formatting a report that contains several pages, at least 2 lines of a paragraph should appear on the bottom of a page, and at least 2 lines should be carried over to the new page.

References—Reference notations to give credit to others for material taken from various sources may be accomplished by the use of internal citations, footnotes, or endnotes. The internal citation method is becoming very popular because it is more efficient to format. Internal citations should include the name(s) of the author(s), the date of the referenced publication, and the page number(s) of the material cited.

All references cited are listed alphabetically by author surname at the end of the report. These references may appear on a separate page or on the final page of the body of the report if enough lines are available.

If a separate reference page is used, the same margins should be employed as on the first page of the report. If the references appear at the bottom of the final page, a quadruple space (QS) should be placed after the last line of the report before centering the heading REFERENCES. A QS should follow this heading. Each reference is single-spaced with a double space between references. The first line of a reference begins at the left margin. All other lines are indented 5 spaces.

Directions for formatting footnotes and endnotes will be given in Unit 14.

44d Problem Formatting

30 minutes

- **Problem 1 -** Personal Business Letter in Modified Block Style, Blocked Paragraphs, Mixed Punctuation

▼ Refer to the steps for format-
▼ ting personal business letters
▼ given on page 99.

Directions: Study the modified block style letter shown on the next page. In this style, the return address, date, complimentary close, and writer's name start at the horizontal center of the paper. This style may have either blocked or indented paragraphs. Also, a letter in this style may be keyed with either open or mixed punctuation. Format a copy of this letter on a full sheet of paper. Follow the instructions shown on the illustration. Since this is a short letter, use 2" side margins. Begin the first line of the return address on line 14 from the top edge of the page.

In mixed punctuation, a colon is placed after the salutation and a comma after the complimentary close.

- **Problem 2 -** Personal Business Letter in Modified Block Style, Indented Paragraphs, Mixed Punctuation

Directions: Reformat the letter shown on the next page. This time, however, use today's date, address it to a different university, and use indented paragraphs. Address it to: Director of Admissions / Utah State University / Logan, UT 84322-3515. Don't forget to change the name of the state in the second paragraph.

- **Problem 3 -** Critical Thinking—Personal Business Letter

Directions: Compose and format a rough draft of a personal business letter of your own similar to the one illustrated on the next page. Choose a college or university where you might have interest in applying. Request whatever information you might want. Use your own return address, today's date, the correct address of the college or university, and your own signature. Choose whatever letter and punctuation style you prefer. Keep your rough draft until the next lesson when you will have a chance to key a final copy.

LESSON 45

45a Keyboard Review

5 minutes

Directions: Key each sentence three times.

1	All letters	Jack Gullway expected to visit the old Bess Quill farm in Switzerland.
2	Number-symbol	Lee & Raye pays $6 an hour for summer work; Coy & Vicker pays only $5.
3	Long reach	My brother, Myron, brought the extra funds Eva needed to pay the debt.
4	Easy	Make a real effort to learn to spell words that give you some trouble.

| 1 | 2 | 3 | 4 | 5 | 6 | 7 | 8 | 9 | 10 | 11 | 12 | 13 | 14 |

- **Problem 1 -** First Page of a Two-Page Leftbound Report

Directions: The illustration on page 89 is the first page of a leftbound report with internal citations. Study the directions given in the example and review those on page 87. Format this first page of the report.

The illustration is shown in pica type. If you are using elite type, do not remove your paper when you finish formatting the first page. Continue with content from Problem 2 until your first page is filled to the 1" bottom margin.

- **Problem 2 -** Second Page of a Two-Page Leftbound Report

Directions: Turn to page 90 and format the second page of the report you began in Problem 1. If you are using elite type, continue page 2 where you left off in Problem 1 above. Notice that this page has references. Refer to the directions given on page 87 for the formatting of references on the final page of a report.

▼ If you are using a computer,
▼ your teacher may give you
▼ additional directions on for-
▼ matting and printing leftbound
▼ reports. These directions may
▼ vary according to your hard-
▼ ware and software.

LESSON 40

40a Keyboard Review

5 minutes

Directions: Key each sentence three times.

1	All letters	Viviane Jacques expected to make weekly flights to Zambia in December.
2	Number-symbol	I was very happy to receive a discount of $385 (4%) on my order #6720.
3	Quotation marks; hyphen	"Batman" and "Jaws" are among the top money-making movies of all time.
4	Easy	I saw a play that he wrote while we were in the city on our last trip.

| 1 | 2 | 3 | 4 | 5 | 6 | 7 | 8 | 9 | 10 | 11 | 12 | 13 | 14 |

40b Technique Builder—Keystroking Fluency

5 minutes

Directions: Key four 1' writings on the paragraph. Try to raise your rate on each writing by 2 to 4 words by eliminating the pauses in your strokes.

60 words
1.1 si

	words
You can key this drill with ease. You can key this drill with	13
ease if you cut out wasted motion. You can key this drill with ease	26
if you cut out wasted motion and keep your eyes on the copy. You can	40
key this drill with ease if you cut out wasted motion, keep your eyes	54
on the copy, and set a goal.	60

- **Problem 2 -** Personal Business Letter in Block Style, Open Punctuation

▼ The / symbol in problem copy
▼ indicates the end of a line in
▼ various letter parts.

Directions: Reformat the letter shown on page 100. This time, however, use today's date, address it to a different person, and use a new salutation. Address it to: Dr. Robert Olney, Professor / Department of Biology / University of California, Los Angeles / Los Angeles, CA 90024-1318 /

LESSON 44

44a Keyboard Review

5 minutes

Directions: Key each sentence three times.

1	All letters	Clifford and Jan had a vexing quarrel about who should keep my zither.
2	All numbers	The scores of the final games were: 95 to 90; 83 to 72; and 74 to 61.
3	br	The bride's brother breathlessly briefed the bridegroom at the church.
4	Easy	We should use clear wording in our letter for our meaning to be clear.

| 1 | 2 | 3 | 4 | 5 | 6 | 7 | 8 | 9 | 10 | 11 | 12 | 13 | 14 |

44b Concentration Practice—Difficult Copy

5 minutes

Directions: Key the following paragraph twice.
Technique Goal: Keystroke with ease and control.

90 words
Difficult copy: 1.6 si
All numbers used

words

New York City is the largest city in the United States.   It has a | 13
population of 7,322,564, according to the 1990 census.   Many people | 27
think of this city as the business and entertainment capital of the | 40
country.   A major landmark in New York which attracts many visitors is | 54
the Statue of Liberty.   This statue was presented as a gift to the | 68
U. S. by France in 1884 in commemoration of the alliance of these two | 82
countries during the American Revolution. | 90

44c Keying from Dictation and Spelling Checkup

5 minutes

Directions: Key the spelling words in 42d, page 98, as your teacher dictates them. Check for correct spelling. Rekey any words in which you have made any error.

Line 13

words

Center title over line
of writing

THE USE OF REFERENCES IN REPORTS

7

QS

Indent paragraphs

The basic purpose of a report is to provide detailed

17

DS

information on a specific subject. Most writers are not

29

able to draw all the needed facts from their own minds or

40

their own experiences. Therefore, they must get help from

52

1" right

1 1/2" left margin

outside sources. This help usually comes in the form of the margin

64

knowledge of others that has been published in books and

76

magazines. If a writer uses information from others, credit

88

must be given to them.

93

Two authorities on report writing (Bovee and Thill,

103

Internal citation with
short quotation
(fewer than four
lines)

1992, 487) believe that "You have an ethical and a legal

114

obligation to give other people credit for their work."

126

Kuiper and Luke (1992, 200) say "An ethical researcher ac-

137

knowledges the sources that have contributed unique infor-

149

mation to a research project." They also suggest that:

160

DS

Long quotation
(four or more lines)

Report writers generally do not cite sources of in-

170

formation that is general knowledge among the primary

181

SS

readers of the report; but the more specific the data

192

are, the greater is the need to provide source ci-

201

Single-spaced and
indented 5 spaces
from left margin

tations.

203

DS

The giving of credit to one's sources is known as cit-

214

ing or documenting. In addition to citing in order to avoid

226

the problem of plagiarism, documenting is done for other

238

reasons. For example, documentation supports statements.

249

Two other experts (Himstreet and Baity, 1990, 542) say that

261

At least 1"

First page of two-page leftbound report with internal citations
(Shown in pica type)

▼ Open punctuation is used in
▼ this letter: no punctuation
▼ follows the salutation or the
▼ complimentary close.

Line 14

words

Return address → **16984 Ridgeview Road** — 4
Los Angeles, CA 90042-5022 — 10
Dateline → **January 26, 19--** — 13

Operate return
4 times (QS)

ZIP code numbers are placed one space
after the state abbreviation.

Dr. Anna Marcus, Professor — 18
Letter address → **Department of Biology** — 23
University of Southern California — 30
Los Angeles, CA 90089-0001 — 35
DS
Salutation → **Dear Dr. Marcus** — 38
DS
I recently read a summary of a speech you gave on — 49
global warming at the United Nations Conference on The — 59
World's Environment at Rio de Janeiro. This aspect of — 70
ecology is of special interest to me, and I hope to — 81
major in a related field in college. — 88
DS
Body of **Global warming is the topic that I have selected for a** — 99
letter → **research project in my biology class this semester.** — 110
Because of your research on this topic, may I come to — 121
your office and interview you for my project? Please — 132
call me and let me know when I could schedule an — 141
appointment. You can reach me at my home any day — 153
after 4 p.m. My telephone number is (310) 256-7784. — 162

1 ½" **I look forward to hearing from you. I believe the** 1 ½" — 172
margin **information you can give me will be very important to** margin — 183
the completeness of my project. — 190
DS
Complimentary
close → **Sincerely** — 192

Operate return
4 times (QS)

Signature → *Michael Harrison*

Typewritten
name → **Michael Harrison** — 195

▼ In the letter address, it is a
▼ matter of courtesy to precede
▼ the name of the addressee
▼ with a personal title such as
▼ Mr., Ms., or Dr. A man should
▼ not use a title before his name
▼ in closing a letter. A woman,
▼ however, shows considera-
▼ tion for the reader when she
▼ uses her personal title (Miss,
▼ Mrs., or Ms.) with her type-
▼ written name. This allows a
▼ person to respond to a
▼ woman's letter appropriately.

Personal business letter in block style (Shown in pica type)

DS   words

"If recognized authorities have said the same thing, your   12

1 1/2" left margin   work takes on credibility; and you put yourself in good   23

company."   25

What is the most effective way to cite material? A   35

writer has the option of using footnotes, endnotes, or any   47

other acceptable method of crediting the contributors who   59

helped provide information for the report. The simplest ap-   71

proach to documentation is internal citation: the last   82

name(s) of the author(s), the date of the publication, and   94

the page number(s) are given within the text material at the   106

point the information is cited. At the end of the report,   118

1" right margin

detailed references are listed alphabetically.   127

The specific method used for documenting is not the   138

most important issue, however. The writer must maintain   149

ethical standards. The main point to remember is that credit   161

should be given where credit is due.   169

QS

Center over line of writing   →   **REFERENCES**   171

QS

Bovee, Courtland L., and John V. Thill. <u>Business Communica-</u>   183
    <u>tion Today</u>. Third Edition. New York: McGraw-Hill,   194
    Inc., 1992.   196

SS   DS

Himstreet, William C., and Wayne Murlin Baty. <u>Business</u>   207
    <u>Communications</u>. Ninth Edition. Boston: PWS-Kent Pub-   213
    lishing Company, 1990.   223

Kuiper, Shirley, and Cheryl M. Luke. <u>Report Writing with</u>   235
    <u>Microcomputer Applications</u>. Cincinnati: South-Western   246
    Publishing Co., 1992.   250

At least 1"

Second page of two-page leftbound report with references
(Shown in pica type)

Formatting Personal Business Letters

Step 1 - Set the line spacing for single spacing.

Step 2 - Set the side margins. These will vary according to the length of the letter. Use 2" margins for short letters (up to 100 five-stroke words in the body); 1 1/2" for average letters (101-200 words); 1" for long letters (201-300 words) and for two-page letters (more than 300 words). The Letter Placement Guide shown below will help you with margin settings.

Step 3 - Space down to line 14 to begin the writer's return address. This is a standard placement suggested for use with personal business letters in this book. However, the number of lines to space down can vary according to the length of the letter. This point can be raised for longer letters or lowered for shorter letters. For a block style letter (see the illustration on page 100), start the return address at the left margin. For a modified block style letter (see the illustration on page 103), start the return address at the center point of the paper.

Step 4 - Place the date (month, day, year) a single space (SS) below the last line of the return address.

Step 5 - Place the letter address on the fourth (QS) line space below the date.

Step 6 - Begin the salutation (greeting) a double space (DS) below the letter address.

Step 7 - Start the body of the letter (message) a double space (DS) below the salutation. In the block style, the paragraphs are always blocked at the left margin. In the modified block style, paragraphs may be blocked or they may be indented. Single-space the paragraphs and double-space between them.

Step 8 - Begin the complimentary close (farewell) a double space below the last line of the body. For block style, start at the left margin. For modified block style, start at the center point of the page.

Step 9 - Key the name of the writer on the fourth line space (QS) below the complimentary close. The writer's handwritten name (signature) should be placed between the complimentary close and the typewritten name.

Step 10 - If something is being enclosed within the letter (check, order form, etc.) key the word Enclosure or Enclosures a double-space below the writer's name.

LETTER PLACEMENT GUIDE

Letter Classsification	5-Stroke Words in Letter Body	Side Margins	Margin Settings	
			Elite	Pica
Short	Up to 100	2"	24–78"	20–65"
Average	101–200	1 1/2"	18–84"	15–70"
Long	201–300	1"	12–90"	10–75"
Two-Page	More than 300	1"	12–90"	10–75"

*plus 5 spaces for end-of-line signal

In open punctuation, there is no colon following the salutation and no comma following the complimentary close.

• **Problem 1 -** Personal Business Letter in Block Style, Open Punctuation

Directions: Study the block style letter shown on the next page. Block is a popular style because of its efficiency. Notice that all elements of the letter begin at the left margin. Format a copy of the letter on a full sheet of paper. Follow the instructions given in the illustration. Since this is an average length letter, use 1 1/2" side margins. Key the first line of the return address on the 14th line from the top.

▼ Your teacher will give you
▼ additional instructions for
▼ the formatting and printing
▼ of letters if you are using a
▼ computer.
▼
▼ Remember to key by your
▼ line-end signal or use your
▼ word wrap.

40c Communication Skill—Titles of Books and Magazines

5 minutes

Directions: Key each sentence three times. The first line gives the rule, and the remaining lines apply it. Capitalize and punctuate the last sentence correctly.

▼ Use the shift lock correctly;
▼ with a computer use a func-
▼ tion key for automatic under-
▼ scoring.

1 Names of books and magazines are underscored or keyed in all capitals.

2 I will use an article from Time and a chapter from Comet for my paper.

3 BACK ROADS OF CALIFORNIA was the book reviewed in SUNSET in September.

4 read the article from newsweek magazine and a chapter from powershift

40d Problem Formatting

30 minutes

- **Problem 1 -** Two-Page Leftbound Report with Internal Citations

Directions: 1. Format the report shown on the next page. Use the directions on page 87 for formatting leftbound reports. **2.** Number page 2 correctly. **3.** Format the problem in rough draft form. Do not correct any errors. When you finish, edit the report carefully and save it. In the next lesson you will be instructed to rekey it in a final form.

Remember that line endings and page endings will vary with pica and elite type. Be sure that you listen for your line-end signal and divide words when necessary. With the computer you will use your word wrap.

- **Problem 2 -** References on a Separate Page

Directions: 1. Format the references shown below for the report you completed in Problem 1 above. **2.** Use a separate page for the references and number it 3. **3.** Use directions as given on page 87. Place the page number on line 7 at the right margin and center the heading on line 13. 4. Format in rough draft form and save your work.

▼ Do not key these references
▼ line for line as shown. Let
▼ your line-end signal be your
▼ guide, or use your word wrap.
▼
▼ References are always listed
▼ alphabetically.

REFERENCES

Graham, Gerald H., Jeanne Unruh, and Paul Jennings. "The Impact of Nonverbal Communication in Organizations: A Survey of Perceptions." Journal of Business Communication, Winter 1991, 45–62.

Hulbert, Jack E. Effective Communication for Today. 9th ed. Cincinnati: South-Western Publishing Co., 1991.

Locker, Kitty O. Business and Administrative Communication. Second Edition. Homewood, Illinois: Richard D. Irwin, Inc., 1992.

Murphy, Herta A., and Herbert W. Hildebrandt. Effective Business Communications. Sixth Edition. New York: McGraw-Hill, Inc., 1991.

Treece, Marla. Successful Communication for Business and the Professions. Fifth Edition. Boston: Allyn and Bacon, 1991.

42d Communication Skill—Spelling

5 minutes

Directions: Key each sentence twice.
Technique Goal: Study the spelling of each word shown in italics.

1 *Aluminum* may be *acceptable*, but *nickel* seems *preferable* and *desirable*.
2 Kim's *exceptional assistant* had *substantial* and *infallible experience*.
3 We are *eligible* for an *eighth extension*, but I do not *foresee* a *ninth*.
4 I might *concede publicly* in *February*, but my *decision* is not *definite*.

LESSON 43

43a Keyboard Review

5 minutes

Directions: Key each sentence three times.

1 All letters   Janis Zier expected to fly to Quebec for a short visit with Kim Grace.
2 Number-symbol   The generous triple discounts of 5%, 7%, and 10% amounted to $238,469.
3 Hyphen   My son-in-law won a hard-earned victory in the coast-to-coast contest.
4 Easy   Good letter format will help us do a better job with the news we send.

| 1 | 2 | 3 | 4 | 5 | 6 | 7 | 8 | 9 | 10 | 11 | 12 | 13 | 14 |

43b Skill Comparison

5 minutes

Directions: Key a 1' writing on each sentence in 43a above. Compare your *gwam* on the four writings.

43c Paragraph Guided Writing

5 minutes

Directions: Set a goal for a 1' writing. Key four 1' writings on the paragraph. Try to reach your word goal just as time is called. Key no faster or slower than is required by the goal you select.

All letters

          Summer might be a good time to try new jobs. Some people have
trouble picking their career. They may have zero knowledge about
varied fields. Working for a few summers could be quite excellent
to do. Clues may be found for the best career as well as the best
degree for one to pursue in college.

60 words
1.3 si

| 1 | 2 | 3 | 4 | 5 | 6 | 7 | 8 | 9 | 10 | 11 | 12 | 13 | 14 |

COMMUNICATING WITHOUT WORDS

▼ Refer to the directions on
▼ page 87 and the illustrations
▼ on pages 89 and 90 as you
▼ format this report.

People spend most of their time in school learning how to communicate verbally--with words--but maybe more time should be spent in learning how to communicate nonverbally--without words. One writer (Locker, 1992, 389) says, "Nonverbal communication--communication that doesn't use words--takes place all the time." She also believes that "Most of the time we are no more conscious of interpreting nonverbal signals than we are conscious of breathing."

Nonverbal communication is also called body language. The way people smile, frown, maintain eye contact, hold their arms, and the tones of their voices all send messages to others. Sometimes the messages that are sent with words and those sent without words contradict each other. Treece (1991, 419) says, "The nonverbal message is likely to be the correct one, and it is likely to be interpreted as the correct one." Therefore, the adage that actions speak louder than words may be quite true.

Perhaps the first aspect of body language that should concern a person is the creation of a good first impression on other people. Hulbert (1991, 381) states:

A favorable impression can do much to build a positive, lasting inter-personal relationship. The impression you create is greatly influenced by nonverbal factors, such as your appearance, your behavior, your voice, your concepts of time and space, and your attitude.

▼ If part of a direct quotation is
▼ omitted, the ellipsis (...)
▼ should be used to show the
▼ omission.

This first impression is especially critical when people give speeches or have job interviews. In these situations, according to Murphy and Hildebrandt (1991, 29), "The eyes and face are especially helpful means of communicating nonverbally. They can divulge hidden emotions . . . . They can also contradict verbal statements." These authors also believe that "Direct eye contact (but not staring) is usually desirable when two people converse face to face."

Research studies have given much information on the importance of nonverbal communication. One study (Graham, Unruh, and Jennings, 1991, 59) of 505 people concluded the following:

Nonverbal communication was important to all surveyed, and most respondents agreed that nonverbal communication would influence their interactions with people more than would verbal content. Better decoders relied most on facial expressions for accurate information while less skilled decoders preferred voice level or tone.

▼ A citation should be given for
▼ paraphrased material as well
▼ as for direct quotations.

We can all improve our nonverbal skills by paying more attention to nonverbal cues, engaging in more eye contact, and probing for more information when verbal and nonverbal signals do not agree. People could also improve their nonverbal skills by being more honest in communicating their emotions (Graham, Unruh, and Jennings, 1991, 60).

> **Directions: 1.** Key 1' writings on the paragraphs that follow. When you can complete the first paragraph in 1', key the second, then the third, and so forth. Climb the speed ladder. See if you can reach the top. **2.** Finally, key two 5' writings over all paragraphs combined. Circle errors; figure *gwam*. Submit the better writing to your teacher.

All letters

gwam

	1'	5'	

¶1
36 words
1.4 si

There are some elements in personal business letters that one should not forget to use when writing. These elements, if used in a proper way, will help the writer do a better job.

12	2	57
26	5	60
36	7	62

¶2
40 words
1.4 si

A good appearance of the letter adds to the reader's image of the writer. A letter should be placed attractively on the page. That is why correct top, side, and bottom margins are so very important.

12	10	65
27	13	68
40	15	70

¶3
44 words
1.4 si

A writer should always place a return address in the top part of the letter. This is quite important if the reader wishes to respond. The return address should include the number, street, city, state, and the zip code.

13	18	73
27	21	76
41	23	78
44	24	79

¶4
48 words
1.4 si

The date of a letter is an important item. It should be placed on the line directly below the return address. A date is also very useful for reference purposes because it is one way, the subject is another, by which a letter may be filed.

13	27	82
26	29	84
40	32	87
48	34	89

¶5
52 words
1.4 si

The part that follows the date is the letter address. This should include the title, name, and address of the reader. The next element is the salutation, and this is followed by the body. The body is the most critical aspect because it contains the message.

12	36	91
26	39	94
40	42	97
52	44	99

¶6
56 words
1.4 si

The last part of the letter includes the close and the writer's matching handwritten and typewritten name. It is extremely vital that the reader know the name of the writer. Since all signatures are not legible, the name should be keyed. It is also signed for a personal touch.

13	47	102
26	49	104
39	52	107
53	55	110
56	55	110

1' | 1 | 2 | 3 | 4 | 5 | 6 | 7 | 8 | 9 | 10 | 11 | 12 | 13 | 14 |
5' | 1 | 2 | 3 |

Directions: 1. Format the title page as shown in the illustration below. This title page is for the two-page report you just completed in Problem 1. **2.** The centering point for each line will be the same as you used in Problem 1. **3.** Follow the directions given on the illustration for spacing. Information for the title page is shown below at left. Key from that copy. **4.** Format this problem in rough draft form and save for rekeying in final form in the next lesson.

COMMUNICATING WITHOUT WORDS

by

Kristin Mulcahy

Personal and Professional Keyboarding

December 15, 19--

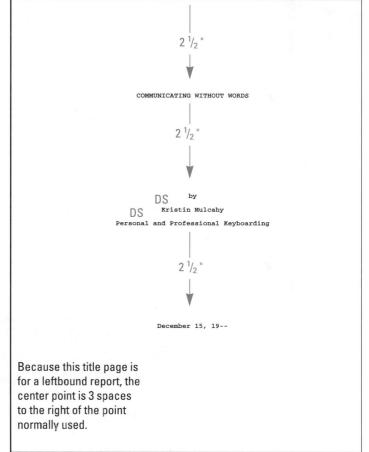

Because this title page is for a leftbound report, the center point is 3 spaces to the right of the point normally used.

UNIT 9 — FORMATTING PERSONAL BUSINESS LETTERS AND ENVELOPES

Lessons 42-46

In this unit you will learn how to format business letters in various styles and how to format envelopes. You will also continue to build your skills in keying, communicating, and critical thinking.

General Directions: For drills and timed writings, use side margins of 1" (elite) or 1/2" (pica). Use default margins and word wrap with a computer, or change default margins. For problems, set margins as directed. SS sentences and drill lines. DS paragraph copy and between groups of repeated lines. Space problem copy as directed. Correct errors in problems if your teacher instructs you to do so.

LESSON 42

42a Keyboard Review

5 minutes

Directions: Key each sentence three times; repeat if time permits.

1	All letters	Joy King's quixotic views of the traffic problem amazed us completely.
2	All numbers	Highest batting averages for our team were .478, .461, .390, and .352.
3	Fourth finger	Paula quickly quizzed the pupils; prizes were awarded for the puzzles.
4	Easy	Check your work with care to see that you do not have too many errors.

| 1 | 2 | 3 | 4 | 5 | 6 | 7 | 8 | 9 | 10 | 11 | 12 | 13 | 14 |

42b Sentence Guided Writings

10 minutes

Directions: 1. Key each sentence for 1'. **2.** Your teacher will call the return every 12 or 15 seconds as a guide. **3.** If you complete the sentence before the guide is called, return and continue keying but pace yourself a little more slowly. If you have not completed the sentence when the guide is called, increase your keying speed.

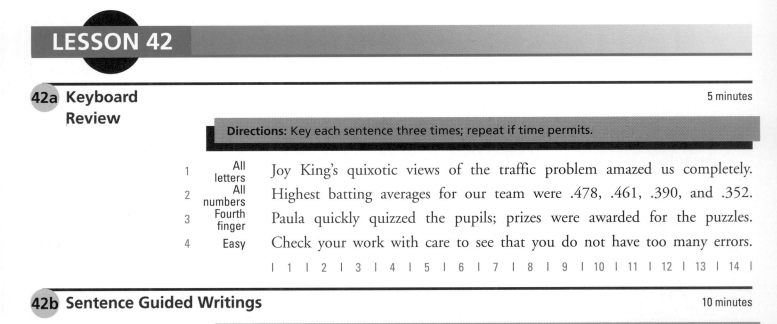

		words	gwam 15" guide	gwam 12" guide
1	Write your letters in a good style.	7	28	35
2	A good style has quite a few techniques.	8	32	40
3	Always spell words correctly in your letters.	9	36	45
4	Your grammar should just be excellent in a letter.	10	40	50
5	Punctuate your letters correctly to help their clarity.	11	44	55
6	Concise sentences are much easier for readers to understand.	12	48	60
7	Emphasize words in your letters that you think your readers know.	13	52	65

| 1 | 2 | 3 | 4 | 5 | 6 | 7 | 8 | 9 | 10 | 11 | 12 | 13 | 14 |

LESSON 41

41a Keyboard Review

5 minutes

Directions: Key each sentence three times.

1	All letters	Cecile Ripley kindly gave them the exquisite old jewelry for a bazaar.
2	All numbers	The sizes of the 100 new houses range from 2,485 to 3,679 square feet.
3	Underline	<u>Oliver Twist</u> and <u>A Tale of Two Cities</u> were written by Charles Dickens.
4	Easy	I saw a big cat on top of my car when I was ready to go to work today.

| 1 | 2 | 3 | 4 | 5 | 6 | 7 | 8 | 9 | 10 | 11 | 12 | 13 | 14 |

41b Technique Builder—Keystroking Fluency

5 minutes

Directions: Key four 1' writings on the paragraph in 40b, page 88. Try to raise your rate on each writing by 2 to 4 words by eliminating the pauses in your keystroking.

41c Sentence Skill Builder—Script

5 minutes

Directions: Key a 1' writing on each sentence.
Technique Goal: Stroke with continuity and without pauses.

words in line

1	You should be trying to attain speed and accuracy in your keystroking.	14
2	Sometimes we should try for speed and not concentrate on our accuracy.	14
3	At other times we must slow down and try to stroke without any errors.	14
4	We have achieved control when our stroking is fast and errors are few.	14

41d Problem Formatting

30 minutes

- **Problem 1 -** Two-Page Leftbound Report

   Directions: From the rough draft copy of the report you prepared in Problem 1, page 91, format a final copy. Proofread carefully.

- **Problem 2 -** References

   Directions: From the rough draft copy of the references you prepared in Problem 2, page 91, format a final copy. Proofread carefully. Attach the reference page to the back of the report you completed in Problem 1 above.

- **Problem 3 -** Title Page

   Directions: From the rough draft copy of the title page you prepared in Problem 3, page 93, format a final copy. Proofread carefully. Attach the title page to the front of the report completed in Problem 1 above.

41e Enrichment Assignments—Reports

- **Problem 1 -** Prepare a two-page leftbound report on the topic "The Value of a Good Education." Use a title page, internal citations, and references at the end.

- **Problem 2 -** Expand the material in 37d, page 83 into a two-page leftbound report. Add other data and use internal citations. Provide a title page and references at the end.

- **Problem 3 -** Format a report that has been assigned in one of your other courses. Prepare note cards, bibliographical cards, a rough draft of the report, and a final copy. Use internal citations, references, and a title page. Edit your draft and proofread very carefully your final copy. Put your report into a heavy paper cover for submission to your teacher.

• APPENDIX •
LEARNING THE NUMERIC KEYPAD

In this section of five lessons, you will learn to operate the ten-key numeric keypad. You will learn the key locations, you will acquire proper techniques for striking the keys, and you will develop speed and accuracy in entering numbers by touch.

GETTING TO KNOW YOUR EQUIPMENT

Located at the right of the alphabetic keyboard of a microcomputer is a special number keypad. This keypad is similar to the one found on a ten-key adding machine. These number keys are used primarily for doing mathematical calculations with certain types of software packages. They may also be used for keying numbers that are found within alphabetical data when no calculations are required. Illustrations of this keypad on various types of computers are shown below. Refer to your user's manual for instructions that apply to your specific equipment and software.

Apple   IBM   Tandy

LESSON 1 4, 5, 6, 0, AND ENTER

1a Using the Correct Position

1. Place your book to the right of the machine.
2. Sit erect with your feet on the floor with your elbows near your body. Use the same position as you do for operating the alphabetic keyboard as illustrated at right.
3. Place the fingers of your right hand over the home keys of the numeric keypad; curve your fingers as you do when you are keying letters:

   first finger (j finger) on 4
   second finger (k finger) on 5
   third finger (l finger) on 6

You will control the 0 key with your right thumb and the ENTER key with your right little finger.

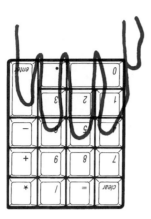

1b Learning to Keystroke 4, 5, 6, (Home Keys) and ENTER Key

1. Place the first, second, and third fingers of your right hand on 4, 5, 6. These three keys serve as the home keys for the ten-key numeric keypad. On some pads, the 5 key will have a raised dot in the middle of the key to help you locate it by touch.
2. Take your fingers off the home keys; replace them. Repeat this process several times to get the feel of these home keys.
3. Strike the 4 with your first finger several times.
4. Strike the 5 with your second finger several times.
5. Strike the 6 with your third finger several times.
6. Hold your right little finger over the ENTER key. Strike the ENTER key several times. At the end of each line, strike the ENTER key to move the cursor to the next line.
7. Key the drill line below three times:

   444455556666Enter

▲ Technique Goal: Strike each key with the tip of the finger.
▲ Use a quick, sharp stroke; release the key quickly. Keep the fingers curved and wrist low.

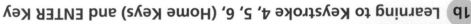

1c Location Drills—4, 5, 6, ENTER

1. Read down the column in A at the right and key each number as it appears. Strike the ENTER key after the final number in each line. (In this drill and those that follow, strike ENTER key twice after keying each group of three numbers.) **2.** Key the numbers in Drills B, C, D, and E. Special software is necessary to calculate—add, subtract, multiply, and divide. The drills in this lesson and those that follow do not involve calculations.

Drill A		Drill B	Drill C	Drill D	Drill E
4	(Enter)	4	44	44	456
4		4	44	45	564
4		4	44	46	645
5		5	55	54	564
5		5	55	55	645
5		5	55	56	456
6		6	66	64	466
6		6	66	65	544
6		6	66	66	655

1d Learning to Keystroke 0

1. Place fingers over home keys (4, 5, 6).
2. Reach to 0 with right thumb.
3. Strike 0 with right thumb several times. Do not move other fingers from home position.

4. Key drill line below three times:

405060400500600Enter

1e Location Drills—0

1. Read down the column in Drill A at the right and key each number as it appears. Strike the ENTER key after the final number in each line. **2.** Key the numbers in Drills B, C, D, and E.

 Technique Goal: Strike the 0 with the side of the right thumb. Release the key quickly.

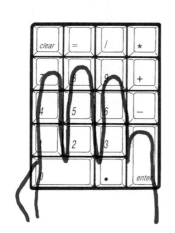

Drill A	Drill B	Drill C	Drill D	Drill E
40	400	404	440	405
40	400	405	450	440
40	400	406	460	406
50	500	504	550	504
50	500	505	540	550
50	500	506	560	506
60	600	604	660	605
60	600	605	650	660
60	600	606	640	604

LESSON 2   7, 8, 9

2a   Number Review

Read down each column in the drills shown at the right. Key the numbers as they appear. Strike ENTER after the final number in each line.

Drill A	Drill B	Drill C	Drill D	Drill E
4	404	450	465	604
5	405	460	564	605
6	406	440	645	606
44	504	540	456	405
55	505	560	564	404
66	506	550	645	406
40	604	404	504	440
50	605	505	505	550
60	606	606	506	660

2b   Learning to Keystroke 7, 8, 9

Reach to 7
1. Place fingers over home keys.
2. Locate **7** on keypad above **4**.
3. Strike **7** with first finger.
4. Touch **474** lightly several times.

Reach to 8
1. Locate **8** on keypad above **5**.
2. Strike **8** with second finger.
3. Touch **585** lightly several times.

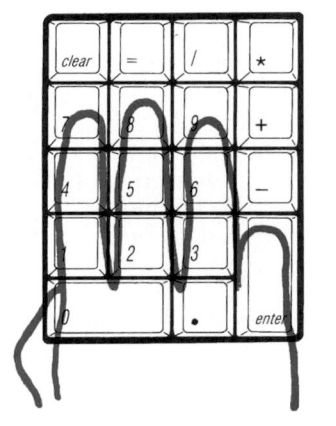

Reach to 9
1. Locate **9** on keypad above **6**.
2. Strike **9** with third finger.
3. Touch **696** lightly several times.

Key drill line below three times:

474474585585696696ENTER

▼ Technique Goal: Key each
▼ number with a quick, sharp
▼ stroke. Hold your wrist low
▼ and steady.

2c   Location Drills—7, 8, 9

1. Read down the column in Drill A at the right and key each number as it appears. Strike the ENTER key after the final number in each line. **2.** Key the numbers in Drills B, C, D, and E.

Drill A	Drill B	Drill C	Drill D	Drill E
47	474	470	770	465
47	747	704	880	897
47	477	740	990	798
58	585	580	740	576
58	858	805	850	495
58	588	850	960	684
69	696	690	706	507
69	969	906	805	409
69	699	960	906	608

3a Number Review

Read down each column in the drills shown at the right. Key the numbers as they appear. Strike ENTER after the final number in each line.

Drill A	Drill B	Drill C	Drill D	Drill E
47	740	745	947	570
58	850	845	957	580
69	960	945	967	590
74	704	757	960	670
85	805	758	850	680
96	906	759	740	690
470	407	847	470	995
580	508	857	480	649
690	609	867	490	785

3b Learning to Keystroke 1, 2, 3

Reach to 1
1. Place fingers over home keys.
2. Locate **1** on keypad below **4**.
3. Strike **1** with first finger.
4. Touch **414** lightly several times.

Reach to 2
1. Locate **2** on keypad below **5**.
2. Strike **2** with second finger.
3. Touch **525** lightly several times.

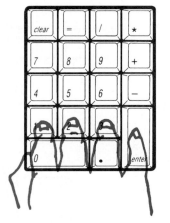

Reach to 3
1. Locate **3** on keypad below **6**.
2. Strike **3** with third finger.
3. Touch **636** lightly several times.

Key the drill line below three times:

`414414525525636636Enter`

▼ Technique Goal: Think and
▼ say each number as you key
▼ it. Keep your eyes on the
▼ book.

3c Location Drills—1, 2, 3

1. Read down the column in Drill A at the right and key each number as it appears. Strike the ENTER key after the final number in each line. **2.** Key the numbers in Drills B, C, D and E.

Drill A	Drill B	Drill C	Drill D	Drill E
41	414	410	110	537
41	141	104	220	428
41	411	140	330	196
52	525	520	140	208
52	252	205	250	107
52	522	250	360	309
63	636	630	105	528
63	363	306	206	471
63	633	360	304	639

LESSON 4 NUMBERS WITH . (DECIMAL)

4a Number Review

Read down each column in the drills shown at the right. Key the numbers as they appear. Strike ENTER after the final number in each line.

Drill A	Drill B	Drill C	Drill D	Drill E
414	426	474	340	349
525	513	414	350	167
636	624	470	360	248
474	696	140	956	268
585	636	250	754	791
696	690	650	864	973
140	585	240	107	560
250	525	250	208	540
360	580	260	309	180

4b Learning to Keystroke . (Decimal)

1. Place fingers over home keys.
2. Locate . on keypad.
3. Reach to . with second or third finger. Use whichever finger is more convenient.

▼ Technique Goal: Keep your
▼ fingers curved and wrist low.
▼ Use a quick, sharp stroke;
▼ release the key quickly.

4. Touch . lightly several times. Key the drill below three times:

5.6.5.6.55..66..5.6.55..66..ENTER

4c Location Drills . (Decimal)

1. Read down the column in Drill A at the right and key each number as it appears. Strike the ENTER key after the final number in each line. 2. Key the numbers in Drills B, C, D, and E.

Drill A	Drill B	Drill C	Drill D	Drill E
5.5	5.50	5.05	14.95	839.27
6.6	6.60	6.05	27.83	643.10
5.5	5.50	5.06	16.70	591.70
6.6	6.60	5.10	75.49	179.62
5.5	5.50	6.10	12.68	380.45
6.6	6.60	6.10	37.90	799.98
5.5	5.50	4.20	28.39	275.14
6.6	6.60	7.18	15.46	460.95
5.5	5.50	9.93	71.50	983.00

5a　Number Review

Read down each column in the drills shown at the right. Key the numbers as they appear. Strike ENTER after the final number in each line.

Drill A	Drill B	Drill C	Drill D	Drill E
517	5.50	95.48	99.79	152.95
539	6.50	73.92	64.98	529.04
528	4.50	10.66	19.90	357.60
482	1.70	15.98	75.70	469.19
681	3.90	12.43	79.17	299.75
279	2.80	76.10	27.79	675.40
170	7.25	39.80	85.80	799.50
280	9.34	17.42	89.18	815.67
390	8.16	52.61	39.28	950.10

5b　Keying Numbers with Commas

Commas are often used to separate numbers (such as hundreds from thousands). They cannot be entered on the ten-key numeric keypad, however.

Ignore the commas as you key the numbers in Drills A–E at the right.

Drill A	Drill B	Drill C	Drill D	Drill E
7,539	1,300	4,301	9,100	30,100
1,468	4,687	9,648	1,489	40,298
9,273	7,395	7,320	7,528	50,367
3,105	3,570	6,257	3,841	1,485.60
8,649	9,699	1,300	5,460	2,379.15
2,860	6,402	3,481	8,435	6,301.95
4,397	5,280	2,496	2,895	92,100.10
5,100	8,493	5,249	4,601	76,385.29
6,428	2,167	8,664	6,419	84,630.75

5c　Skill Measurement

1. Take several 1' timings on Timed Copy A and B shown at the right. Strike ENTER twice after each group of three numbers. 2. If you finish the first column before time is called, continue to the second column.

▼ Goal: Try to complete keying at least one column of numbers accurately in one minute.

Timed Copy A		Timed Copy B	
594.10	2,789	749.82	3,240
247.65	7,530	635.70	5,097
810.73	1,406	186.09	7,861
614.83	9,275	387.40	4,260
370.25	3,460	294.86	1,389
957.10	8,100	510.39	8,507
415.20	4,207	976.50	9,349
173.98	6,810	421.83	6,510
708.65	5,394	805.97	2,078

BACKSPACE—to move the print carrier, print point, or cursor to the left by striking the BACKSPACE or back arrow key once for each character or space.

CENTERING—the placing of text so that half the copy is on each side of the center point.

CONTROL KEY (CTRL)—a special key that is pressed at the same time another key is struck, causing that key to perform a specific function.

CURSOR—a lighted point on a display screen where the next character or space can be entered.

DEFAULT SETTINGS—preset specifications in the word processing software that control line lengths, spacing, tabs, etc.

DISK (DISKETTE)—a magnetic record-like disk encased in a protective cover used for recording, reading, and writing by a computer's central processing unit. Common sizes are 5 1/4" and 3 1/2".

DISK DRIVE—the unit of the computer into which a disk is inserted for reading or writing.

DOCUMENT—formatted information such as a letter, memorandum, or report.

DOUBLE-SPACE (DS)—to use vertical line spacing that leaves one blank line space between each printed line of copy.

EDIT—to arrange, change, and correct existing text.

ELITE—a type size that prints 12 characters to an inch.

ESCAPE KEY (ESC)—a key that lets the user cancel a function or exit one segment of a program and to go to another.

FORMAT—the arrangement, placement, and spacing of a document; also to arrange a document in proper form.

FUNCTION KEYS—special keys on a computer that are used alone or in combination with other keys to perform special operations such as setting margins, centering copy, etc.

GWAM (GROSS WORDS A MINUTE)—a measure of the rate of keyboarding speed; *gwam* equals total standard 5-stroke words keyed divided by the time required to key those words.

HARDWARE—the physical equipment that makes up a computer or word processing system.

KEY—to strike keys to print or display text and data; also called enter, key in, keystroke, input, and type.

MARGINS—blank space framing a document.

MEMORY—data storage location in a computer, word processor, or electronic typewriter.

MENU—a listing of available software options that appears on a display screen.

NUMERIC KEYPAD—an arrangement of figure keys and special keys to the right of most computer keyboards.

OPERATOR'S GUIDE (USER'S MANUAL)—instructions accompanying hardware and software that tell and/or shows how various features are made to work.

PICA—a type size that prints 10 characters to an inch.

PROOFREAD—to compare copy on a display screen or a printout to the original or source copy, and to correct errors or mark them for correction.

PROOFREADER'S MARKS—notations used to indicate changes and corrections needed to convert draft copy to final copy.

QUADRUPLE-SPACE (QS)—to use vertical line spacing that leaves 3 blank line spaces between each printed line of copy.

RETURN—to strike the RETURN or ENTER key to cause the print carrier or cursor to move to the left margin and down to the next line.

SINGLE-SPACE (SS)—to use vertical line spacing that leaves no blank space between each printed line of copy.

SOFTWARE—instructions or programs that tell a computer or word processor what to do; may be contained on a disk or on computer hardware.

VARIABLES—information, such as names and addresses, that is inserted in standard documents to personalize messages.

WORD PROCESSING—the act of writing and storing documents on a computer, electronic typewriter, or word processor; may also include printing of the final document.

WORD WRAP—a word processing feature that permits information to be keyed on successive lines without having to strike the return key at the end of a line.